PAC-10 FOOTBALL

PAC-10 FOOTBALL
AL MOSS

Crescent Books
A Division of Crown Publishers, Inc.
A Bison Book

Published 1987 by
Crescent Books, distributed by
Crown Publishers Inc.

Produced by Bison Books Corp.
15 Sherwood Place
Greenwich, CT 06830, USA

Printed in Hong Kong

ISBN 0-517-63353-1

h g f e d c b a

PHOTO CREDITS

All photographs courtesy of the Bill Mesler collec-
tion except:
© American Graphic Systems: 2–3, 66 (right), 68
(top), 88, 181 (right), 184–185
Arizona State University: 154, 155, 176 (top), 177,
178, 179 (top and bottom)
Cornell University: 36
Notre Dame University: 39, 49
Oregon State University: 78, 106, 120, 121
Stanford University: 35, 37 (left and right), 41, 58
(all), 59 (all), 62, 73, 74 (all), 75, 76–77, 95, 96
(left and right), 97 (top), 107, 152 (top and bottom), 153 (all), 180–181 (left), 187
Tournament of Roses: 81
University of California, Berkeley: 25, 27, 29, 30,
32–33, 51 (bottom), 52, 68 (bottom), 69, 83,
84–85, 86 (top and bottom), 89 (top and bottom), 110, 146 (left), 146–147 (right), 186, 188–
189 (left), 189 (right)
University of California, Los Angeles: 70 (left and
right), 79 (top), 82, 100, 101 (bottom), 102, 107
(bottom), 172–173 (left), 173 (right)
University of Oregon: 1, 4–5, 18–19, 22 (left), 22–
23 (right), 91, 105, 109, 111, 183 (bottom)
University of Michigan: 13 (right)
University of Southern California: 31, 47, 48, 50

(top and bottom), 51(top), 71, 79 (bottom), 90,
97 (bottom), 98, 99, 101 (top), 103 (top), 118,
119, 126, 127, 145, 148, 149, 156 (top and
bottom), 157, 158 (top and bottom), 159, 183
(top)
University of Washington: 7, 17, 20, 44, 45, 65, 66
(left), 92 (left), 92–93 (right), 113, 114, 115,
116–117, 122, 123, 124–125, 150, 151 (top),
160, 161 (top and bottom), 162–163, 164–165
(left), 165 (right), 166 (left), 166–167 (right), 182
Washington State University: 21, 55, 174–175,
176 (bottom)
Yale University: 9, 10, 11, 14 (top and bottom)

Page 1: University of Oregon back Chris
Miller lifts his hands in the victorious glow of
a touchdown achieved.

Pages 3–4: Washington confronts the mighty
Cal Bears in an intense scene typical of Pac-
10 football action.

These pages: The past glories of the Pacific
Coast include coach Hugo Bezdeck (*at extreme right*) and the very successful University of Oregon team he coached to a 14–0
Rose Bowl win over the University of Pennsylvania in 1917.

Contents

The Beginning	6	The New Rose Bowl	80
The Real Game Emerges	16	Stanford, USC and UCLA	94
The Golden Age	24	The End of the PCC	104
The Pop Warner Years	34	Rising from the Ashes	112
Howard Jones and the		The Trojan Dynasty	128
Thundering Herd	46	Pac-10: The Seventies	
Stanford's Vow Boys	54	and Eighties	144
Washington, Cal and UCLA	64	That Wild Win	170
The Wow Boys and the		Statistics	190
T-Formation	72	Index	192

The Beginning

It was hardly an auspicious hallmark for collegiate football in the West.

On 19 March 1892, Stanford University and the University of California were to meet on the football field, not only the first meeting between those two schools but the first confrontation involving two major universities on the West Coast. The atmosphere surrounding the game was a harbinger of what was to become one of the game's greatest rivalries, the Big Game. Fans made what was then the long trek from Berkeley and Palo Alto to San Francisco, partied late into the night and then invaded the Haight Street Baseball Grounds in totally unprecedented and unexpected force.

Estimates ranged as high as 20,000 people. Far too few tickets had been printed, and Herbert Hoover, the Stanford manager and the one most responsible for arranging the game, and his California counterpart, Herbert Lang, stood at the gate collecting coins in every available box and wash tub. The two teams took the field for the kickoff—and there was nothing to kick.

No one had remembered to bring a football.

That gaffe usually is blamed on Hoover—it somehow lends romance to the moment to claim that a future President of the United States forgot the ball. But whether or not he was at fault, it was Hoover who sprang into action. He grabbed David Goulcher, owner of a sporting goods store from whom Hoover, politician to be, had cajoled $250 worth of uniforms and equipment on credit. Goulcher agreed to fetch a ball, jumped on his horse and rode to his shop in downtown San Francisco.

There he found a ball, but no bladder to fit inside. Looking around frantically, he found the bladder from a punching bag, which he managed to fit, more or less, into the football. During the course of the game, that ball took some very strange-looking bounces.

No, not an auspicious debut at all.

American football began—depending on which account you choose to believe—in either 1869 or 1874. The official version is that Rutgers and Princeton met in the first collegiate football game on 6 November 1869, at New Brunswick, NJ, but that was in truth merely a soccer match, played with 25 men per side and no running with the ball allowed. Most of the Ivy League schools continued to play that way, and in 1873 Yale invited Harvard, Princeton, Rutgers and Columbia to a convention in New York to form an Intercollegiate Football Association. Harvard refused to attend—if it had, college football probably would now be the soccer variety.

Harvard was playing its own game—'Boston Rules,' in which the round ball was used and there was still considerable kicking, but picking up the ball and running with it was allowed. In May of 1874 Harvard and McGill University of Montreal played a two-game series: one under Boston Rules and the other under the rules of the similar and much older game of Rugby football,

played with an oval ball and with far more emphasis on attacking. Harvard was impressed enough with Rugby to incorporate many of the aspects of the English game into its own, then convince other Ivy League schools to follow suit.

On 13 November 1875, Harvard and Yale met for the first time in a game that was largely Rugby, included some soccer variations to satisfy Yale, and was played with Rugby's 15 per side: American football was born.

It was not immediately welcomed to the campus with open arms. When Cornell players asked permission to travel to Cleveland to meet Michigan in an informal, 30-a-side match in 1873, President White of Cornell made a classic decision:

'I will not,' he said, 'permit 30 men to travel 400 miles merely to agitate a bag of wind.'

But the game grew nevertheless, and it was bound to reach the Pacific Coast before long. California was the first to take it up; a Rugby game was played at Berkeley in 1881, between the Class of 1880 and Class of '81, and Rugby it remained through the next three years as Cal played sporadic games—two or three a year—with local club teams. But in 1885 Oscar Shafter Howard, who had played football at Harvard, brought the American game to the West Coast. He convinced California to switch from Rugby—and offered to coach not only the University, but any Rugby club in the Bay area that would make the change.

Over the next six years California played 25 games—the entire 1889 season was rained out—against clubs and, occasionally, Hastings College of Law, and won 20 of them.

In the fall of 1891 Stanford students approached John R Whittemore, who had attended school in the East, and convinced him to form a team there. It seemed only natural that Stanford should play California, but Whittemore felt his young charges weren't ready for so experienced a foe that soon, so when the Bears issued a challenge for Thanksgiving Day of 1891, Whittemore turned it down.

Meanwhile, other schools—in what would a quarter century later become the first Pacific Coast Conference—were picking up the game. The University of Southern California had started a team in 1888 but had no coach for several years and was limited to two or three local games a year. In Seattle a University of Washington team was formed in 1889 but the only available opponent the first season was the alumni, and Washington too had to settle for one or two games a season for awhile; it was one of the more progressive programs, however, and by 1900 was playing not only Washington Agricultural College and School of Science—later Washington State—but also the University of Oregon and Oregon Agricultural College—later Oregon State.

At right is one of Gil Dobie's fearsome and very physical University of Washington teams mauling an opponent in the early 1900s, at the Huskies' Seattle Center field. *Note* the face guards worn by two of the players for protection of their broken noses.

The Territorial Normal School of Tempe, Arizona (which later would become Arizona State) started the sport in 1896 but had only prep school and club opponents until the University of Arizona took it up three years later.

This was not football as we know it today. John W Heisman—a famous player, coach and athletic director, and the man for whom the coveted Heisman Trophy is named—described early football thusly: 'The length of the field between goal lines in the old days was 110 yards, not 100 as at present. That made longer runs possible. There were no five-yard stripes running across the field. There were no linesmen, and no line sticks. The referee kept track of distance by just dropping a handkerchief where he guessed the ball was last put into play. The players of both sides would slyly try to move that handkerchief, while some teammate engaged the referee in a discussion of the rules. So we varied action by kicking a handkerchief as well as a football.

'We had gotten down to 11 men on a team even so long ago as that (Heisman first played college football in 1887) but, as a rule, teams carried only four substitutes, even while on a trip, and trips sometimes meant playing two or three games on successive days so as to be sure to take in enough money at the gate to defray the expenses of the trip.

'The time of the playing halves of a game in those days was 45 minutes, not 30 minutes as now.... Players of my time had to be real iron men, because we played two games each week—Wednesdays and Saturdays. Once a game started, a player could not leave unless he actually was hurt, or at least pleaded injury. Accordingly, whenever the captain wanted to put a fresh player into action, he whispered, "Get your arm hurt, or something." In one game my captain whispered to me: "Get your neck broke, Heisman."

'We wore jerseys and shorts of great variety. We had no helmets or pads of any kind; in fact, one who wore homemade pads was regarded as a sissy. Hair was the only head protection we knew, and in preparation we would let it grow from the first of June … .

'In those pioneer years, arguments followed almost every decision the referee made. The whole team took part, so that half the time the officials scarcely knew who was captain. More than that, every player was privileged to argue as much as he pleased with any and every player of the opposition.'

Sound chaotic? It was an even stranger game the Westerners were playing—a mishmash of Rugby and football. There is a story that in 1893 the University of Idaho and Washington Agricultural arranged to meet in a game—but not until the referee called the team captains together moments before kickoff was it discovered that while Idaho was ready for a football game, the new Washington team had been practicing Rugby. The kickoff was held up for an hour, while the Idaho players taught their opponents the basics of the American game.

Coaches were few and far between, and those who were available were generally volunteers who may or may not have known anything about what they were coaching. In 1898, for example, Washington Agricultural brought in its first real coach, Frank Shively, a Nez Perce Indian trained at the famous Carlisle Indian School in Pennsylvania. But that was such a departure from acceptability that College President E A Bryan was moved to report later: 'Mr. Shively was not regularly employed, for at that time the employment of an athletic coach from public funds would have been a scandal, but his service was largely gratuitous and inspired by his love for the great college game.'

Eligibility rules were nil. Coaches sometimes played in games. It was not unusual for players to compete for three or four colleges,

Football teams of the 1870s got possession of the ball by engaging in disorganized rugby scrum-like formations *(lower left)*. Famous Wild West artist Charles Remington played football for Yale in the late 1870s under team captain Walter Camp. His illustration of 'the straight arm' *(above left)* and 'the lateral pass' *(above)* reveal some of the playing tactics of those days. The first Harvard-Yale football game was played in 1875, and was actually a compromise between rugby and soccer. *Below*: Harvard runs for the ball.

often without registering at any of them. W W 'Pudge' Heffel-finger, who later coached for one season (1893) at California, played for the University of Minnesota while still a senior in high school, then went to Yale and became an All-American guard who was called by Walter Camp and Grantland Rice 'the greatest player of all time.' John Heisman played at Brown University in 1887-88 and then at the University of Pennsylvania for three more years. In the West, a youngster named Charlie Haigler enrolled at Arizona State at age 17, played there for six seasons, becoming that school's first real star—and then was recruited by USC for four more years.

But the game was taking shape—and California and Stanford were in the forefront. When they met in March of 1892 it was a milestone for the West—the first real game of more-or-less American football between two major Pacific Coast universities.

Their records were not imposing. California had won four of its five games, but the wins were over local prep schools; Stanford had wins over two of the same prep schools, and both teams had lost to the Olympic Club by six points. Cal, having played the game for awhile, was a heavy favorite.

Stanford, surprisingly, won the first half 14–0, with Carl C Clemans contributing two touchdowns—which then were worth four points apiece. California dominated in the second half, but missed some kicks (while its fans complained loudly about David Goulcher's lopsided ball)—and the Bears finally lost, 14–10.

Obviously, a rematch was in order. It was set for 17 December 1892 and this time they took things seriously.

Above: **Yale's 1879 team, with Walter Camp, the Father of American Football, holding the ball.** *At the extreme right* **of the front row is Frederick Remington. Walter Camp** (*at right,* **in 1879) molded what had been a mishmash of sports into one of the greatest sports.**

For one thing there actually was a set of eligibility rules drawn up—perhaps the first of their time. Players had to be bonafide students at the respective schools, attending at least five lectures per week for at least six weeks before the game.

Finally, the punting, an important part of football, was wholly ignored, neither side thinking it worthwhile to send the ball downfield on a third-down situation. Such policy is entirely unaccountable and, from a football standpoint, indefensible.

With the exception of these few criticisms, the play would have been intensely interesting had it not been for the inexcusable delays which marred the flow of the contest most atrociously.

Then there was the coaching. After the first game, Whittemore had written to the famous Yale coach Walter Camp, asking him merely to recommend someone to coach the Stanford team. He was amazed when Camp volunteered his own services, without pay, after Yale's season ended. California countered by bringing out a teammate of Camp's at Yale—Thomas Lee McClung.

Walter Camp had been a fine halfback, earning seven football letters at Yale. But it was as a coach that he quite literally and totally revolutionized football.

Camp was largely responsible for setting up the line of scrimmage and for introducing the system of 'downs'—a certain num-

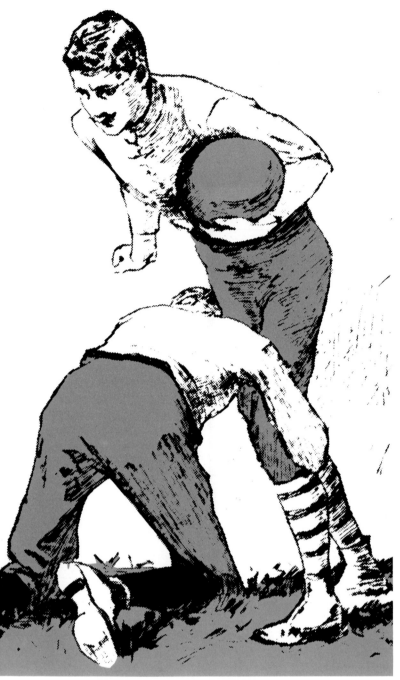

Among several illustrations of the 1887 Yale-Princeton game, this one *(above)* was entitled *A Foul Tackle, Too Low. Facing page— upper left:* Fielding H 'Hurry-up' Yost, Stanford and Michigan coach par excellence; *upper right:* Alonzo Stagg who coached inventively for 70 years; and *(bottom)* a diagram from Stagg's 1893 book.

ber of plays to gain a certain number of yards, rather than the Rugby system of continuous play and tactical kicking back and forth. He invented the quarterback position. He spearheaded the change from 15 players—another Rugby holdover—to 11. He wrote the first football book ever published, in 1901. He was quite justifiably called 'The Father of American Football.'

That December the Stanford-California game ended in a 10–10 tie. 'For the most part, it was as effective as the quality played back East,' Camp told reporters after his first look at Pacific Coast football. 'The general tricks need work, however; their efficiency depends too much upon the very uncertain defensive tactics opposed to them and the lamentably high tackling indulged in by both sides....The push work was as good as that used in the East and crowded the runner oftentimes a good distance. The tempo, although occasionally fairly fast, was, on the whole, far slower than any good football in the East, and the lining up was less sharp and quick. Individual runs were quite up to the average of Eastern play, but here again it was frequently poor tackling which allowed the runner to make his gain.

When Camp was named to the National Collegiate Football Hall of Fame, it was not because of his career at Stanford. He was there for only three years: 1892 and then again in 1894-95, after another Yalie, Pop Bliss, had coached the Cardinals to an 8–0–1 record in 1893. Camp's overall record there was 12–3–3, including a win and two ties with California. But that was beside the point: his contribution was far greater than any won-lost record could possibly reflect. When he came West he brought with him national attention and the aura of respectability. Pacific Coast football had arrived.

A few years later another nationally known coach, Fielding H 'Hurry-Up' Yost, came to Palo Alto. When he arrived at Stanford in 1900 he was barely into his career; he had played football and earned a law degree at West Virginia, but decided to coach instead and went 7–1–1 at Ohio Wesleyan in 1897, 7–1–1 again at Nebraska the next year and 10–0 at Kansas in 1899—coaches didn't stay in one place very long in those days.

Yost coached the Cardinals to a 7–2–1 record in 1900, including a win over California, but after that season he was gone again. There are conflicting versions of the reason: One story says that Stanford (and California as well) passed a rule making it mandatory that the universities hire a graduate to coach their football teams—costing an irate Yost his job. The other side says that the rule was adopted because Yost left after just one year.

Whatever the reason, Stanford had not heard the last of Fielding Yost. While at Stanford, he also had coached Lowell High School in San Francisco, a school team in Ukiah and San Jose Normal (now San Jose State University) in addition to the Cardinals. When he left Palo Alto for Michigan, he took several of the San Jose players with him, including Willie Heston, who was to become one of the all-time great running backs at Michigan.

Yost had an incredible career at Michigan, coaching there (with one year out to serve as athletic director) until 1926. His success was immediate; his 'Point a Minute' teams from 1901 to 1904 had 43 wins and one tie in 44 games and outscored opponents by the staggering total of 2,326 points to 40.

His was an innovative football mind. His offense incorporated just about everything that is now seen in modern football except the forward pass, which was still illegal; his players would call each play, almost before the previous one had ended, and would sprint to the scrimmage line—hence the nickname 'Hurry-Up.'

In 1901, his Wolverines, led by Heston, had a 10–0 record and scored 550 points. The opposition scored none—absolutely zero– and Michigan was invited to the first Rose Bowl game.

The opponent, fittingly enough, was Stanford.

The Pasadena Tournament of Roses Committee had decided to hold an 'East-West' football game as a climax to its Tournament of Roses celebration of 1 January 1902. Michigan was a natural enough selection as the East team. But Stanford, with 1896 team captain Charlie Fickert guiding its destinies as the first of the graduate coaches, had finished the season with a mediocre 3–1–2 record, including a loss (albeit by only 2–0) to California.

The Bears seemed the obvious choice. Two years earlier, they had taken an unbeaten, unscored-upon team to play the powerful Carlisle Indian School (which later produced Jim Thorpe) and lost by only 2–0, earning national respect for West Coast football for perhaps the first time. In 1901, California compiled a 9–0–1 record and beat Nevada and a Southern California all-star team in addition to Stanford. Yost reportedly favored California as an opponent, hoping to meet what he considered the best in the West. But for some unknown reason the administration at Berkeley said no. It would be Yost against Stanford.

It was a mismatch. Stanford played hard and (for awhile at least) reasonably well. But Heston gained almost 200 yards, Neil Snow

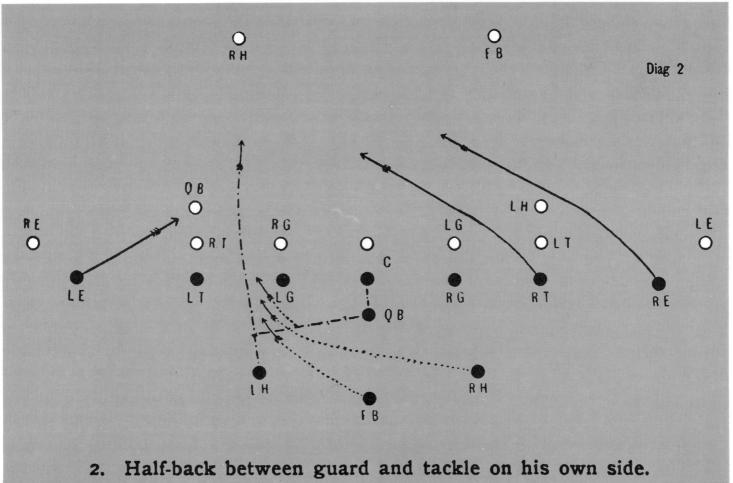

2.   Half-back between guard and tackle on his own side.

Seen *below,* the original Flying Wedge formation, used in the Yale-Harvard game of 1892, was widely imitated in the following year, only to be banned as 'too dangerous' in late 1893. *Above:* Yale players in a wedge in 1893. Football in the 1890s became such a game of pushing, pulling and punching that casualty counts became *de rigueur* for football games. In 1905, President Theodore Roosevelt, shown *at right* acting along with a tide of popular and intra-football outrage, demanded that changes be made, and they were.

scored five touchdowns for the Wolverines, and when the score reached 49–0 with eight minutes still remaining, Stanford captain R S Fisher simply surrendered and the game was stopped.

The Easterners, who felt the football world revolved around the Ivy League and ended somewhere around the Great Lakes (remember that the Big Ten originally was called the Western Conference), were smug. 'The score is quite in proportion to the general superiority of the Eastern men at the game of football,' the *New York Times* wrote—somewhat unfairly, since Michigan also had defeated its Eastern opponents by an average score of 55–0.

But one-sided or not, it was the beginning of something big— even though the next Rose Bowl football game would not be held until 1916. Some 8500 people showed up for that first game at Tournament Park, which seated 1000. Lon F Chapin, publisher of the *Pasadena News*, wrote:

'Several thousand Dutchmen and Britishers engaged in several years of bloody fighting for the possession of a government (the Boer War) and don't get an encore. Twenty-two striplings argue for an hour over the progress along the ground of an inflated hog's hide, and law-abiding citizens bound up and down on the seats of their trousers, while demure maidens hammer plug hats down over the ears of their escorts with their parasols.'

But the football picture was not—if you'll pardon the pun—all rosy. The game was rough and dangerous. Stanford guard W K Roosevelt, a second cousin of President Teddy Roosevelt, had broken his leg in the Rose Bowl game—and then continued to play for another 15 minutes until he got his ribs broken, too, and had to leave the field. The vicious 'flying wedge' was the epitome of the game: line up in front of the ball-carrier and simply run over the defense.

In 1905, Amos Alonzo Stagg, another of the great early-day coaches, criticized football in an article in the *Chicago Tribune* claiming that in that season alone, there had been 18 fatalities and 15 serious injuries in the game. In the preceding five years, it was reported, there had been 71 fatalities in college and high school football.

Teddy Roosevelt called the presidents of Harvard, Yale and Princeton to the White House and gave them an ultimatum: 'Remove every objectionable feature to save the game,' or it would be outlawed. In December of 1905, representatives of 62 colleges met and made a number of major revisions to eliminate brutality from the game, most of the changes suggested by Walter Camp and John Heisman. Among the changes: The halves were shortened to 30 minutes (from 35 at that time), a neutral scrimmage line was established and three downs were allowed to gain ten yards.

Most of the Pacific Coast schools followed these new rules, but at Stanford and California, which in those early days had been the pioneers in Far West football, Roosevelt's dictum came too late. David Starr Jordan, the president of Stanford, and his California counterpart, Benjamin Ide Wheeler, had discussed the possibility of abolishing American football after the 1904 season, and decided during the following season to switch to Rugby—although they wisely waited until the 1905 season was concluded to announce their decision.

Students and alumni protested bitterly—especially at Stanford, where the Cardinals had just finished a perfect 8–0 season of football under coach Jim Lanagan, capped by a 12–5 victory in the Big Game. But Jordan and Wheeler prevailed, and for the next nine years these two schools played Rugby.

American football in the West was on hold.

The Real Game Emerges

When the two most prominent teams on the Pacific Coast chose in tandem to give up the game, it could have been a terrific setback for American football in the West. California and Stanford had dominated the Western American game before they elected to switch to Rugby beginning in 1906. Cal had been the first real collegiate football team on the Coast, and from the time the Bears started playing the game under Oscar Shafter Howard in 1885 until the change in '06, they compiled an even 100 wins, 22 losses and 22 ties. Stanford had nearly as good a record, 75–21–15.

But other programs were beginning to emerge. The University of Southern California had begun a team in 1888, but for many years rarely had a coach and never played more than five or six games—usually less. Finally, in 1904 they brought in their first 'long-term' coach, Harvey Holmes; in his four years there the Trojans won 19, lost five and tied three. Virtually all of the games were against local high schools and small colleges—although Holmes' team did meet Stanford in 1905, losing 16–0. It was hardly yet the USC dynasty of years to come, but it was a start.

Not long afterward, the Pacific Coast's first real dynasty did appear—and it was in neither Los Angeles nor the San Francisco Bay Area.

The University of Washington, in Seattle, had aimed high from the beginning of its program. In 1893 for example, Washington played a touring Stanford team in the Huskies' first actual intercollegiate sports event; the Cardinals won 40–0, but it was one more early step toward real collegiate competition in the Wild West. By the turn of the century, Washington was playing perhaps the most complete schedule against major schools of any college team on the Coast.

Then, in 1908 the Huskies hired Gil Dobie as their head coach. The dour Dobie was not a likeable character; he was a pessimist and a perfectionist, subject to spells of acute depression and irrationality, who lived by himself in a room cluttered with books, papers and football diagrams. He was extremely unpopular. Often, during games, Washington fans would boo their own coach; throw fruit and vegetables at him from the stands and cheer for the opponents.

On his first day at Washington, Dobie barred everyone but players from practice; he nearly got into fist fights with a former mayor and the postmaster. He told team captain and local hero Pete Teutmeir that he was 'yellow' and quarterback Wee Coyle that he played 'like a man devoid of a brain' who wouldn't even be on the team 'if I didn't have so many cripples.' He kicked a key player, Penny Westover, off the field for missing an assignment and told him never to come back—and yet when Westover (who spent the night musing over terrible things he should have done to Dobie) returned the next day the coach promptly stuck him back on the first team. 'I knew that he had too much pride to stay away,' Dobie said with a thin smile.

Charley Hunt, who played tackle at Annapolis for Dobie and once had to restrain a teammate from punching the coach, said Dobie 'was no leader—only a slave driver.'

He was in danger of being fired virtually every season he was at Washington, simply because of his personality, but one overriding factor dictated against that: in nine years, Gilmour Dobie's teams did not lose a single game. Their record was 58 wins, three ties, no losses.

When he finally did leave, under a cloud, to take the head coaching job at the Naval Academy, a writer on the student newspaper who was given to sarcasm said this:

'The disagreement between Dobie and (University) President Suzzolo is caused by a misunderstanding on the part of the president. In some manner, Suzzolo has gotten the idea that the educational functions of the University are of more importance than the football team. The error of judgment, while regrettable, is excusable. For nine long years, spurred on by Dobie's zeal and profanity, Washington has waged successful football warfare. Any fan will tell you that the University has grown and prospered solely because of the wonderful record which Dobie has achieved. Now, with a president who puts mathematics over muscle, brain over brawn, the future of the University is indeed shrouded in uncertainty.'

Gil Dobie was not generally known as a great innovator, although he occasionally pulled a trick out of the bag and his players had more respect for his ingenuity than did the press and

Power football specialist Gil Dobie *(right)* was so well disliked by almost everybody, that even Huskies fans regularly pelted him with fruit, even though in his 1908-16 coaching career at the University of Washington his teams won 58 games and lost none.

public; he was simply an outstanding teacher and drillmaster who specialized in power football. 'Dobie's style of offensive football,' George Pfann, one of Dobie's greatest players (at Cornell in the early 1920s) once told Allison Danzig of the *New York Times*, 'was power with timing, mixed with just enough passing and deception to keep the secondary from moving immediately toward the ball carrier, thereby keeping the defense sufficiently off-balance to give his power plays a chance to develop.'

Grantland Rice, one of the all-time great sportswriters, recalled in his autobiography, *The Tumult and the Shouting*, a conversation with Dobie when the latter was coaching at Cornell in 1925. Dartmouth, using the forward pass liberally, walloped Cornell 62–13, but afterward Dobie told Rice, 'Well, we won, 13–0.

'What about Dartmouth's 62 points,' Rice asked.

'I don't count those scores made by passing,' Dobie replied. 'That isn't football.'

But whatever Dobie's style, it worked. He won nearly 80 percent of his games in a coaching career that spanned 33 years.

Despite Dobie's doomsday philosophy, he had a human side. His few close friends insisted he was articulate, well-read and humorous—especially after a glass or two. And he could be friendly and helpful when the mood took him.

In 1915, California had returned to American football, and Jimmy Schaeffer, who had been successful as the Rugby coach at Berkeley since 1909, was convinced to stay on and coach what was to him a new sport. Stanford still was playing Rugby and in addition had broken relations with Cal the year before over the question of freshman eligibility—Stanford favored it; the Bears

did not. With USC's program still developing, there was no major collegiate opponent available to take Stanford's place in a 'big game' except the Northwest schools. Dobie was in his heyday, and either because of that or despite it, California chose Washington and a home-and-home series was arranged.

Schaeffer had played one season of American football as a freshman at Berkeley, but major rules revisions in 1906 and again in 1912 had made it a far different game. So, in an effort to learn the intricacies of the sport, Schaeffer packed his bags, headed for Seattle, walked unannounced into Dobie's office and asked that forbidding individual to teach him all about American football. And surprisingly, Dobie did—spending the next three days teaching the upstart from California everything he could cram into the brain of the young coach who would, in a few weeks, be his opponent.

It would be the height of drama to say that California then went out and beat Washington. Hardly. The first game was played in Berkeley—and the Huskies won 72–0. Only once in their history have the Bears ever suffered a worse defeat, that by 74–0 to USC in 1930. However, Dobie may not have been a bad teacher at that; in the very next game, the return match in Seattle, Washington had to scramble to win by 13–7.

California's return to football coincided with a momentous event on the Pacific Coast, although it's a bit difficult to ascertain whether the Bears' decision prompted the formation of a new league or vice versa. On 2 December 1915, Professor C M Lynch, the faculty athletic representative from Cal, invited representatives from three Northwestern schools to meet with him at the Oregon Hotel in

Portland. Dean Arthur R Priest of Washington, Dean A B Cordley of Oregon State and Colin Dyment of Oregon answered his summons, and Professor Lynch told them:

'Gentlemen, the time has come to organize our own conference and to broaden the scope of college athletics in the Far West. It has become perfectly clear that the problems are awesome.'

They certainly were that. One of the major problems was eligibility; despite the massive overhauling of the rules in 1906, that area remained much as it had before the turn of the century. In other words, there were no rules and no National Collegiate Athletic Association yet to make and enforce them.

The new league was named the Pacific Coast Intercollegiate Athletic Conference, and the one-day meeting in Portland established the first set of rules. By current standards they are fairly simple, but at the time they contained some pretty revolutionary ideas:

1. Each of the schools shall appoint an athletic committee to supervise and enforce rules regarding football and all intercollegiate athletics.

2. No one may participate in athletics unless he is a bona fide student doing full work in a regular or special course as defined in his college's curriculum. No transfer student who has played for another college will be eligible to participate at your school until he has been registered for six months.

3. No athlete will be allowed to participate in college sports if he accepts any gift, remuneration or pay for his services on the college team.

4. Any student of any institution who shall be pursuing a regularly prescribed resident graduate course within such institution, whether for an advanced degree or in one of its professional schools, may be permitted to play for the period of the minimum number of years required for securing the degree for which he is a candidate.

5. No professional athlete shall be allowed to participate in college sports.

6. No student shall play in any game under an assumed name.

7. No athlete who is found by the faculty to be delinquent in his classroom work shall be permitted to play in any intercollegiate contests.

8. All games shall be played on grounds either owned by or under the immediate control of one or both of the colleges involved in the contest and all games shall be played under student management exclusively.

9. The election of managers and captains of teams in each college shall be subject to the approval of its athletic committee.

10. College teams shall not engage in games with professional teams.

11. Before every intercollegiate contest a list of men proposing to play shall be presented by each team to the other or others, certifying that all the members are entitled to play under conditions of the adopted rules. Each team captain must enforce this rule.

Below: **The Rose Bowl of 1917 pitted the University of Oregon against the mighty University of Pennsylvania team, which had a 7–2 record for the regular season, but the Ducks beat Pennsy 14–0. Pennsylvania wore jerseys with striped arms, Oregon wore the plain.**

Captain of the 1907 Washington Huskies in 1907, Enoch Bagshaw (above) posed for this period photo in full playing regalia. His uniform's knee padding would have been considered 'sissy stuff' 10 years earlier. The 1916 Rose Bowl pitted the University of Washington against Brown University, as per the program cover at right.

12. We shall call upon the expert managers of football teams to so revise the rules as to reduce the liability of injury to a minimum.

That was the beginning of the Pacific Coast Conference. A year later, at a meeting in Seattle, Stanford and Washington State were selected for membership—although Stanford, because of the changeover from Rugby and the intervention of World War I, did not play football within the league until 1919. Southern California and Idaho joined the PCC in 1922, Montana in 1924 and finally, in 1928, UCLA became the tenth member.

It was also at about this time that the Tournament of Roses Committee decided, after a 15-year hiatus, to again hold a football game on New Year's Day as part of its celebration. Ironically, it was not a member of the new Pacific Coast Conference that

got the bid as the Western team, but Washington Agricultural College (later Washington State)—which wouldn't join the league until the following year.

The Aggies were coached by one of the more colorful characters in the history of West Coast football. William H 'Lone Star' Dietz had been a tackle and the captain on the 1911 Carlisle team under coach Glenn 'Pop' Warner (whose influence on Pacific Coast football was yet to come). Carlisle beat such Eastern powers as Penn, Harvard, Brown and Pittsburgh during Dietz's senior year. In 1915 he became the second of four Indians from Carlisle to coach at Pullman, following Frank Shively and preceding Gus Welch (1919–22) and A A Exendine (1923–25).

Dietz was half Ogalala Sioux. He was a talented artist and had a flair for acting; he showed up for the squad picture for the Rose Bowl wearing top hat, tails, gloves and spats and carrying a cane. When Washington Agricultural went to Pasadena, Dietz spent part of his time coaching and part of it acting in nearby Hollywood and he managed to get some of his players bit parts in a football movie, 'Tom Brown of Harvard.' It wasn't exactly 'Gone With the Wind,' but it did earn the boys $100 a day—which, one story says, they pooled and bet on themselves in the Rose Bowl game, thus taking home a healthy chunk of cash. It might have been more but the movie company fired them when they made the mistake of roughing up the star in a 'scrimmage.'

But don't be fooled: Lone Star Dietz also was a canny coach. Using Warner's double wing formation as a basis and adding wrinkles of his own, he built a powerful team in his first year at Washington Agricultural that in seven games went unbeaten and outscored the opposition by 204 points to 10.

He had considerable talent on that team (some of it assembled by his predecessor, John R Bender)—brothers Dick and LeRoy Hanley, center Asa V Clark, sophomore end Clarence Zimmerman, blocking quarterback Arthur 'Bull' Durham, a well-known Admiral in World War II, and bruising runners in Carl Dietz (no relation to the coach) and the beautifully named Benton Bangs.

Their Rose Bowl opponent was Brown University, which had just a 5–3–1 record and was picked despite the fact that several Eastern teams had better records; Syracuse had been the first choice of the committee, but had declined to make the long trip. Brown had the first black All-American, speedy Fritz Pollard, but a wet field slowed Pollard (he gained just 46 yards in 15 carries) and the far bigger Washington players just wore down the Easterners to win 14–0. Carl Dietz scored a touchdown and was named the game's most valuable player, and the *Los Angeles Times* put it this way: 'The western backs, with five and six men ahead of them, literally tore the right side of the Brown line to shreds during the last half when all of the scoring was done.'

One of the outmanned Brown players, incidentally, was a young guard named Wallace Wade; he would return to the Rose Bowl five times as a coach.

The following season Oregon went undefeated (with one tie) in eight games and was chosen as the Western team in the Rose Bowl on 1 January 1917—the first to officially represent the Pacific Coast Conference. But this time there was no question of a weak opponent—Brown may have been a second-rate selection the year before as some had claimed, but Pennsylvania finished the 1916 season with a 7–2 record and was considered one of the strongest teams in the East.

'Scared of 'em?' recalled John Beckett, Oregon's star tackle and halfback, years later. 'We were scared to death of 'em. They came out here with quite a reputation.'

But when the Ducks repeated Washington State's victory by the same 14–0 score, the Eastern football establishment began to realize that they'd better take Pacific Coast football seriously.

50¢

Oregon was coached by another unusual character, Hugo Bezdek. Bezdek, who was born in Czechoslovakia and raised in the roughhouse South Side of Chicago, had played at the University of Chicago under Amos Alonzo Stagg. Although he was a rough, belligerent man who wasn't above a little chicanery—he was known to put onions on his cheeks to bring the tears for pregame fight talks—he also was a sound football mind.

Bezdek first coached Oregon in 1906 (his team going undefeated) then moved to Arkansas from 1908–12 and had an undefeated season there in 1909 before returning to Oregon from 1913–18. With help from Stagg and former Chicago star quarterback Walter Eckersall, Bezdek made Arkansas one of the earliest teams to really utilize the forward pass and he was a pioneer in exploiting spread formations for passing and screen passes. He also had a lot to do with developing the spinner plays that 'Pop' Warner later perfected at Stanford.

During his second term at Oregon, Bezdek's teams provided the stiffest competition for Gil Dobie's Washington powerhouses—that one tie marring the record of the Rose Bowl-bound Ducks in 1916 was with the Huskies. After leaving Oregon, Bezdek had a successful 10-year tenure at Penn State, and wound up with a 127–58–15 record in 24 years of coaching and a spot in the College Football Hall of Fame. He also was a major league baseball manager with the Pittsburgh Pirates from 1917–19—at the same time that he was coaching football on the West Coast.

Bezdek drove his players hard, scrimmaging virtually every day during the week and on occasion even holding a full practice under the stands immediately before a game. Often his own players took sides—some for him and some against. 'I don't know any man who could make as bitter an enemy as Bez had the knack of doing,' Pittsburgh sports columnist Chet Smith once said—and he was a friend of Bezdek's.

Harvard beat Oregon 7–6 in the 1920 Rose Bowl game pictured *at right*. Hugo Bezdek *(above)* coached Oregon State in two widely-spaced intervals—an undefeated season in 1906 and, after turning Arkansas into the first forward passing 'bomb' squad (with help from Alonzo Stagg), helped dampen Dobie's Ducks in 1916.

Hugo rarely praised a player—'Your best is not good enough! I want something better,' he was fond of shouting. Opposing coaches were all villains, spies and cheats while he and his team were poor little put-upon lambs. When he found that Penn was favored in their Rose Bowl game, Bezdek was overjoyed. 'I've got only overgrown high school boys,' he was quoted as saying—ignoring the fact that his team had outscored opponents by 244–17—'while Penn can field a varsity of big university strength. We haven't got a chance.'

And while Bezdek was conducting his own practices in secret, he wasn't above accepting an invitation from Pennsylvania coach Bob Folwell to visit a Penn practice.

'Bezdek asked Folwell if he would show him our reverse-pass play,' recalled Bert Bell, the All-American quarterback on that Quaker team who later was Commissioner of the National Football League. 'Folwell told me to run it and I complied, reluctantly. Imagine what we thought—and said—when Oregon scored its first touchdown against us on our own play.'

In addition to Bell, Penn had another man who was to become a big name in football—All-American tackle Lou Little, who coached Columbia to a 7–0 win over Stanford in the 1934 Rose Bowl. But in this game Beckett and tackle Ken Bartlett outplayed Little, and the brilliance of All-American Shy Huntington and his brother Hollis (in the Oregon backfield) turned the game.

Bezdek coached in two more Rose Bowls. In the 1917 season Washington State again had gone undefeated, but because of World War I two service teams were invited to Pasadena, and Bezdek's Mare Island squad beat Camp Lewis, 19–7. He also was the Penn State coach in the 1922 game against USC and challenged Trojan coach Gus Henderson to a fist fight in the middle of the field before the game when Henderson took Hugo to task for bringing his team to the game an hour late for kickoff.

When Washington State gave up football (as did many collegiate teams) in 1918 because of the War, 'Lone Star' Dietz succeeded Bezdek as coach at Mare Island. At the same time one of his stars from Pullman, Dick Hanley—who later became one of the nation's most respected coaches himself at Northwestern—joined the Marine Corps and became Dietz's captain and quarterback. They led Mare Island to the 1919 Rose Bowl, where they lost in another all-service match to a loaded team from Great Lakes Naval Training Center. George Halas—who was to become the owner, coach and life force of the Chicago Bears and one of the guiding lights of the NFL—returned an intercepted pass 72 yards and also scored a touchdown on a pass from Paddy Driscoll to lead Great Lakes to a 17–0 victory.

The following year the Rose Bowl was returned to the colleges. Shy Huntington (one of the Oregon stars in the 1917 Rose Bowl) had taken over as head coach of the Ducks the next year, and though they finished the 1919 regular season with just a 5–1 record including a loss to Washington State, they won the PCC title by virtue of a win over Washington (which also finished with one loss) and were invited to Pasadena. They lost that game 7–6

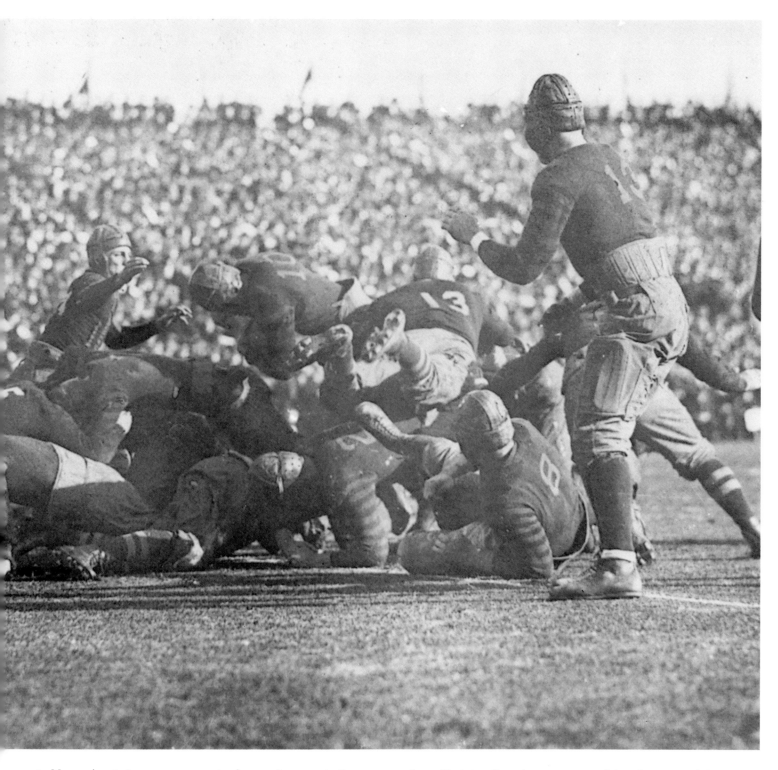

to Harvard, missing seven separate chances to score in the game. It was 38 years before an Oregon team again played in the Rose Bowl.

Meanwhile, California and Stanford were working their way back to the top of the heap. Following Stanford's Rugby win in the 1914 Big Game—a season in which the Cardinals went undefeated and Cal lost only one game in 15 games—the two schools had their falling out over the question of freshman eligibility. Stanford continued to play Rugby and went undefeated again in the 1915 season under the same coach, Floyd Brown. Cal returned to American football and was 8–5 in 1915 under Jimmy Schaeffer, including the two losses to Gil Dobie and Washington.

Stanford had joined the Pacific Coast Conference but World War I curtailed sports at the university in 1917 and 1918. In 1918 they played California, but Cal had a 7–2 record and won the PCC title, while the Cardinals fielded an SATC (Student Army Training Corps) team, many of the players not full-time students. The Bears won in a runaway 67–0, with Pesky Sprott scoring seven touchdowns, but not even rabid California followers ever have considered that an 'official' Big Game.

In 1919 this great rivalry finally was resumed. Brick Morse, who had been a football star at Cal before the turn of the century and later was a *San Francisco Chronicle* sportswriter, summed up just how much the Big Game had been missed: 'Many of us (Cal people) realized for the first time that we loved Stanford, although we hated her worse than poison.'

California won that game, 14–10, and its varsity finished the season with a 6–2–1 mark, but that was almost incidental. The Bear Cubs—the freshman team—of that 1919 season finished with a 10–1 record, with their only loss coming by one point (13–123) to the Nevada varsity. Andy Smith was beginning to make his presence felt. The Golden Age of Sports was at hand and for the University of California it was going to be just Wonderful.

The Golden Age

Although Jimmy Schaeffer was a highly successful coach (if not a household name) in his seven years at the University of California, the most important thing he ever did for the Bears was to listen to the advice of a Chicago bartender.

The official version is that Andy Smith became the California football coach after the usual 'comprehensive nationwide search' by the athletic department administration. But in his book, *The Big Game*, John Sullivan tells a slightly different story.

When, prior to the 1915 season, Cal decided to switch from Rugby back to American football, Schaeffer hit the road to try to learn the new (at least to him) game. He was immediately successful with his approach to Washington's great coach Gil Dobie, and emboldened by that he spent the summer touring the Midwest looking for more help. Coaches there were far more reticent to part with information but Schaeffer's odyssey was a good human-interest yarn and was widely reported in Midwest newspapers, often accompanied by his picture.

One afternoon he paused for a small libation in a Chicago tavern and was recognized by the bartender, who asked him how his quest was coming. The discouraged Schaeffer told him and the bartender said, 'They've got a sharp young coach at Purdue, name of Andy Smith; why don't you go see him?'

Schaeffer and Smith hit it off immediately. Smith was even more helpful than Dobie had been and during one all-night session in Schaeffer's hotel room, Jimmy brashly offered Smith the coaching job at Cal—an offer which of course he had no authority to make. Smith accepted—not for the upcoming 1915 season because he still had a contract at Purdue—but for 1916. All that remained was for Schaeffer to return to Berkeley and convince the school officials to follow through.

To their everlasting relief, they did.

Andrew Latham Smith had been an All-American fullback on the University of Pennsylvania team that compiled a 12–0 record in his senior year. He became head coach at his alma mater in 1909, built a 30–10–3 record in four years there, then moved to Purdue in 1913 and was 12–6–3 in three seasons there.

Smith taught fundamental football—solid blocking and tackling, a good running game—and he taught it extremely well. 'Andy,' said Dr John W Wilce, the coach of the Ohio State team that lost to California in the 1921 Rose Bowl, 'brought to a Rugby-steeped West Coast, then relatively backward in football, a brilliance of all-around coaching knowhow which, combined with the great Coast material, left an indelible record in the total annals of football.'

Lee Cranmer, a guard on the great Wonder Team of 1920–22, described Smith thusly: 'One thing that made Andy Smith so great a coach was his ability to inspire a team in a few words, but that was not all. Andy knew football so completely that, in his blackboard talks and lectures before any specific game, he would tell us just what to expect. He never missed. Andy sized up everything that was ever sprung on us by another team and warned us about it in advance. He seemed to have analyzed the character of the other coach and to know exactly what kind of football he would use.'

In Smith's first speech to the California student body, he said: 'There are four mental qualifications necessary for success—aggressiveness, obedience, concentration and determination. Add to this harmonious cooperation and you have the making of a real team.'

It took Andy some time to build that kind of a team, however; he was not an immediate success. The inexperienced Bears had a 6–4–1 record in his first year in 1916, losing both 'big games' to Washington; in 1917 they were 5–5–1 and although they won the Pacific Coast Conference championship in 1918 with a 7–2 record and beat Stanford 67–0, it was a war year and the opponents were primarily service teams or college squads loaded with part-time students who were taking military training.

Jimmy Phelan, another great coach and a friend of Smith's, was visiting Andy in Berkeley after the 1919 season. Although the Bears had edged Stanford 14–10, and finished with a 6–2–1 record, they had lost to Washington and Washington State and Phelan warned Smith of the persistent rumors that Andy would soon be fired.

'I'm not worried,' Smith told Phelan. 'Next year I'll have 'em where I want 'em.'

How true! In 1918, Smith had hired as his assistant coach Clarence 'Nibs' Price, a high school coach in San Diego. In 1919 Price recruited a bevy of high school stars, including one Harold P 'Brick' Muller; within a year, that group would become one of the great collegiate football teams of all time.

Freshmen were not eligible for varsity play in 1919 but the Bear Cubs made their mark nevertheless, finishing the season with a 10–0 record marred only by a 13-12 loss to the Nevada varsity.

Ironically enough, that almost was the end of an era rather than a beginning. During the 1919 season, the freshmen were practicing with the varsity and Smith was so overwhelmed with

Andy Smith (*right*) coached the *Wonder Team* to a 1920–1922 sprint of 27-1-0, compiling 1220 points to their opponents' combined 81.

the amount of talent on hand that he had an 'elimination day' practice—a brutal scrimmage ladled with heaping helpings of verbal abuse—to find out which were his best players. Following that, many of those outstanding freshmen, led by quarterback Charley Erb, decided not to return to Berkeley. But between seasons Smith and Price visited Erb and convinced him to return, bringing his teammates with him. And Price convinced Smith that 'elimination days' were better eliminated.

Over the next three years, that group compiled a record of 27 wins, no losses and one tie, scoring 1220 points to just 81 by the opposition. No wonder Brick Morse, the former California football star who by then was a San Francisco sportswriter, dubbed the group 'The Wonder Team.'

Smith did not care for the appellation, fearing that his players would become bigheaded. He actually called Morse, the most loyal of Old Blues, to complain about the disservice he had rendered. But Smith didn't really have much of a case and, to Andy's chagrin and history's delight, the nickname stuck.

Smith's fears may, however, have had some foundation at that. Cranmer once told *Portland Oregonian* sportswriter L H Gregory: 'As good as the 1921 team was, and its successors, to my mind none of them quite came up to the 1920 eleven. What made the 1920 team so great was the fire and inspiration of youth, plus fine material and the most wonderful collective team spirit I believe ever existed on a football eleven. The difference between that team and the one of 1921 was that in 1920 we knew we were good, that we had the stuff, but we were out to

demonstrate it. In 1921, we knew we were good—so good that we sometimes felt we didn't have to prove it. The 1921 team felt its oats at times and was hard to handle…. In 1920 we listened to everything Andy told us. In 1921 we were so good, and knew we were so good, that Andy had his troubles.'

Smith had a number of great players in that era. Stan Barnes, who played all the line positions at one time or another and tackle Dan McMillan both are in the National Football Foundation Hall of Fame; there were other linemen like Cort Majors, Cranmer and Fat Latham, and backs such as Pesky Sprott, Crip Toomey, Archie Nisbet, Duke Morrison and Charley Erb, a 132-pound quarterback of whom Cranmer said later: 'When the Bears went on the field, running the team was in the hands of Charley, and it was Charley who called every play. One reason why Erb was such a great quarterback was that Andy Smith, after the game started, left him absolutely alone.'

But there was nobody like Brick Muller.

First of all, Muller was a big man for the era. Legends grow as the years go by, and he now is often referred to as 'six feet two or three and 210 or 215 pounds'; six feet and 190 pounds or so probably was closer to the truth, but then, few players were over 200 pounds in those days. More importantly, Muller was a great athlete. He had sprinter's speed and in the 1920 Olympic Games at Antwerp, Belgium, he had won the Bronze Medal in the high jump.

Brick was named to the third team All-America as a sophomore in 1920 by Walter Camp, the only one who picked such a team, and it was generally felt that only the Eastern disdain for West Coast football kept Muller off the first team. Camp remedied that in both of the next two years, putting Muller on his first team in 1921 and '22. A quarter-century later, in 1946, he was chosen to the All-Time All-American team by *Colliers Magazine*.

Southern California coach Gus Henderson called Muller simply, 'The best man I have ever seen put on a football suit.'

Muller played end and he could of course catch the ball well; he had the huge, sure hands of a surgeon—which he later was. In addition, he was a deadly tackler on punt coverage, a fine defensive end and an outstanding blocker. But he also was a great passer; in the modern game, quarterbacks think nothing of throwing the ball 50 or 60 yards in the air, but remember that the football in the 1920s was far harder to throw than today's streamlined version. 'Brick is easily the greatest player I've ever seen on either end of a forward pass, throwing or catching,' Andy Smith said. 'He probably can throw a football farther and with flatter trajectory than any other player the game has ever seen.'

If Muller is remembered for one play, it would be that pass in the 1921 Rose Bowl. Following a 1920 regular season in which California went 8–0, allowed only 14 points (while scoring 510) and beat St Mary's by 127–0, Pacific Coast Conference champion Bears were naturally enough invited to the Rose Bowl, to meet Ohio State.

California pretty well dominated the game and beat the Buckeyes, 28–0, but was leading only 7–0 in the second quarter when fullback Archie Nisbet plunged into the line for a short gain. He got up slowly and stood for a few moments, talking to some of the other Bears on the line of scrimmage. The other three backs stood casually behind the line, hands on hips; Muller wandered off to their left.

Suddenly Nisbet stooped and flipped the ball back to Pesky Sprott. He faked a run, then lateraled the ball to Muller who was

Brick Muller (right) was the wonder man of the Wonder Team. Muller could block and kick, and could pass the blimp-like football of his day with consistent accuracy and range.

STANFORD
CALIFORNIA
FOOTBALL GAME

STANFORD STADIUM
2:30 ● P·M·
NOV·25·1922

PRICE TWENTY FIVE CENTS

circling from the left side toward his right. Brick drifted well back, to his own 47-yard line. Erb and Crip Toomey went a few yards downfield as pass receivers, but they were just decoys; meanwhile, right end Brodie Stephens was flying down the field.

Pete Stinchcomb, the Ohio State star halfback who was playing safety, simply didn't believe anybody could throw the ball that far and as Stephens ran past, Stinchcomb asked disdainfully, 'Just where do you think you're going?' But Stephens just kept running; at the goal line he turned, and Muller's pass—which had traveled 53 yards in the air and never much more than ten feet off the ground—hit him right in the chest in full stride.

That 53 yards, incidentally, seems to be the accurate distance—although some semi-hysterical reports of the moment called it 70 yards and more. Later in the game, Muller also completed a 55-yarder but that was called back by a penalty; in addition, he completed two other passes in the game, caught two for 33 yards, made several tackles on the dangerous Stinchcomb on punt returns and several times stopped Buckeye sweeps for no gain from his defensive position.

The 1921 season was more of the same for the Wonder Team. They were again undefeated and untied during the regular season, capping it with a 42–7 win over Stanford in the first game ever played in Stanford Stadium. A crowd of 62,740—largest ever for a sporting event in California up to that time—was on hand and following the game even the Stanford Daily had to give credit to its archrival:

'No one will deny, after Saturday, that the Bruins (meaning Cal—UCLA was not yet in the picture) have a "wonder team." They had no plays that surprised the Cards. They did not need them to gain. They would not need them against any team in the country. Their touchdowns are a record of a fast tractor moving over all obstacles until the goal line is reached.'

Following the 1921 season, Smith was asked to name an All-Coast team. He chose 11 Bears. 'I doubt if California could be improved by substituting a man from any other West Coast team,' he said.

But the Bears were about to get a comeuppance. They were, of course, again invited to the Rose Bowl and the selectors chose as their opponent a Pennsylvania school of some 500 students named Washington & Jefferson. The selection caught everyone by surprise, including Cal and the Washington & Jefferson team itself. The Presidents were a good team; they had finished with a perfect 10–0 record, had beaten Eastern powers Syracuse, Pittsburgh—coached by Pop Warner—and West Virginia and had several outstanding players including All-American tackle Russell Stein. But on the West Coast they were strictly an unknown quantity.

'All I know about Washington and Jefferson,' one reporter wrote, 'is that they're both dead.'

California was a huge favorite. Another writer said 'On a dry field Cal would have defeated Stanford close to 100–0....When you have a fighter like (Jack) Dempsey or a football team like California, it doesn't really matter how good the other fellows are, does it?'

That was hyperbole, but maybe the Bears believed it. Apparently the only one who was ready for what happened was Andy Smith, who proved himself a great prophet as well as a great coach. It had rained heavily in the days before the game, and the night before they were to play Smith stuck his head out the window, looked at the weather and told some friends: 'We'll kick.... The score will be nothing to nothing.'

Presidents' coach Greasy Neale, a one-time major league outfielder with the Cincinnati Reds who many years later coached the Philadelphia Eagles to a National Football League champion-

Twenty-five cents bought the program *(left)* for the (Cal 28-0) 1922 Big Game. Brick Muller *(above)* even *looked* like a giant!

ship, brought just 16 players West with him. Only 11 played, all going the full 60 minutes. And little Washington & Jefferson totally dominated the mighty Wonder Team.

California made only 49 yards and just two first downs in the entire game—both of them, incidentally, right over the All-American, Stein. W&J actually scored in the third period on a 35-yard run by Wayne Brenkert, but Stein was offsides, nullifying the touchdown and that was the only threat of the day. With the field muddy and slippery, there was a lot of kicking on first down—as Smith had predicted. Stein tried several long field goals, but failed to connect, while the proud Bears disdained several easy field goal attempts—any one of which would ultimately have won.

The game ended exactly as Smith had said—in a 0–0 tie, in what would be the only blemish on the Wonder Team's record in three full years.

While the game might not have offered much in the way of offensive football, it certainly was a study in the psychological

'Did you ever see a rottener college outfit than that one of mine?' 'Gloomy Gus' Henderson *(opposite)* was sure to say that opposing teams would make dishrags out of his phenomenal Trojans. *Above:* All-American center Edwin C 'Babe' Horrell captained Cal in 1924.

aspects of the game. Neale had the Presidents talking and needling constantly, anything to take their opponents' minds off the game. For example, Muller did not start because of a severe attack of boils, but entered the game in the second quarter. When he lined up, his clean uniform highly visible among the others caked with mud, one of the W&J players approached him—most reports say it was Stein who started the whole thing, but another historian credits end Herb Kopf. Whoever it was, he said to California's famous All-American, 'I'd like to shake your hand, but oh, I'm all muddy'—whereupon he reached over and wiped his hands on Muller's clean uniform. Every single one of the other Presidents players then followed suit.

The idea, of course, was to rattle Muller, perhaps even to the point of causing him to swing and be thrown out of the game. Brick was fuming, all right, but he took it without a word.

California lodged complaints with the Rose Bowl Committee over the selection of the Presidents, but it wasn't because of their muddying of Brick Muller or the 0–0 tie; rather, the Bears seriously questioned the eligibility of some of Washington & Jefferson's older players, a complaint that according to some Eastern writers of the time was probably well-founded. Getting no satisfaction, school officials notified the committee that the University of California would not be available for future Rose Bowl games and, in spite of some excellent records in the interim, the Bears didn't return to Pasadena until 1929.

The Rose Bowl may have been left to other teams, but that didn't mean Smith was about to give up that conference championship so easily. In 1922 (the final year for Muller's class) the Bears won all nine games and only three teams even scored against them: Santa Clara (a 45–14 Cal win), Washington (45–7) and Nevada (61–13). The only thing resembling a close game was against Rose Bowl-bound USC (12–0), and Stanford fell 28–0.

With Muller and the original Wonder Team gone (although the undefeated '23 and '24 teams continued to carry the nickname

with dignity), 1923 was supposed to be a rebuilding year, but they recorded an amazing nine shutouts in their ten games. Ironically, one of those shutouts wasn't enough; Nevada managed a 0–0 tie. The Bears were such heavy favorites in that game that, to spare Nevada embarrassment, it was agreed before the kickoff to shorten the quarters to ten minutes each. And Smith, confident of an easy victory, skipped the game in order to go to Palo Alto and scout Stanford, even though the Big Game was three weeks away.

Southern California again gave the Bears their toughest match, losing 13–7. California defeated Andy Kerr's Stanford team—the last Big Game Cal would win until 1931.

The next season was yet another undefeated one, although there were ties with Washington and Stanford; for the years 1920–24, Smith's teams won 44 games and tied four without a single loss. There were more great players—the best of them All-American center Edwin C 'Babe' Horrell, who captained the 1924 squad.

'Ball-carriers folded like an accordion when Babe tackled 'em,' Smith said, and Southern California coach Howard Jones added, 'Horrell approaches each game as though it's a world war. He has football instinct, courage and intelligence. He is one of the finest centers ever to play this game.'

But California was not to have things its own way for much longer; other coaches were beginning to build their own dynasties at other schools. The legendary Pop Warner arrived at Stanford in 1924 and immediately went undefeated, tying Cal 20–20 in one of the greatest Big Games of all time and the first game ever played in the Bears' Memorial Stadium. Fittingly, Babe Horrell scored the first touchdown in the new stadium by blocking a punt.

At Washington, Enoch Bagshaw was quietly building a powerhouse that would generate two conference titles in three years. And in Southern California some people were deciding that big-time college football was just the ticket.

The Trojans had been adequate but generally undistinguished during their early years, but *Los Angeles Express* sportswriter Harry Grayson began a campaign to change all that. When Mark Kelly, sports editor of the rival *Examiner* agreed, they approached USC officials and with their blessing began to line up civic support and look around for a coach. Grayson made contact with Elmer C 'Gus' Henderson, then a highly successful coach at Broadway High School in Seattle. Henderson was just what the Trojans were looking for—especially when he promised to bring most of the best players from his powerful high school team with him to Los Angeles.

Howard Jones, who followed Henderson at USC, is generally acknowledged as the man who put Trojan football on the map—but don't overlook Henderson. In six years, 'Gloomy Gus' won 45 games, lost only seven, took Southern California to the first of its many Rose Bowl victories and left Jones, who arrived in 1925, with a powerful nucleus that included All-Americans Brice Taylor and Mort Kaer, among others.

In 1919, Henderson's first year, his team played only five games but won four of them—losing only to Cal 14–13 and beating Stanford and Utah. In 1920 the Trojans were 6–0 (they did not play the Wonder Team) and in each of the next two years they were 10–1 with the single loss each season coming of course, to California. In 1922 that loss was by just 12–0 and since the Bears had taken themselves out of Rose Bowl consideration in their spat with the bowl committee the previous year, USC got the bid. The opponent was Penn State, coached by a man who was very familiar with Pasadena—Hugo Bezdek.

It was a hectic year for the abrasive Bezdek. He had a great team at Penn State in 1921 and actually received the Rose Bowl invitation then—nearly 13 months before the game was played—

since the Nittany Lions were expected to be even stronger in 1922. But one of his assistants, Dick Harlow, left during the off season to become head coach at Colgate and took six promising sophomore players who were mad at Bezdek with him. In the second half of the '22 season it caught up with the Lions. They lost to Navy—ending a 30-game unbeaten string—as well as Penn and Pitt, and were tied by Syracuse.

So when Bezdek—who had coached Oregon in the 1917 Rose Bowl and the Mare Island Marines in the 1918 game and won with both—returned to Pasadena, he was looking for any kind of edge he could get.

This 1 January 1923 game was the first played in the Arroyo Seco and the first actually given the name Rose Bowl. It drew 52,000 fans and the kickoff was set for 2:30 pm but when that hour came, there still was no sign of the Penn State team. Bezdek claimed the team buses had gotten tied up in traffic; others said it was a warm day and he wanted to wait until the sun had gone part way down—and perhaps until USC had worn itself out warming up.

The Trojans had indeed warmed up strenuously and Gloomy Gus Henderson was getting gloomier by the minute until finally, at 3:15 pm, a Penn State manager informed him that the Penn

State starting team had arrived. Henderson went to the middle of the field to meet Bezdek. The conversation reportedly went like this:

Henderson: 'Your manager tells me your first team has arrived. Don't you think you've delayed the game long enough? Let's get going.'

Bezdek: 'All of my players are not here, and I don't like it any better than you do. If you say I am responsible for delaying the game, you're a liar.'

Henderson: 'I only know what your manager said, and he seems to know what he's talking about. That makes you out a pretty good liar, and you can take it any way you want.'

Bezdek: 'You're not calling me a liar. Take off your glasses and we'll settle this thing right here and now.'

Unfortunately for the fans, perhaps, all they saw that day was a football game. Henderson had been suffering from the flu and more to the point, he said, 'I knew that Bezdek had earned his way through the University of Chicago fighting as a pro under an assumed name, so I decided it would be wiser if the two teams decided the issue.'

Wise move. Southern California won, 14–3. Following the game, both coaches—still angry—barred writers from the dressing rooms.

Henderson's Trojans continued to win in his final two years. They were 6–2 in 1923 but unfortunately both of the losses were in the conference—to California and to Washington (which went to the Rose Bowl that season). In 1924 USC came close to winning another Rose Bowl bid, even over unbeaten Stanford— which the Trojans did not play—but a 7–0 loss to Cal was followed immediately by a damaging 14–10 loss to St Mary's and Southern California finished 9–2.

Perhaps one other indication of Henderson's success may be found not in his wins but in his losses. California was rolling over everybody on the Pacific Coast by huge scores, yet four of the five games Henderson's Trojans played against the Bears—the exception was a 38–7 drubbing in 1921—were decided by a total of only 26 points.

With this kind of opposition springing up, California's string was destined to end. And in the third game of the 1925 season, after 50 straight games without defeat, the Bears finally fell to the Olympic Club of San Francisco 15 – 0. Then after shutting out the next four opponents, Cal also saw its string of five straight Pacific Coast Conference titles (won or shared) ended by a 7–0 loss to Bagshaw's Washington Huskies. In the next game the Bears also lost to Warner's Stanford team 27–1, as the great Ernie Nevers scored two touchdowns for the Cardinals in his final college game.

That made the Bears' season record 6–3, and Smith's ten–year mark at California 74 wins against just 16 losses and seven ties. What it might ultimately have become, nobody can ever know— because on 9 January 1926, Andrew Latham Smith, visiting in Philadelphia, died suddenly of pneumonia. He was just 43 years old.

In keeping with Smith's wishes, his ashes were scattered from an army plane over Memorial Stadium—the stadium he had been so instrumental in building—as a mourning student body led by the members of the Wonder Team looked on.

More than half a century later the Andy Smith Eulogy still is spoken at every California Big Game rally. And in Memorial Stadium, on the sideline right in front of the California rooting section, now stands a stone players' bench—the *Andy Smith*.

California Memorial Stadium *(at right)*, on the University of California campus in the Berkeley hills, can hold 76,780 football fans.

The Pop Warner Years

Andy Smith had come to the Pacific Coast as a promising young coach. Not so Pop Warner—when he arrived at Stanford in 1924, he already was recognized as one of the most innovative minds in the history of college football.

Warner had begun coaching in 1895—almost immediately after taking a law degree from Cornell. He had four straight unbeaten seasons—from 1915–18, during a long and successful tenure at Pittsburg. When Stanford approached him in 1922 he still had two years remaining on his contract with Pitt.

However, Warner accepted the Stanford job on the understanding that the Cardinals would have to wait until 1924. Meanwhile he sent two of his assistants, Andy Kerr and Tiny Thornhill, to Stanford to begin the building process.

Andy Kerr was to become a great coach in his own right. The little Scotsman had assisted Warner for seven seasons at Pitt, and he had learned (there were those who would tell you that Kerr taught Warner's double-wing formation better than Pop himself). Following two years as Stanford's head coach and two more as Warner's assistant there, Kerr became head coach at Washington and Jefferson. He went on to coach football until he was 71 years old, including many years as coach and advisor to the East team in the Shrine East-West charity game in San Francisco. He was named to the Football Hall of Fame in 1951.

So this was not a mere lame duck coach that in 1922 took over a happy-go-lucky Stanford team that was sadly lacking in discipline. In Kerr's first season the Cardinals finished with a 4–5 record—including season-ending losses to Smith's Cal Wonder Team and Warner's own Pittsburgh squad. In 1923 Stanford finished 7–2, the only losses being to USC and California. But far more importantly, he was installing the single and double-wing offenses that Warner had invented 15 years earlier, paving the way for his mentor's arrival.

Then, in 1924 Pop Warner came West and Pacific Coast Conference football immediately took on a decidedly Cardinal tinge.

Glenn Scobey Warner was the head coach in 451 collegiate games during his 44-year career. He won 313 of them, falling just one win short of the record of 314 then held by the immortal Amos Alonzo Stagg. (Stagg's record was broken by Bear Bryant in the 1970s and that mark in turn fell to Grambling's Eddie Robinson in 1985.) Warner's winning percentage (313–106–32) was .729.

However, Pop Warner contributed far more to football than a dazzling won-lost record. Stagg himself called Warner 'one of the excellent creators.' Pop was the first to use headgear (at Carlisle), the first to use the huddle and he invented the single and double-

wing offenses—with one or two wingbacks outside the ends and the other two backs taking the snap from center. If you think that's all outdated now, take a look at the 'new' formations in the National Football League: the shotgun, the three-wide-receiver alignments, the one-back offense. Right the first time! Those are nothing but variations—and sometimes not even variations—of Warner's old alignments.

He was the first to use trap plays and screen passes effectively and he used bewildering sets of spins, reverses, double reverses, fake reverses, runs from fake passes and passes from fake runs.

Allison Danzig of the *New York Times*, one of the great chroniclers of collegiate football, wrote of Warner:

'He was not the magnetic, vibrant personality that was Knute Rockne, but he was a dominant, forceful leader of men .... Contemplative, deliberative, a tinkerer who worked on car engines—dismantling them and then putting them back together again. He was one of the two most fertile and original minds football has known—the other being Amos Alonzo Stagg. Warner was preeminently a creator, and his fame is secure as one of the trailblazers who led football out of the wilderness of massed, close-order, push-and-pull play and into the open game of speed, deception and brains.... His was one of the more intelligent and visionary minds that helped to bring about the evolution of football from a mere physical test of unimaginative brute strength to a contest of skill.'

Warner's use of those tricky spins and reverses is the stuff of legend. In 1928 for example, Stanford played heavily-favored Army at Yankee Stadium in New York; the Cardinals won, 26–0, and one New York writer attempted to describe a key play where quarterback Herb Fleishhacker took the snap from center, did a half spin, faked to two wingbacks crossing behind him, then smashed up the middle. Sound simple? Just listen.

'Fleishhacker took the ball from Hoffman and gave it to Sims, who gave it to one of the guards pulling out of the line,' the befuddled reporter said. 'The next thing I knew, Fleishhacker had the ball again and was 20 yards down the field. How the hell he got the ball I'll never know.'

During his stretch at Carlisle, Warner's team was playing Harvard and the Crimson (who ultimately won the game, 12–11) had just scored. Jimmy Johnson took the ensuing kickoff for Carlisle and, as the usual wedge of players formed in front of him, Charlie Dillon turned to face his own goal line—and Johnson stuffed the ball up the back of Dillon's jersey, where a rubber strip had been

Pop Warner (right) was one of football's master strategists and innovators. Alonzo Stagg called Pop 'one the excellent creators.'

been sewn to hold the ball in place. The wedge, including the now humpbacked Dillon, charged up the field into the Harvard defenders, who struggled to get at the Carlisle player they thought had the ball—actually, it was his helmet—tucked under his arm. Dillon casually detached himself from the melee and trotted toward the sideline, then suddenly broke into a run toward the goal line, followed by referee Mike Thompson, who had been alerted before the play.

'I went flying behind him,' Thompson said later. 'The Harvard team ignored us, and many of the 25,000 spectators thought I was chasing Dillon off the field for some infraction of the rules.' When the crowd detected the hump on Dillon's back, however, the roar grew and the Harvard players finally caught on; they gave chase, but in vain.

Harvard complained bitterly, and finally insisted that such a play was 'not honest' and a rule should be written against it. There soon was.

In fact, Stagg once said that Warner was more responsible than any other man for the enactment of rules that improved football. 'Glenn was never very active on the rules committee, but we'd make a rule and Glenn would think up a way to get around it within the rules and we'd have to meet his challenge. He kept us on our toes, I can tell you.'

In 1926, California had a guard named Bert Schwartz; he would become an All-American, but in the Big Game that year he was just another overzealous sophomore and time after time Warner exploited his eagerness with a trap play in which Dick Hyland would block Schwartz from the blind side, then roll away as the fullback smashed up the middle.

The Bears just couldn't figure out what was happening. After he had been trapped thusly for about the fourth time, Schwartz pulled himself up to his knees, looked up at the 80,000 fans in Memorial Stadium, raised both hands to the heavens and screamed: 'God Almighty, please tell me where they're coming from.' A lot of Pop Warner's opponents in 44 years felt that way.

Don't get the idea that Warner was unethical, however—just tricky. His tricks were all within the rules and he never condoned dirty play. 'I don't believe anyone can play two kinds of football, good and dirty, at the same time,' he once said. 'I want my boys to play good football.'

And before the 1927 Rose Bowl game against Alabama, Pop told his players: 'Last year Alabama played Washington here. It was a rough game. We don't want Wallace Wade (the Alabama coach) and his boys to think all Coast football is played like that. The first man I see doing anything he shouldn't will come off the field and he's through.'

'Glenn Warner was one of the finest coaches of our time, and of all time,' Wade said many years later. '... A very popular, attractive man. His players loved him and his opponents respected him.'

Warner had lettered in football (as a guard), baseball, boxing and track at Cornell, where he earned his nickname because he was a few years older than the average student. But he was far more than just an athlete; his hobbies included tinkering in the workshop, songwriting and painting, and although there's no record of him ever selling an invention or a song, he did sell several watercolors (mostly landscapes). Following his 1895 graduation, he passed the New York bar, opened a law office, and decided almost immediately that he'd rather coach a football team—or more precisely—two football teams. In 1895 and '96, he coached Iowa State from August 15 until the first game, then immediately shifted to Athens, Georgia, to coach the University of Georgia for the rest of the season.

Above: Glenn 'Pop' Warner is shown here, already (in 1894) exuding confidence and leadership as a member of the Cornell squad.

Following his term at Georgia, he coached at Cornell, Carlisle and Pittsburgh before moving to Stanford. He immediately set the Pacific Coast Conference on its ear.

Warner's first Stanford team, in 1924, was unbeaten going into the final game with California, despite the fact that the Cardinals had not had their great junior fullback, Ernie Nevers, for most of the season; he broke his ankle before the first game, did not return until the sixth game against Utah and almost immediately broke the other ankle. To make matters worse for the Cardinals, their fastest back and best punter, Norman Cleaveland, was declared ineligible by a Stanford faculty committee two days before the Big Game.

Andy Smith's Cal team also was unbeaten, and it was the first game ever played in the Bears' new Memorial Stadium. Scalpers were getting $100 for a pair of tickets—and remember, this was 1924, when a dollar was worth something. There were 73,000 fans jammed into the stadium, and thousands more dotting the now-famous 'Tightwad Hill' that overlooked the field.

In a rivalry that has seen many great games, this was one of the greatest. Both Warner and Walter Camp, who was on hand, called it the most dramatic football game they'd ever seen.

California led 20–6 with just ten minutes to play, but Stanford, led by reserve Ed Walker and Murray Cuddeback, came roaring back. Walker passed to Ted Shipkey for one touchdown and then,

Two of Pop Warner's best at halfback—and possibly two of the best ever, and anywhere: Ernie Nevers *(above)*, who was Stanford's Blonde Block Buster of the mid-20s, and who Pop himself chose as 'the greatest football player of all time' over Jim Thorpe *(above right)*, who, by a national sportswriters' poll in 1969, was voted the Number One backfield star of football's first 50 years, and has been said by many to be the best all-around athlete of all time.

with less than three minutes remaining the Cardinals drove 81 yards, capped by Walker's 34-yard touchdown pass to Cuddeback. Cuddeback also kicked the conversion—his 14th point of the day—and the game ended in a 20–20 tie.

Still unbeaten (8–0–1), Stanford seemed the logical choice for an invitation to Pasadena, especially since California (8–0–2) still was feuding with the Rose Bowl Committee. There was considerable political pressure in Southern California to get USC into the Rose Bowl again, but Gus Henderson's Trojans had lost to California and also to St Mary's. Stanford was invited to the bowl, while California invited Eastern power Pennsylvania to a 1 January 1925 game in their new stadium.

The Bears won that 14–0, but all eyes that day were on Pasadena, where it was Stanford, Pop Warner and Ernie Nevers against Notre Dame, Knute Rockne and the Four Horsemen—a classic confrontation with the National Championship at stake. The Fighting Irish won the game 27–10—their first bowl appearance ever and their last for another 45 years—but that Rose Bowl will forever be remembered for one man: Ernie Nevers.

Warner coached too many great players to even list, including Jim Thorpe at Carlisle. But to Pop, Nevers was his greatest.

'Many veteran coaches argued my selection of Ernie Nevers as the greatest player I ever coached, when I also coached the great Jim Thorpe,' Warner said many years later. 'I still pick Ernie, be-

cause I never saw him do anything but his best, in any situation. He was always putting on the pressure, whether it was a big game or a little one, or a drill against the subs. He knew only one way to compete, and that was all out.

'Jim, on the other hand, would ease up when he felt safe in doing so. Sometimes he found it wasn't as safe as he thought it was, and this made him a bit of an in-and-outer. I'll pick the all-outer over the in-and-outer any day, if their skill is about the same.'

Nevers still was recovering from his broken ankles as the Rose Bowl approached; he had the casts removed just ten days before the game, and even one day before they were to play he told Warner, 'How can I play? I can't even walk.' A set of braces that Warner, the inveterate tinkerer, made in his workshop out of inner tubes was no help, but Pop still was adamant: Nevers would start, even if he could only play a few minutes.

Nevers played the entire game, 60 minutes. With both ankles so tightly taped that he had virtually no feeling below the knees, he carried the ball 34 times for 114 yards—more than all four of the famous Four Horsemen combined. He passed for a touchdown. He punted for a 42-yard average. He blocked like a madman and was in on three-quarters of the tackles on defense. He intercepted a pass to set up a touchdown.

Stanford outgained the Irish by more than 100 yards. 'We spotted Notre Dame 21 points,' Warner said afterward (referring

STANFORD
vs
NOTRE DAME

Jim Lawson
STANFORD CAPTAIN

Adam Walsh
NOTRE DAME CAPTAIN

Pasadena Rose Bowl
January 1st 1925

Official Souvenir Program

Published by the Board of Athletic Control
Stanford University

Price 25c

Notre Dame's backfield was known as the 'Four Horsemen,' but to their loved ones they were (above right, left to right) Don Miller, Elmer Layden, James 'Sleepy Jim' Crowley and Harry Stuhldreher. At left: The 1925 Rose Bowl game program. This game pitted Knute Rockne's Four Horsemen against Pop Warner's Ernie Nevers. Notre Dame won 27–10, despite spectacular Stanford yardage.

to two pass interceptions and a fumble recovery that gave the Irish three touchdowns). 'Except for those errors we completely outplayed them. Notre Dame was great, but I think I had the better team.'

Rockne, the Irish coach whom Warner once called 'the greatest football coach of all time,' agreed that 'Stanford might have won except for several unwise quarterback calls (referring to two flat passes by Nevers that were intercepted by Elmer Layden and run back for touchdowns).'

But whichever was the better team, Warner had the best player. 'No one on the field today performed more brilliantly than Nevers,' the Associated Press report of the game said. 'Except for one occasion when he was halted on the eight-inch line, the Notre Dame line was unable to stop his terrific smashes that carried the force of every ounce of his 200 pounds.'

After the game, Rockne wrote in a newspaper article: 'In Ernie Nevers, Stanford has as formidable a triple threat as any have ever seen. A powerful line smasher, he ripped off yards and yards almost every time he was given the ball. He also passed with an uncanny accuracy and with rifle-like speed. It was no fault of Nevers that Stanford is not tonight the recognized football champions of the country.'

Adam Walsh, the Notre Dame captain and All-American center, was somewhat less flowery. 'Nevers was tremendous,' he said. 'He gained enough ground that day to win ten ball games, but it was between the 20-yard lines. I was black and blue for ten days from contact with him.'

Rockne started his substitutes, his shock troops, which was a

not-uncommon maneuver at that time, to feel Stanford out before bringing in his starters. The Four Horsemen was the nickname hung on the quartet of Harry Stuhldreher, Don Miller, Elmer Layden and Sleepy Jim Crowley by Grantland Rice after their great upset win over Army; the Notre Dame line then, naturally enough, came to be known as the Seven Mules.

Layden scored the first of his three touchdowns on a short run, then intercepted a Nevers pass and returned it more than 60 yards (estimates at the time, when statistics were more guesswork than anything, ranged up to 85 yards) for another score. Stanford mounted a drive but fumbled at the Notre Dame 10-yard line late in the first half, and the Irish had a 13–3 lead at intermission. Another Stanford fumble led to another Notre Dame score in the third quarter, and the Cardinals trailed 20–3.

It looked bleak, but then Nevers went to work. He intercepted a pass at the Irish 29-yard line to set up a touchdown and make the score 20–10 and then, after another Stanford interception deep in Notre Dame territory, he helped the Cardinals move to a first down at the six-yard line. What followed is one of the most famous sequences in Rose Bowl history. Nevers carried twice, got five yards and it was third down at the one-yard line, two tries to make one yard and the touchdown that would turn it into a close ball game.

Nevers tried again. Half a yard. On fourth down he carried yet again; it was so close that Walter Eckersall, the head linesman who was used to being a referee in the Midwest, threw his hands in the air to signal touchdown.

Later he said, 'I wasn't the referee, it wasn't my call,' and refused to second-guess.

And Nevers was ruled down—some said eight inches away from the goal, some said one inch. It might as well have been a mile. Instead of the score being 20–17, it was still 20–10, and another interception and touchdown by Layden turned the final score into a very non-indicative 27–10.

Ernie Nevers was originally from Willow River, Minnesota—a big blond Scandinavian who came West to Santa Rosa, California, and attended high school there. He played in the line on a team that was so new, with a coach so inexperienced, that Nevers diagrammed most of the plays. He was so talented a runner—with power to spare and enough speed to run away from the defense as well as over it—that it was only a matter of time until he became a fullback.

He was selected as a first team All-American by Grantland Rice in 1924—even though he played only briefly because of the ankle injuries—and again in 1925. After leaving Stanford, Nevers not only played professional football for the old Duluth Eskimos and the Chicago (now St Louis) Cardinals of the National Football League, but he also was a major league pitcher for the St Louis Browns. When Babe Ruth hit his record 60 home runs in 1927, two of them were hit off of Nevers.

Ernie was nicknamed 'Big Dog' because he was so easygoing off the field, but that attitude didn't carry over when he put on the pads. Enoch Bagshaw of Washington, another of the many fine coaches in the Pacific Coast Conference in that period, had this to say after Nevers was literally knocked out of the Stanford Washington game in 1925, which decided the PCC title:

'You had to admire that Nevers. On defense he was everywhere, tackling behind the line or knocking down passes in the secondary. He's an all-time master. And tough? I'll never forget seeing him throwing his helmet to the sidelines and playing bareheaded in a fury of determination when the going got tough. He can run like a sprinter through a sliver of an opening or plow like a battleship through a mass of tacklers. His punts always seem on the verge of sailing out of the stadium, and he never admits defeat.'

Washington won that game with Stanford 13–0 on a muddy field, and with it their second Rose Bowl trip in three years. The Cardinals finished with a 6–2 record that year, beating California for the first time since the Rugby days 27–14, as Nevers scored two touchdowns in his final college game. Stanford also met UCLA—which was not to enter the PCC for three more years—for the first time.

The final score was Stanford 82, UCLA 0. Welcome to big-time football.

That relatively poor year (how many coaches would love to have a 6–2 record?) was simply a short hiatus for Warner, however; in 1926 Stanford again was undefeated, capping a 10–0 season with a 41–6 rout of California and then tying Wallace Wade's Alabama team in the Rose Bowl. Warner, ever full of those tricks, introduced silk pants in that game, and although it earned a lot of catcalls and insults from the 'Bama players, it also made the Cardinals extremely hard to tackle. Stanford outgained the Crimson Tide by 305 yards to 98 and was in command all the way, but Alabama blocked a punt at the Cardinal 14-yard line to set up a last minute touchdown and forge the tie.

In 1927 Stanford's record fell to 7–2, but that was good enough for yet another Rose Bowl invitation—this time against Pittsburgh. The Panthers were coached by Jock Sutherland, who had played guard for Warner on the 1916 Pitt team that many consider Pop's greatest squad ever.

Warner claimed that that 7–6 Rose Bowl win over Pittsburgh was the toughest game any team of his ever played. 'I have seen many games where one team or the other played itself to exhaustion, but in yesterday's contest both sides fought with equal fury, and when the last whistle blew, every player on the field was well used up,' he said.

Frankie Wilton, whose blocked punt set up Alabama's tying touchdown the year before, appeared on his way to being a goat again—he fumbled early in the game to give Pitt a 6–0 lead. But following the ensuing kickoff, he helped lead a drive to the Panther two-yard line. From there, Bob Sims caught a pass in the flat, but fumbled; Wilton outwrestled three Pitt players for the ball, picked it up and dove over the goal line with it. Biff Hoffman then kicked the winning conversion.

This game was yet another tribute to Warner's ingenuity. Stanford ran for 203 yards and a lot of it came on a play that Pop had put in especially for Hoffman—and aimed especially at Pittsburgh left guard Alec Fox. Hoffman would take the snap from center and then stand straight up with his arm raised as if to pass. Sometimes he did throw, but he also had the option of using the old Statue of Liberty play with wingback Dick Hyland taking the ball. And most often of all, Hoffman would just tuck the ball away and drive into the line—right over the retreating Fox's spot.

'Dammit, if I didn't know enough to back out when I see a pass coming, Hoffman would not have made a yard,' Fox told Hyland after the game. Told of that comment, Warner smiled: 'You know,' he said, 'I scouted their (Pitt's) game with Penn State. That Fox fellow seemed to handle himself very well. Sometimes you put in a play to fool a smart player that a dumb one would not react to. I thought Fox was pretty smart.' And that, as well as anything, reflected Pop Warner's coaching philosophy.

That was Warner's last Rose Bowl, although the Cardinals continued to win. In 1928 they had an 8–3–1 record, but were very unpredictable—they lost to USC 10–0 for example, although outgaining the Trojans by more than 500 yards to 125—primarily because they fumbled five times inside the USC five-yard line in the first half alone. In 1929 Stanford was 9–2, including a 57–0 romp over UCLA (the Bruins were getting closer, however); in 1930 the Cards were 9–1–1 and in 1931 were 7–2–1, including a 6–0 loss to Cal—Warner's first defeat in eight Big Games.

In 1932 Stanford won its first five games, but finished with a 6–4–1 record and following that season Warner, then 61 years old, announced he was leaving Stanford for Temple. His record in nine years at the Cardinal helm was 71 wins, 17 losses and eight ties, but football coaching is the most tenuous of professions; he had lost five straight times to Howard Jones' USC teams, and the alumni were grumbling. The players petitioned Warner to stay, but Pop always liked a challenge and Temple was elevating its football program; besides, that string of defeats by Southern California—four of them shutouts—had about convinced him that Stanford's personnel would have trouble continuing to win consistently in the ever-improving PCC. And so he left the Cardinal fortunes to his long-time assistant Tiny Thornhill and the Vow Boys.

Warner coached six more years—five of them winning ones—and his Temple team played in the first Sugar Bowl game following the 1934 season.

Glenn Warner could be an irascible old soul; he smoked heavily, was known to take more than a nip of whiskey and had a vocabulary charitably described as colorful. In his book on Stanford athletics, *The Color of Life Is Red*, Don Liebendorfer, long-time Stanford sports publicist and a close friend of Pop's wrote:

'Warner was a strangely contradictory character, whose gruff, sometimes almost surly and sullen exterior concealed a big and very warm heart. The great coach was penurious and "tighter than the paper on the wall" about little things. But let a former player or associate come to Pop with a hard-luck story, and the purse strings loosened immediately. A fierce competitor, both as

Ernie Nevers (right) was Stanford's very great fullback, and led Stanford's defeat of Cal in 1926. In the 1925 Rose Bowl, he ran for 114 yards and punted for an average of 42 yards—with two broken ankles! Pop Warner said 'Nevers always gave 100 percent.'

NOVEMBER STANFOR

STANFOR

The 21 November 1931 Big Game program cover *(these pages)* featured Pop Warner's Indians jousting with Bill Ingram's Bears. Cal 'unhorsed' their opponents 6–0, handing Pop his first defeat in eight Big Games—on home turf (ouch!), too.

STANFORD

At left: The 'Boy Plunger' grew up, and with a commandingly scepti-cal glance, fixed his future as the University of Washington football coach from 1921-29. With terrific players like super star George Wilson *(above)*, Washington was a terror in the '20s.

a player and as a coach, he came up with surprising exhibitions of compassion, and never poured it on.'

When Warner's Stanford team wasn't going to the Rose Bowl in that stretch, it seemed that Enoch Bagshaw's Washington Huskies were. Bagshaw was following a tough act at Seattle—Gil Dobie, who had been undefeated in 61 games as the Washington coach. Ray Eckman, an All-Coast halfback who years later served as the Huskies' athletic director, described the situation thusly: 'The situation here was practically impossible for any coach. The alumni and citizens are used to winning … years in a row. If a ball game is lost, it's "Well, what's wrong?"'

Eckman was talking about Claude Hunt, who had replaced Dobie following the 1916 season. Because of the war, the Huskies only played six games total in the next two years. In 1919 Hunt went 5–1 and tied for the PCC title, but didn't get invited to the Rose Bowl and the alums were livid. He resigned. Stub Allison, who much later was to coach California, held the job for one year—and simultaneously was the basketball and baseball coach—but had a losing record that obviously was not acceptable.

Following that season the Huskies formed a massive committee and staged a month-long, nation-wide hunt for a new coach. They found him right in their own backyard, at Everett High School—just north of Seattle. Enoch Bagshaw had taken the Everett job immediately after graduating from Washington, where he had captained the football team; in 12 years at Everett, his teams scored more than 3000 points and allowed just 375.

He had just a 3–4–1 record in 1921, and lost to California's Wonder Team, 72–3. That was a bitter pill for Husky followers to swallow, but this time they knew they had the right man to rebuild the program in the 'Little Giant,' a loud, outspoken taskmaster. In 1922 the Huskies were 6–1–1, again losing to Cal and in 1923 Bagshaw's 'Super Sophs' went 10–1 during the regular season, beating Gus Henderson (who had been considered for the Washington job before Bagshaw was chosen) and his defending Rose Bowl champs from USC, and losing only to unbeaten California, 9–0. With the Bears out of the Rose Bowl

picture by their own choice, Washington was invited to Pasadena to meet Navy.

The Midshipmen, who had accepted the bid before the season even began, finished 5–1–2 under Bob Folwell (who had coached Penn in a previous Rose Bowl). Navy used a wide-open passing game, and completed its first 14 passes to take a lead, but George Wilson, who would become one of Washington's greatest players, scored one touchdown and a trick pass to All-Coast guard James Bryan, who lined up as an end, brought the Huskies back. Les Sherman kicked both extra points despite a broken toe and the game ended in a 14–14 tie.

Washington finished 8–1–1 the next year, and tied powerful Cal, but lost to Pop Warner's first Stanford team and had a 0–0 tie with upstart Oregon (just how big an upset that was is demonstrated by the two teams' games against a mutual opponent—Oregon had a 0–0 tie with Willamette, the same team that Washington had beaten 57–0). If there was any unrest in Seattle over that season, however, the 1925 team stilled it.

Those 'Super Sophs' were seniors now, and George Wilson was an All-American halfback. Teamed with powerful fullback Elmer Tesreau, Wilson gave the Huskies one of the finest backfields in the nation. They led the country in scoring with 480 points to just 59 for the opposition; they ended Cal's PCC win streak with a 7–0 win on Tesreau's 26-yard scoring run and Andy Smith said afterward, 'We have no alibi, we will have none. Washington was the stronger team.' A 6–6 tie with Nebraska was the only regular-season blemish and whereas two years earlier it had been a struggle for the Huskies to get into the Rose Bowl, now they were doubly blessed.

Not only did they receive an invitation to Pasadena, but they were courted by a rival post-season game (which never really got off the ground) to showcase the new Los Angeles Coliseum. At first, Washington refused the Rose Bowl bid but pleas from fans, alumni and the Rose Bowl Committee got the Huskies to change their minds, and they went south to meet Alabama.

This was the first bowl appearance by the Tide and the first of many as a coach by Wallace Wade. As late as 1951, a poll still ranked the game among the ten greatest of all time.

Washington took a quick 12–0 lead, and at that point the two conversions they missed didn't look important. Wilson, the Huskies' great triple-threat, intercepted a pass and then ripped off a 25-yard run to set up the first score and his 36-yard run set up his own touchdown pass for the second. But Wilson, who had problems all season with the aftermath of a pneumonia bout the previous summer, was carried off the field, exhausted and with a rib injury in the second quarter, and Alabama roared back for three touchdowns and a 20–12 lead in the third period.

Wilson returned in the fourth quarter and threw his second touchdown pass of the game, but it wasn't quite enough and 'Bama hung on, 20–19. For the day, Wilson had 134 yards in 15 carries in addition to his two touchdown passes and while he was out of the game, Washington gained a total of just 17 yards.

One of the stars of that Alabama team, incidentally, was halfback Johnny Mack Brown, who later became a Hollywood cowboy star.

That was the last title for Bagshaw's Huskies. From 1926–28 they went 8–2, 9–2 and 7–4, but unfortunately all eight of those losses were to PCC opponents and the grumbling was getting louder. Following a 2–6–1 season in 1929, Bagshaw resigned and entered private business.

The balance of power in the Pacific Coast Conference was moving south again, and this time it didn't stop at Berkeley and Palo Alto. The Thundering Herd was beginning to gather at Southern California.

Howard Jones and the Thundering Herd

The 1920s were known as the 'Golden Age of Sports' and so far as Pacific Coast Conference football was concerned, that certainly was the case.

Some of the greatest players in the history of the game—Ernie Nevers at Stanford, Brick Muller and Babe Horrell at Cal, Morley Drury at USC, George Wilson at Washington and innumerable others—were performing for some of the greatest coaches. Pop Warner and Andy Smith each was in his own way unique, but they were not the only exceptional coaches around.

Howard Jones came to Southern California in 1925 and stayed for 16 seasons. During that time his teams compiled one of the most impressive records in the game: seven Pacific Coast Conference titles, three national championships (and chosen by at least some polls for that spot in three other years) and five Rose Bowl victories in five tries. Jones' overall record with the Trojans was 121 wins, 36 losses and 13 ties. Gloomy Gus Henderson had brought USC to the top; Howard Jones cemented the Trojans' spot in national football prominence.

Unlike Warner with his tricky spins and reverses, Jones was a strict traditionalist. The USC game was power; the left halfback carried the ball almost exclusively with the other three backs as blockers—and they ran to the strong side perhaps 90 percent of the time. When the starting left halfback got tired, Howard simply put in another one and ran him for awhile—a pattern, incidentally, that has remained a big part of USC football for more than half a century.

He emphasized line play. 'Lick a man and hold your position,' was his theory. 'You have a spot about a yard or two either side of you to see that nobody gets through. No matter who winds up with the ball, they won't go anywhere if you guard your own small territory and don't get faked out, trying to find where the ball is.'

Jones lived on that philosophy throughout his coaching career. Joe Shell, captain of his next-to-last team in 1939, once noted, 'More than 60 percent of our total practice time was involved with purely fundamental blocking and tackling positions.'

Jones also recognized the fundamental principle that good players make good coaches, and he knew how to get them. He had 19 All-Americans in his time at Southern Cal. Babe Hollingbery, another of the great coaches of the era, at Washington State, once said, 'The Trojan practice field looks like Churchill Downs on Derby day—and Howard knows what to do with his thoroughbreds, too.'

No wonder they called those Southern California teams of the late '20s and early '30s 'The Thundering Herd.'

Jones occasionally played golf or bridge, or fished—but virtually all of his waking hours were put into devising formations, plays and defenses. He would get so preoccupied that he sometimes got lost driving home, and often he had to be asked questions two or three times because his mind was on the game.

'Howard lived and breathed football,' Al Wesson, the USC sports publicist during that period, once said. 'If it were not for football he would have starved to death—he couldn't possibly have made a living in business. His assistants tried to get him to organize the practices and let them do most of the heavy work: he'd promise to do it but after 15 minutes on the field he'd be down on the ground showing them personally how to block, following every play on the dead run and acting as though he were still playing end at Yale.

'His putting so much into the game was undoubtedly the cause of his premature death from a heart attack in 1941, at the age of 56. He just couldn't relax and let others do the heavy work.'

Howard Harding Jones was born in the aptly-named town of Excello, Ohio, in 1885. He played end at Yale; his brother Tad, who also became an outstanding coach, was the quarterback on the same team and got far more notice—but that was just fine with Howard, a shy man who hated publicity.

At right: **Howard Jones meant business when it came to football—his Trojans won seven Pacific Coast Conference titles, five Rose Bowls, three national championships (and were nominated for three more). Jones literally lived football, and loved the 'nitty gritty.'**

Howard Harding Jones *(above)* **had been a star end at Yale (1905–07), and became Yale's first paid football coach. He was so deeply centered on football that he forgot socks and keys, was oblivious to appointments and traffic signals, and in short, gave his all to football.** *Opposite:* **Notre Dame's great football coach, Knute Rockne.**

As conservative off the field as on—again the antithesis of the colorful Pop Warner—Jones was a humorless man, inwardly sensitive but with a forbidding exterior. He never drank, although he was a nervous smoker, and his strongest expletive was 'Dad burn it.' He was seldom demonstrative—although he did kiss his captain, Stan Williamson, on the field after the great 1931 victory over Notre Dame—and he was against anything that he felt interfered with an athlete's dedication to the sport, even dancing.

His nickname at Yale was 'Mother.' It's easy to see why.

One of Jones' greatest admirers was Bob Zuppke, the fine coach at Illinois, who admired Howard's thoroughness. One day in 1935 Zuppke and Jones visited Grantland Rice, and during their conversation Zuppke told Jones, 'You are a great coach, Howard, but you'd be an even greater one if you'd take a drink once in awhile. You'd have more imagination.'

'I never heard of a drink yet figuring out a play,' Jones retorted.

'You never did?' Zuppke asked. 'Well, I've just had two drinks and I've figured out three new plays.... I'll diagram them for you. I'm going to use them next fall when Illinois meets Southern California.'

Zuppke did use all three plays. All three scored. Illinois won 19–0. What a setback for sobriety.

But for all his social stiffness, Jones was a great coach. He began his career at Syracuse in 1908; coached Yale to an unbeaten, untied and unscored upon season in 1909; was at Ohio State in 1910 and returned to Yale as its first paid coach in 1913. In between he tried his hand at business but as Al Wesson would have predicted, Jones' heart was not in it. He committed himself fully to coaching in 1916 at Iowa and built a powerful program, going unbeaten in 1921—when his team beat Knute

Rockne's Notre Dame squad to end a 21-game Irish unbeaten streak—and again in 1922, building a 20-game undefeated string of his own that finally was ended in 1923 by Illinois and a sophomore named Red Grange.

After one season at Duke, Jones replaced Elmer Henderson at Southern California in 1925. He coached there until his early death. Overall, his coaching record was 194–64–21.

And Jones was not picking on patsies. With all of the great coaches around at that time, he held a winning edge on every one of them except Rockne; Notre Dame beat Howard four times in six tries—but three of the losses were by one point.

Consider Jones' five Rose Bowl victories. In 1930, USC beat Pittsburgh, coached by Jock Sutherland, 47–14; in '32, it was Tulane and Bernie Bierman who fell 21–12; and in '33, another rout of Sutherland's Pitt team 35–0; in 1939, a 7–3 victory over Duke and Wallace Wade; and in 1940 USC beat Tennessee and General Robert Neyland 14–0. Every one of those coaches is in the Football Hall of Fame.

But Jones perhaps liked to beat Warner best of all. 'Howard had great respect for Pop Warner,' Wesson said, 'and he always worked his hardest to get ready for Stanford.'

The two first met when Jones was at Syracuse and lost to Warner's Carlisle team. Pop barely beat USC in Jones' first two years there, 13–9 in 1925 and 13–12 in 1926. They tied in 1927 13–13, but Jones' innovative defense caught up with the double wing at that point and Warner never defeated him again. In their final five meetings before Pop left Stanford, USC won four by shutouts—and the other by a 41–12 score.

Jones also had a great rivalry with Notre Dame and Rockne. In November of 1924 Stanford and California both terminated relations with USC; that altercation was patched up within a year, but in the meantime sportswriters Harry Grayson and Mark Kelly, who had begun the campaign to make USC a football power in 1919, were looking for a 'name' opponent to fill the gap. They contacted Rockne and a great series was begun.

Two of the most memorable games between the two great powers were in 1930 and '31. In 1930 USC had lost to Rose Bowl-bound Washington State in the third game of the season, but had walloped everybody else until the final game of the season, when they met the Fighting Irish. That Notre Dame team, quarterbacked by the brilliant Frank Carideo, was unbeaten and Pop Warner said it 'ranked with the greatest teams of all time,' but several players were injured by the time they got to Los Angeles. Rockne, master psychologist that he was, wasn't going to let the Trojans forget it.

At a USC rally the night before the game, Rockne spoke; he painted a dismal picture of his team, and offered the hope that the big strong Trojans wouldn't be too hard on his poor little players—to at least spare them serious injury. The Trojans swallowed it whole. Notre Dame won, 27–0.

That turned out to be Knute Rockne's last game. Four months later, on 31 March 1931 he died in the crash of a private plane in a Kansas wheatfield.

The 1931 rematch, at South Bend, Indiana was one of the classic football games of all time. Both teams were undefeated, Notre Dame—now coached by Hunk Anderson—sporting a 26-game unbeaten string. Southern California, on its way to the Rose Bowl and a national championship, had eight current or future All-Americans on the field. This is how Allison Danzig reported it in the *New York Times*:

'One of the greatest winning streaks compiled in football since the time of Michigan's Point-a-Minute teams of a generation ago came to an end with one minute to play today as Notre Dame's all-conquering horde, unbeaten in three years, went down in

Irving 'Cotton' Warburton *(at top)* a 146-pound star quarterback in 1932-33, figured heroically in many of Cal's victories. He spent half of one game in a daze, making a 63-yard touchdown run that he later could not remember. Morley Drury *(above),* 'The Noblest Trojan of Them All,' was one the Thundering Herd's best halfbacks.

stunning defeat before one of the hardest running, fiercest tackling elevens that ever stepped upon a gridiron.'

The Irish had taken a 14-0 lead into the last quarter, but USC battled back to score two touchdowns and trail 14-13. All-American guard Johnny Baker had missed one of the conversions, which looked disastrous, but in the final minute of play Baker—who had never kicked a field goal in a game before—booted a 33-yarder to give the Trojans the 16-14 victory.

Danzig's 1930s prose was up to the occasion: 'That pigskin parabola through the air, which gave Southern California its first victory over Notre Dame in three years, and a thoroughly

deserved one, if leonine courage, berserk tackling and reckless abandon in running are football virtues, left the great throng stunned and overwhelmed with despair, save for the handful of Trojan rooters, who were fairly delirious with joy.'

Wow!

The Southern Californians spent little time celebrating in the dressing room. Within hours after the end of the game, Howard Jones had sought out Knute Rockne's gravesite, and he and the entire USC team were gathered there for an impromptu memorial service.

The Trojans went unbeaten for the rest of the season, including a post-season but pre-Rose Bowl game against Southern power Georgia. Granted that the Bulldogs were battered and road-weary from a hard schedule, USC's 60-0 win certainly clinched its National championship, especially when it was followed by a 21-12 victory over Tulane in the Rose Bowl. In Jones' first Rose Bowl, the 1930 romp over Pittsburgh, it had been the passing game that won; Russ Saunders and Marshall Duffield combined to throw for 279 yards and four touchdowns, with Saunders' first three passes in the game all going for TDs. This time it was the running game—Erny Pinckert raced 25 and 30 yards for scores to provide the difference.

The following year, in the 1 January 1933 Rose Bowl, it was 146-pound sophomore Cotton Warburton who was the hero with two touchdowns in the 35-0 win over Pittsburgh. That team may have been the greatest of Howard Jones' many great teams at USC; after losing the opening game of the 1931 season to St Mary's, the Trojans won their next 25 in a row, were tied 0-0 by Oregon State and then beat California before the undefeated streak finally ended at 27 with a 13-7 loss to the Stanford Vow Boys midway through the 1933 season.

It is hard to single out Jones' greatest player—there were so many. Mort Kaer, in 1925, was the first Trojan All-American and the first of seven halfbacks to make national honors under Jones. The best might have been Morley Drury, the 'Noblest Trojan of Them All,' who finished his career in 1927 with a 180-yard, three-touchdown effort against Washington that drew an incredible ovation from the packed stadium. Drury set what were then USC records in his senior year with 223 carries and 1163 yards in addition to passing, punting, calling signals and playing strong defense. Had he not been sidelined with a knee injury in the 13-12 loss to Stanford in 1926—USC's only loss of the year until the final game against Notre Dame—the Trojans might have been in the Rose Bowl that season.

If Drury was indeed Jones' best player, Irving 'Cotton' Warburton must have been the most colorful. The little quarterback was an All-American in 1933, but it would have been hard to equal his sophomore year the season before. He scored the touchdown that beat Washington 9-6; he was the star of a 13-0 win over Notre Dame; his two touchdowns broke open the Rose Bowl game against Pitt. But the best run of all might have been the one that beat California.

Warburton had been knocked out while making a tackle in the first half and was taken to the locker room. When the team went out for the second half, he was just sort of overlooked; assistant manager John Lehners, returning to look for him, found that Cotton had showered and was sitting naked on a pile of blankets, trying to get dressed and convinced that the game was over. Lehners finally convinced him that they were still playing, got him back into uniform and out onto the field, where the second half already was well under way.

'I asked Dr Packard Thurber, the team physician, to take a look at Cotton,' Lehners recalled later. 'Quite frankly, I had no idea they'd allow him back into the game. The next time I looked up, there he was running for the touchdown; I was never so surprised in my life.' Warburton's 60-yard touchdown run gave USC a 6-3 victory over the Bears and preserved the Trojan unbeaten streak at 27, although Stanford ended that the next week.

Cotton never did remember that touchdown run, or much of anything else about the game.

Not all of Jones' famous players were All-Americans; some made their mark elsewhere. One was a rangy tackle—six feet, four-inch, 205-pound Marion Morrison, nicknamed Duke. 'He has the perfect build for a lineman,' Jones said. 'He's strong, he's aggressive, he's not shy about slugging it out. He can help us.' Morrison never became a great football player, but he did all right in Hollywood after he changed his name to John Wayne.

Morrison had a summer job as an extra at Fox Studios, and he once rounded up some of his teammates for a football movie. One of them, a boisterous 220-pound tackle who, the Duke insisted, talked a better game than he played, caught the eye of a director who thought he was just ugly enough to be an actor. His name was Wardell (Ward) Bond.

That 1928 Trojan team isn't just remembered for its contributions to the silver screen, however; it compiled a 9-0-1 record including a 27-14 win over Notre Dame, and won its first national championship behind All-Americans Jess Hibbs at tackle and Don Williams in the backfield. But the players voted among themselves not to go to the Rose Bowl.

They didn't know it at the time but they were contributing—albeit indirectly—to one of the most famous and bizarre Rose Bowl games of all time.

USC had beaten heavily-favored Stanford, 10-0, that year— Howard Jones' first win over Pop Warner—but had played a 0-0 tie with California on a muddy field. Clarence 'Nibs' Price, who is more famous in Cal annals as a basketball coach, had taken over as head coach of the Bears, after Andy Smith's untimely death, and—after a poor first year (3-6 in 1926)—the top of the Pacific Coast Conference. Unfortunately, Jones and Warner were in the way, but the Bears went 7-3 in 1927 and then in 1928, had a regular-season mark of 6-1-2, losing to the Olympic Club and tying both the Trojans and Stanford. When Southern Cal turned down the Rose Bowl bid, the Bears were asked to Pasadena.

The tie with Stanford was another one of those incredible Big Game finishes. The Bears led 13-0 at halftime, and a disgusted Pop Warner put in a number of substitutes in the second half. Two of them, Lud Frentrup and Bill Simkins, got the Cardinals back in the game and in the closing minutes Cal was hanging on for dear life. Then, on fourth down and with just seconds to play, Simkins passed 24 yards to Frentrup for the tying touchdown and the Stanford partisans among the 82,000 fans went crazy. Seconds later it was California's turn to roar as tackle Frank Fitz blocked the conversion to save the tie—and also Cal's trip to the Rose Bowl.

It was a solid Bear team that went to Pasadena. The offense had been shaky all year, but the defense was outstanding—shutting out six opponents and allowing only 28 points all year. End Irv Phillips was an All-American and there were two other future All-Americans on the line, guard Bert Schwartz and the center (and 1929 Bear captain) Roy Riegels.

Roy Riegels would be an All-American the next year. Remember that. No one else did.

Riegels was about to become involved in the most famous play in the history of the Rose Bowl, and perhaps in all of football. Georgia Tech was leading the game 6-0, when it happened. The *New York Times* described it thusly:

'Captain-elect Roy Riegels of the Golden Bears, playing center, snatched up a Tech fumble in the second quarter and started

Six-foot, four-inch, 205-pound USC tackle Marion Morrison took a summer job as an extra at Fox movie studios, kinda got the hang of it and, heck, changed his name before anyone knew it—and before long, plenty of people knew him as John Wayne *(at top)*. Benny Lom *(above)* was the Cal halfback who turned Roy Riegels' wrong-way run around.

toward the Tech goal.

'Tech men sprung up in front of him and in eluding them Riegels cut back across the field. He turned again to escape and in so doing apparently became confused and started toward his own goal, 60 yards away. As he pounded down the sideline both California and Tech players stood amazed in their tracks.

'Benny Lom, halfback for the Golden Bears, sensed the situation and sprang into action. Down the field he went after the flying Riegels, who only put on more speed as he heard feet pounding in the turf behind him. Finally Lom grabbed hold of his mate at the California three-yard line and turned him around. Making interference for Riegels, Lom started back up the field, but a wave of

Tech tacklers hit Riegels before he could more than turn around, hurtling him back to the one-yard line.

'California immediately took up the punt formation, but Riegels, at center, was nervous and Lom, receiving the ball to kick, was little steadier. As the ball was snapped, (Vance) Maree, the Georgia Tech tackle, stormed through and blocked the punt. The ball rolled out of the end zone, but the officials ruled that (Harold) Breakenridge, the California quarterback, had touched it and that a safety would be scored against California.'

Ironically, a blocked punt helped lead to Georgia Tech's touchdown in the third quarter. Cal finally scored in the final period on a long drive—starting, strangely enough, when Riegels blocked a punt and ending with Lom passing to Phillips for the touchdown. But the Bears still lost 8–7—by the margin of that safety.

It just wasn't California's day. A Bear receiver dropped a pass when he was alone on the Tech goal line, two others slipped just as they were about to catch passes in the open field, Lom ran 60 yards with a fumble recovery but it was called back because the referee said he blew the whistle an instant before the fumble. One time Lom punted the ball—and it went flat in mid-flight.

But those are all forgotten; it's 'Wrong Way Roy' Riegels they remember.

'Kids who were in the womb 20 years after I made the run know about it,' Riegels said years later. 'I've never hit anyone (who jibed him about it), but there were times I wanted to kick some people in the butt. However, most people aren't critical. What I did was just an oddity, not the first and certainly not the last.'

In the 1929 Rose Bowl game against Georgia Tech (see the game program cover *at right*), Bears team captain Roy Riegels *(above)* got turned around while eluding tacklers and sprinted to within one-half of a yard from his own goal post before Benny Lom set him straight. Derided as 'wrong way Reigels' for years afterward, he nevertheless was a fine center, and was voted All-American in 1930.

At the time, Riegels said, 'It was a terrible boner. I don't know how it happened. I can't even think of a decent alibi. I just bounced out with the ball, saw a pair of goalposts and headed for them.'

Later, he admitted, 'I could hear him (Lom) shouting at me when I got about 30 yards from the goal, although I couldn't make out what he was saying.' When Lom finally caught up and grabbed Riegels' arm, 'He shouted at me, "Stop, you're going the wrong way." I thought "what's the matter with him?" … I'm sure that Benny would have caught me sooner, except he was using all his breath to shout at me. When I realized what I had done, I thought, "This couldn't be true."'

Following the game Georgia Tech center Peter Pund, an All-American himself, paid Roy this compliment: 'That was a tough break for Riegels. But don't get the idea he isn't a wonderful center. He is the best center I've played against all year. He's a battler, and he never quit. Some boys might have folded up under the situation, but Riegels didn't. I admire him for it.'

That was California's last Rose Bowl visit for nine years. The Pacific Coast Conference now belonged to Howard Jones, Stanford's Vow Boys—and a coach who never went to college.

JAN. 1929

GEORGIA TECH vs. CALIFORNIA

Stanford's Vow Boys

Howard Jones left his mark on USC and the Pacific Coast Conference for decades to come, but he didn't have things all his own way during that period of Western football.

Stanford's Vow Boys—who it might be said were a product of Southern California's success—were to dominate the mid-1930s, and several other coaches made their mark on the league in that stretch, notably Babe Hollingbery and Bill Spaulding.

Oren E Hollingbery was certainly the most colorful of the group; his background alone would have taken care of that. For when Washington State hired Babe in 1926, he not only had never coached a college team, he had never even attended college. He got his training—both as a player and as a coach—with the powerful Olympic Club team in San Francisco. He actually had begun coaching at Lick-Wilmerding High School there, played—at all positions, but primarily end—for the Olympic Club from 1915-21 and then became their player-coach.

His most notable achievement during that time, and probably the one that most attracted Washington State when it went shopping for a new coach, came in 1925. The Olympic Club not only beat Pop Warner's Stanford team 9–0 (the Cardinals' only other loss, remember, was to Washington in the Rose Bowl decider), but whipped California 15–0, ending Andy Smith's unbeaten streak at 44 games.

Hollingbery coached the first East-West Shrine all-star game in San Francisco that year and one of his players was a big center from the Olympic Club (who prior to that had been an All-American at Texas A&M), named Arthur (Buck) Bailey. Following that 1925 season Hollingbery went to Pullman, Washington. He took Bailey with him as line coach and for 17 years, until 1942, they were the entire Washington State football staff—with Bailey doubling as baseball coach—where he won 14 Northern Division titles.

In Hollingbery's first season the Cougars (who had not had a winning team in five years) went 6–1, losing only to USC. For nine years—think about that, nine full seasons—the Cougars did not lose a home football game. In his 17 seasons, 14 of them winning ones, Babe Hollingbery compiled a 93–53–14 record and in addition coached the West in nine East-West games, winning six.

He earned nation-wide respect for himself and for Washington State football. When California was searching for a new coach to succeed Nibs Price after the 1930 season, Knute Rockne, the famous Notre Dame coach, told them: 'If it's a winner you're after, if you want a coach who can put points on the scoreboard, then go after Babe Hollingbery at Washington State.'

Hollingbery had a strange collection of players on his early teams, including Frank Stojack, a fine guard who later became a world wrestling champion and Butch Meeker. Meeker, who stood five feet, four inches and weighed less than 140 pounds, had planned to go to Washington but coach Enoch Bagshaw told him he was too small to play for the Huskies. So in true Horatio Alger fashion, he crossed the state, became a star halfback for the Cougars—and scored the winning touchdown on a sensational run to beat Washington in his junior year. That was such fun that he did exactly the same thing to the Huskies again in his senior year.

However—Hollingbery's greatest teams were the 1929–1930 squads led by three future All-Pro linemen: Mel Hein, Glen 'Turk' Edwards and George Hurley. In all there were six future pros on that team, and remember the National Football League was a far smaller and more select group than it is today. Hein was a charter member of both the College and Professional Football Halls of Fame and in 1969 was chosen as the best center in the first 100 years of football.

Hein was six feet, three inches tall, weighed 200 pounds and was amazingly fast, and in Hollingbery's words, 'Mel loved and lived for contact.' He covered the field brilliantly as a linebacker and when he got to the ballcarrier he knew what to do. 'I tried to stiff-arm him,' one Oregon halfback said of Hein after playing Washington State, 'and you know what he did? He picked me up and slung me eight yards backward and then sat on my face! What did he do in high school, bite off their arms?'

In 1929 the Cougars finished with a 10–2 record, but one of the losses was 27–7 to Southern California—the game that put the Trojans in the Rose Bowl and kept Washington State at home. Nineteen thirty was a different story. The Cougars won nine straight and while they boasted three first-team All-American linemen—Hein and tackles Edwards and Harold Ahlskog and a second team All-American fullback in Elmer Schwartz—it was the kicking of end Lyle Maskell that gave Washington State its first Pacific Coast Conference championship. He kicked the extra point that beat USC, and his 43-yard field goal was the only score in the 3–0 win over Washington that finally clinched the title.

Southern California had another great team—that was the only time in a four-year span the Trojans didn't go to the Rose Bowl—led by Erny Pinckert, Irv Mohler and Gus Shaver. But when they met in the third game of the season, Washington State's great

Babe Hollingbery (right), former player and coach for the Olympic Club, built Washington State into a winner, especially in 1929–30.

WASHINGTON STATE COLLEGE

UNIVERSITY OF CALIFORNIA

line shut down the high-powered USC running game (which had scored 76 points against UCLA in the opener) and Maskell's conversion was the difference in a 7–6 Cougar victory. USC did not lose again until the 27–0 rout by Notre Dame in the season finale—Rockne's last game before his tragic death.

So it was the unbeaten Cougars in the 1931 Rose Bowl against Alabama, also unbeaten (9–0) and in its last year under Wallace Wade, who already had announced he was moving to Duke. Washington State came out in all-red uniforms, from helmets to socks, but the effect was not what had been desired; one writer said at day's end that the Cougars looked 'like bottles of raspberry pop that had lost their fizz.' Alabama also had some great players: Johnny 'Monk' Campbell was the Rose Bowl MVP and Jim 'Hurry' Cain had a great day punting and passing. They were on the bench, however, when the game began. Wade started his 'shock troops' to feel out the Cougars, then inserted his regulars in the second quarter and that's when Washington State really got a shock—Alabama scored 21 points, and had no trouble thereafter coasting to a 24–0 victory.

That was the Cougars' first visit to the Rose Bowl since the first renewal of the game in 1916; they haven't been back since.

Bill Spaulding did not coach in a Rose Bowl in all of his 14 years at the helm of the UCLA team, but there is no question that he was the one man who built the foundation for future Bruin successes.

Spaulding came to Westwood as football coach and athletic director after three years as Minnesota coach. At the time, UCLA was just six years old and had been playing in the Southern California Conference against schools like Whittier, Pomona and Occidental—without much success; the Bruins record was four wins, 30 defeats and four ties. By the time Spaulding retired as football coach (remaining as athletic director) following the 1938 season, UCLA had been in the Pacific Coast Conference for 11 years and had progressed to the point that (in Babe Horrell's first year as coach succeeding Spaulding) the Bruins could go unbeaten and share the PCC title with USC. Three years later they had their first outright title and first Rose Bowl bid.

Bill Spaulding was one of the most respected and beloved men in the college game. In his first year at UCLA an old friend, Pop Warner, tried to do Spaulding a service by giving him a game with Warner's Stanford team. It was no favor, as it turned out—Stanford won 82–0—but it introduced the Bruins to big-time college football.

Despite that mismatch, UCLA had winning seasons in Spaulding's first three years. Then in 1928 the school joined the PCC—and for awhile the going was extremely rough. USC, trying to build up the natural cross-town rivalry, agreed to meet the Bruins in 1929 and 1930 but Howard Jones' Trojans were simply too powerful for the new kid on the block, winning by 76–0 and 52–0. The rivalry was then discontinued until 1936.

But Spaulding was too good a coach to let that go on. In 1931 UCLA played Stanford for the first time since that 1925 debacle—and this time barely lost (12–6), when Stanford scored on a 50-yard pass play as time was running out. The next week the Bruins upset nationally-ranked St Mary's 12–0. In 1932 they beat Oregon for their first major PCC victory (they had beaten Montana 14–0 in 1929), two weeks later finally beat Stanford (in Warner's final season) 12–6 and wound up with a 6–4 overall record and a 4–2 league mark for their first winning record since joining the PCC.

At left: The 15 October 1932 Cougars versus Bears game program. Up to this point, Cal had won nine of 11 contests with Washington State. Bill Ingram's thoughts were also, no doubt, on other arenas—the Big Game versus the 'Vow Boys,' for instance. *At right:* Typical early '30s program art.

UCLA was 6–4–1 in 1933, 7–3 in 1934 and finally in 1935, it really came together. The Bruins beat Stanford 7–6, the Rose Bowl-bound Cardinals' only loss of the season; that helped give UCLA an 8–2 record overall and a share of the league championship with Stanford and California. The Bruins had definitely arrived as a full-fledged threat in the Pacific Coast Conference.

The real story of that decade, however, was Stanford's Vow Boys. On 26 November 1930 the team had officially become the Indians, but it did nothing to improve Stanford's football fortunes. Pop Warner was on the way out; USC was establishing what seemed like permanent tenancy in the Rose Bowl and California was taking even the local spotlight away from Stanford.

Nibs Price had resigned at California following a 4–5–0 record in 1930; the Bears had hired Bill Ingram, the successful Navy coach, and he brought in as assistants Stub Allison and Frank Wickhorst—both of whom would later be head coaches at Berkeley. They immediately turned things around, compiling an 8–2 record in 1931 and beating Stanford 6–0—Warner's first Big Game loss in seven tries. Ingram also gained a bit of Blue and Gold revenge in the final game of the season when Cal beat Georgia Tech, its 1929 Rose Bowl tormentor, 19–7.

The following year Stanford opened the season with five straight wins, but they lost to USC and UCLA—for the first time—and tied

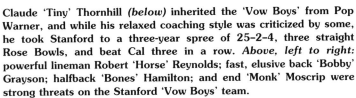

Claude 'Tiny' Thornhill *(below)* inherited the 'Vow Boys' from Pop Warner, and while his relaxed coaching style was criticized by some, he took Stanford to a three-year spree of 25–2–4, three straight Rose Bowls, and beat Cal three in a row. *Above, left to right:* powerful lineman Robert 'Horse' Reynolds; fast, elusive back 'Bobby' Grayson; halfback 'Bones' Hamilton; and end 'Monk' Moscrip were strong threats on the Stanford 'Vow Boys' team.

California 0–0 to finish 6–4–1. Warner, frustrated by the Indians' inconsistent play and harassed by some grumbling alumni, left The Farm to become the coach at Temple.

It was, he said many times later, 'the worst mistake I ever made.'

He left behind a 1932 Stanford freshman team that was, in a word, loaded. Three of them—tackle Bob Reynolds, fullback Bobby Grayson and halfback Bones Hamilton—are members of the College Football Hall of Fame and end Monk Moscrip joined that trio of legitimate All-Americans.

In that '32 season the Indian varsity lost to Southern California 13–0, continuing Howard Jones' mastery over Warner. The following Monday that was the Number One topic of conversation among the freshmen, and quarterback Frank Alustiza said something about that group never wanting to lose to the Trojans. Hamilton suggested they make it a vow.

Such things often happen in locker rooms; most of them are forgotten the next day, and that one might have been too but for two San Francisco newspapermen, Bud Spencer and Harry Borba (both, incidentally, Stanford alumni). They heard about it and made a human interest story of it, mistakenly enlarging Hamilton's pledge to include the promise never to lose to California. The Vow Boys were born.

They were as good as their word. As freshmen they finished with a 7–0–1 record, tying Cal 7–7—and walloping the Southern California frosh 33–6. Warner left Stanford and his long-time assistant, Claude 'Tiny' Thornhill took over the head coaching job.

Thornhill was far more relaxed and low-key than Warner had been—he once was photographed lying flat on his back on the practice field, a football serving as a pillow. Ultimately that may have helped cost him his job at Stanford—for when he started to lose, some alumni complained that he 'didn't take the job seriously

enough.' But for the close-knit, fun-loving Vow Boys, his style was perfect; the chemistry was there.

'Thornhill wasn't as strict or as distant as Warner,' Bob Reynolds said later. 'He made us into a friendly, cohesive group.'

That cohesive group wasn't so friendly to the opposition. In the next three years the Indians won 25 games—20 of them by shutouts—lost only four and tied two. They went to three straight Rose Bowl games, they beat California three straight years—as sophomores, they had rashly enlarged their vow to include the Bears on the eve of the Big Game—and most important, they never lost to Southern California.

The Vow got its sternest test in 1933. The Trojans were 6–0–1 on their way to a 10–1–1 season and had a 27-game undefeated string working. Stanford had five wins but had been tied by Northwestern 0–0, and then lost to Washington 6–0. In addition a train accident delayed the Indians on their trip to Los Angeles, and they already were tired when they ran into the Coliseum—to be confronted by a huge crowd, most of them screaming for Southern California. Cotton Warburton ripped off a 43-yard touchdown run in the first quarter and guard Bill Corbus—yet another All-American and Hall of Famer from that team but already a senior by 1933—missed two field goals to make things even darker for the Indians. Corbus made good on two kicks and that was the margin in a 13–7 Stanford victory. So far, so good.

Stanford capped its regular season with a win over a good California team in one of the more exciting Big Games ever. With the Bears leading 3–0, Frank Alustiza connected with Al Norgard on a 57-yard pass late in the game for a 7–3 lead. Cal immediately drove back 73 yards to the Stanford four-yard line, but Bones Hamilton intercepted a pass with three minutes left to save the win and the Rose Bowl bid for the Indians.

Their opponent in Pasadena was Columbia, and to say the

Lions were not the first choice would be an understatement. They were 7–1, losing only to unbeaten Princeton, but many of their wins had been over lesser teams—they narrowly beat West Virginia, a team that had lost to Ohio State by 75–0. Princeton however, had an agreement with Yale and Harvard which precluded bowl games for the 'Big Three'; Army and Duke both were unbeaten and either could have had the bid by winning its final game, but the Cadets lost to Notre Dame and Duke fell to Alabama. The Rose Bowl berth went—almost reluctantly—to Columbia.

Stanford had a big edge and was rated a huge favorite—three touchdowns at least. Columbia halfback Al Barabas, who was on the verge of football immortality if he'd only known it, put up a brave front; 'We fully expected to win,' he said later. 'I think that's a common feeling among football players.... We had a good team that year.' But the truth was that even the Eastern press conceded the Lions no chance at all.

The game was played in a terrible storm. The field was completely submerged the day before and the Pasadena Fire Department worked all day pumping water—one report insisted it was two million gallons—out of the stadium. Only about 35,000 fans showed up (the previous year's game between Pitt and USC had drawn 74,874) and they all expected Stanford to win.

It came down to one play—probably the most famous set of numbers in Rose Bowl history—KF79. All kinds of rumors grew up around that trick play and to this day Columbia and its coach, Lou Little, may be better known for that than for anything else they ever did on a football field. When Leonard Koppett, the fine New York sportswriter, moved to the West Coast a quarter century after that game, he immediately ordered personalized California license plates with that number, 'KF79.'

In point of fact it was a fairly elementary play with three options

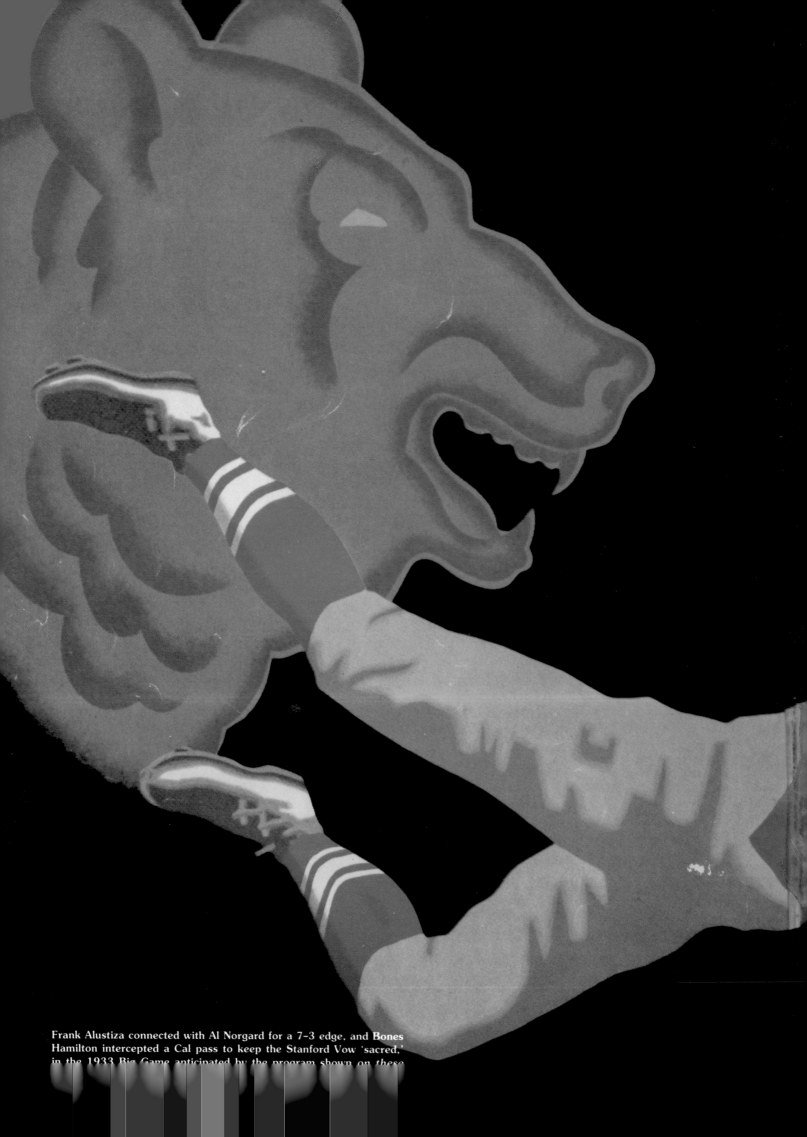

Frank Alustiza connected with Al Norgard for a 7-3 edge, and **Bones** Hamilton intercepted a Cal pass to keep the Stanford Vow 'sacred,' in the 1933 Big Game anticipated by the program shown on *these*

which Columbia had used many times before—including at least three times previously in that very Rose Bowl game, one of them employing the same option, with Barabas carrying—that was later used for the winning touchdown. On those earlier occasions, however, the play gained only minimal yardage and so they were later forgotten. 'I remember a couple of (practice) sessions where Little would run the damn play 50 times in a row,' Barabas recalled later.

KF79 was simply a direct snap to Cliff Montgomery, who then spun completely around and ran into the line. He had three options; hand it to Barabas after a half spin, hand it to another back as he completed the spin or keep it himself. On this occasion he gave it to Barabas, who, unprotected and hiding the ball on his hip, ran around the left end. The lone Stanford defender who wasn't fooled by Montgomery's faking—the man who had tackled Barabas when they tried the play earlier—this time was blocked out and Barabas waltzed untouched into the end zone.

The play became more famous with the years. At the time, Columbia's six goal-line stands, coupled with eight fumbles and some key penalties by Stanford, were considered more important. The *New York Times* report of the game said:

'So magnificent were these defensive stands of the Lions that they overshadowed the lone touchdown of the day, which Barabas scored on a 17-yard dash that still has the California fans baffled, not to mention Stanford.'

For the Indians the game was an unhappy repeat of the 1925 Rose Bowl match between Ernie Nevers and Notre Dame's Four Horsemen. Again Stanford outgained the opponent and again its All-American fullback was stopped on one key goal-line series that could have changed the game. This time it was Bobby Grayson (who had been compared to Nevers) who ran the ball three times (and reversed it to Bones Hamilton on the other of the four plays) from the Columbia three yard line—and was stacked up every time. On the last, he was hit just short of the goal by Al Ciampa, a 165-pound reserve center, fumbled and Barabas recovered.

And like Nevers, that failure did not diminish Grayson's great performance. He ran for 152 yards—45 more than Columbia

gained, total, rushing and passing. 'My boys were the most underrated team in America,' Little said afterward. 'I felt all along Stanford was in for a rude shock, and I was right. But that Bobby Grayson, he's something else. He's the best back in the country.'

The following year was more of the same for Stanford: An unbeaten regular season (9–0–1) in which the Indians gave up just 14 points, seven of them in a tie with Santa Clara; another win over Cal, 9–7 (after which Bear coach Bill Ingram resigned); a victory, of course, over USC, which had fallen on hard times; another Rose Bowl invitation.

And another Rose Bowl loss.

This time, however, there was no question that the opponent was a good one. Alabama was unbeaten, with nine wins and had scored 287 points while allowing just 32. It was the Crimson Tide's fourth trip to Pasadena; they had lost to Washington and George Wilson in one of the great Rose Bowl games in 1926, tied Stanford in 1927 and beaten Babe Hollingbery's Washington State team in 1931.

In that 1927 game Stanford's Pop Warner had introduced the zone pass defense and Alabama had thrown just one pass all day, completing it. There was no danger of the Tide repeating that performance when it rolled into Pasadena on 1 January 1935— not with Dixie Howell and Don Hutson in the lineup.

Stanford was prepared to stop the running game. They were not prepared for Don Hutson, who was to go on and become perhaps the greatest end in football history, and they were not prepared for Millard 'Dixie' Howell, who put on what Grantland Rice called 'one of the great all-around exhibitions that football has ever known.'

Howell, like Hutson a member of the Football Hall of Fame, accounted for 341 yards in the game—107 rushing, including a 67-yard touchdown run that put Alabama into a 16–7 lead and broke the game open, 74 yards on punt returns, 160 yards on passing (he completed nine of 12). As Associated Press described the performance, 'He passed, ran, kicked (a 44.8 punting average), intercepted passes, backed up the ends and tackled in the open.'

At that he barely overshadowed his batterymate, the 'Alabama Antelope.' Hutson caught six passes for 164 yards including a 54-yard touchdown pass from Joe Riley, Howell's replacement, and a 59-yarder from Howell for the final score of the game. 'I couldn't recognize Hutson if I met him face to face,' Bones Hamilton said after that frustrating afternoon, 'because I spent all afternoon chasing him. The rear view, I will never forget.'

'We didn't know the speed of Hutson or the potential throwing ability of Dixie Howell,' Stanford tackle Bob Reynolds said later. 'They had some fine ballplayers up and down their whole lineup, and Bear Bryant was a damned fine end.'

Yes, *that* Bear Bryant. The man who would become an Alabama legend as one of the great coaches in football history was the end opposite Hutson on that Tide team. Although he called himself 'a very ordinary member of the team,' he caught some key passes on Alabama's first two scoring drives. But he was facing a great player in Reynolds; 'I don't think I blocked Reynolds all day,' Bryant said years later. 'I held him a couple of times, but don't think I ever blocked him.'

Stanford led the game 7–0 early in the second quarter—before Howell got started. He passed 'Bama down the field twice, leading to his own five-yard touchdown run and a field goal for a 9–7 lead. A few minutes later he ran 67 yards for another TD. Shortly after that, Riley hit Hutson on the 54 yard line and it was 22–7— 22 points in 13 minutes. Alabama went on to win without much trouble, 29–13.

The Vow Boys were doing all they had promised but they still hadn't won a Rose Bowl.

They had one more chance, but the 1935 season didn't look like it was going to be so successful. There were a lot of injuries including All-Americans Bobby Grayson and Bones Hamilton— and Alustiza, who suffered a detached retina in the UCLA game and was finished for the season. UCLA upset the Indians 7–6 and Hamilton reinjured his ankle in that game and missed the next three games.

Stanford won all three, including a 3–0 win over USC on Monk Moscrip's field goal in the final minute. Ironically, both Hamilton and Alustiza, the men responsible for that freshman pledge, missed that game, but the Vow was kept.

The Big Game that year really was big. Stub Allison had succeeded Bill Ingram as Cal coach and the Bears were unbeaten, untied and ranked fifth in the nation coming into the game against Stanford. Cal would tie for the PCC title even if it lost, and many felt the Bears would get the Rose Bowl bid regardless of the outcome.

But with the exception of Alustiza, Stanford was healthy for almost the first time all year. The Indians drove 80 yards for one touchdown— most of it on Grayson passes to Hamilton and runs by the two great backs — Grayson ran in the touchdown. Two plays after the ensuing kickoff, Cal's Sam Chapman, an All-American and later a major league outfielder with the Philadelphia Athletics, fumbled and Indian center Wes Muller recovered at the Bear 29. Moments later Jimmy Coffis scored on an eight-yard reverse and Stanford had a 13–0 victory.

And, it turned out, one more shot at a Rose Bowl victory.

The opponent that year looked like the toughest one of all— Southern Methodist, 12–0, ranked Number One in the nation, had allowed just 38 points all year including 14 to Texas Christian and its great quarterback Sammy Baugh. But Stanford had one more trick up its sleeve—the team was not called the Vow Boys for nothing.

'Just before the game,' wrote Maxwell Stiles in his book *The Rose Bowl,* 'these same men—the eight who remained—who had vowed as freshmen never to lose a game to USC, and who didn't, took another vow. This time they pledged themselves not to lose another Rose Bowl game. And they didn't.'

Quarterback Bill Paulman set up a first-quarter touchdown with his 62–yard quick kick, then scored it himself on a one-yard run and that was that. The Mustangs did penetrate to the Stanford five-yard line once but then tried some razzle-dazzle that didn't fool center Wes Muller for an instant; he caused a fumble, then recovered it himself and the Indians were home free. It ended 7–0.

SMU's All-American back Bobby Wilson was held to 21 yards by the fine defensive work of ends Moscrip and Keith Topping; SMU was equally tough defensively, stopping Grayson with 27 yards in 18 carries and Hamilton with 21 in 15 tries. But none of that meant anything: Stanford had its Rose Bowl victory.

The Indians had a number of outstanding players in that stretch but the best may have been Bob 'Horse' Reynolds—the six foot, four inch, 230-pound tackle from Oklahoma who played *every* minute of all three Rose Bowl games—and Grayson—who was called by Ernie Nevers 'the best back I've ever seen, and I've seen a lot of good backs.'

He not only was a fine runner with power—at six feet and 190 pounds—and speed—he had been a high school sprint champion in Oregon—but he could pass *and* he was a fine defensive player. One year Washington got the idea that Bobby was weak on pass defense, so the Huskies tried to throw over him; he intercepted four passes that day, returning two of them for touchdowns.

Quentin Reynolds, a famous New York sportswriter, put Grayson's ability in perspective when he wrote, 'Grayson is a carbon copy of Red Grange when the old redhead was doing his stuff for Illinois—except that Bobby actually is faster than Red ever was.'

But now the Vow Boys were a part of history. There was Thunder on the horizon again—and this time it didn't all come from Howard Jones' Herd at Southern California.

Washington, Cal and UCLA

With the talented nucleus of the Vow Boys gone, Stanford fell (if only temporarily) on hard times—the Indians won only two games in 1936 and only 10 total in the four years that Tiny Thornhill remained on The Farm.

But there was no dearth of talent in the Pacific Coast Conference. Howard Jones was still at USC, rebuilding toward two more Rose Bowls; there were rumblings in Berkeley; a coach at Oregon State College named Lon Stiner was beginning to make his presence felt, and Jimmy Phelan had the team he wanted at Washington.

Phelan had been a fine quarterback at Notre Dame and had coached both at Missouri and at Purdue—where he had crossed swords with Howard Jones—then at Iowa; when he and Jones both moved West their feud moved with them.

Enoch Bagshaw had won 52 games against 11 losses and three ties in the six seasons prior to 1929, and took the Huskies to two Rose Bowls. But football coaching, like no other job, is a case of 'What have you done for us lately?' When he finished with a 2–6–1 record in 1929, Bagshaw was out and Washington hired Jimmy Phelan.

In the next 12 seasons (through 1941) Phelan compiled a record of 65–37–8. He had winning teams his first few years but the PCC power then was in Los Angeles and Palo Alto and nobody was paying much attention to the Huskies. In 1934, however, Washington beat the Trojans—a particularly sweet win for Phelan, who disliked Howard Jones intensely—and finished with a 6–1–1 record. The following season the Huskies lost to Stanford, California and Oregon, but in 1936 Phelan was ready.

The Huskies were not a high-powered offensive team; despite the presence of All-American Jimmy Cain in the backfield, they scored only 148 points in nine regular-season games that year. But the defense was something else. Led by consensus All-American guard Max Starcevich and tackles Vic Markov (a member of the College Football Hall of Fame) and captain Chuck Bond, the Huskies shut out six opponents including a good California team and USC—Phelan's third straight win over Jones. Washington finished with a 7–1–1 record—a surprising 14–14 tie with Stanford and a season-opening loss to Number One-ranked Minnesota 14–7. After 11 years the Huskies were back in the Rose Bowl.

It was not a productive visit to Pasadena. Their opponent was an outstanding Pittsburgh team coached by Jock Sutherland and led by the great Marshall Goldberg, who finished third in the Heisman Trophy balloting that year and second the following season. The Panthers had finished 7–1–1, identical to Washington, and had beaten Notre Dame by 26-0 but they were not a popular choice because of previous Rose Bowl failures; that criticism stung Sutherland, and he worked the team extremely hard in preparation for the game. In addition, it rained heavily the night before, which probably aided Pitt, a straight-ahead power team; Bobby LaRue slashed through the Washington defense for 199 yards on just 15 carries and Pitt won easily 21–0—only 14 points less than the Huskies had allowed total in the previous nine games.

Phelan had another good defensive team the following year, registering five shutouts and allowing only 33 points in nine regular-season games and battling to a 0–0 tie with unbeaten and Rose Bowl-bound California. However, the Huskies also tied Washington State and again were upset by Stanford 13–7 and had to settle for third in the PCC. That, however, earned them an invitation to Honolulu to play in the Pineapple Bowl; they demolished the University of Hawaii 53–13 and then stayed long enough to whip an all-star team of sorts called the Honolulu Townies 35–6.

The spotlight shifted back to the San Francisco Bay Area at this point—but it was on California this time, not Stanford. The Bears had been a strong team for most of the previous decade; Bill Ingram, who became head coach in 1931, had four winning years and two All-American halfbacks, Rusty Gill in 1931 and Arleigh Williams (who later became dean of men at the University) in 1934.

Perhaps one of those winning years needs an asterisk—in 1934 the Bears lost to Stanford 9–7, giving them a 6–4 record, and Ingram then resigned. Assistant coach Leonard B 'Stub' Allison took the team to Honolulu for two scheduled post-season games and Cal lost both, winding up the year at 6–6.

The following season Allison, who had come to Berkely with Ingram in 1931, became the full-time head coach. His record on the West Coast was hardly encouraging—he had served one year at Washington way back in 1920 and finished with a 1–6 record and then had lost the two games in Hawaii at the end of 1934.

But this time Stub was an immediate success. His 1935 team, led by All-American tackle Larry Lutz and a fine sophomore center named Bob Herwig, shut out its first five opponents, beat USC 21–7 and UCLA 14–2, and then shut out Washington and Pacific. Going into the Big Game the Bears were 9–0, had clinched at least a share of the title and were inches away from the Rose Bowl.

Jimmy Phelan *(at right)* **took over the University of Washington reigns from Enoch Bagshaw, and produced two great season in 1936–37.**

That was a Big Game that really was big; that was the last of the Vow Boys teams and although they lost to UCLA 7–6, they shut out seven of their nine opponents—including California 13–0 and Southern Methodist in the 1936 Rose Bowl 7–0. The Bears would have to wait for two more years.

Cal started the 1936 season with two more shutouts but lost four of its next five games. At this point, however, Allison started to experiment, and what he came up with was good enough to beat USC, Oregon and then a very down Stanford team 20–0. The Bears finished 6–5 (including a season-ending intersectional loss to Georgia Tech), but something far more important had happened during that late-season burst.

The nucleus of the Thunder Team had come together—and they were all coming back in 1937.

It was a great collection of players. Five of them made at least one All-American first team that year—halfback Sam Chapman, who made most of the teams; end Perry Schwartz; quarterback Johnny Meek; guard Vard Stockton and Herwig, who was honored for the second straight year. Vic Bottari, a junior halfback, was ignored that year but was to be a near-unanimous All-American the following season.

The Bears blasted through the schedule, scoring 214 points and allowing just 34; only UCLA scored more than seven points against them, the Bruins losing 26–14; only four of their opponents scored at all. Nobody came closer than two touchdowns except Phelan's strong Washington team, which held California to a 0–0 tie. Stanford, still struggling and with the dissatisfaction with Tiny Thornhill growing by the day, fell to the Bears 13–0 in a heavy rain.

This was a team that relied on power and running and tough, opportunistic defense, grinding out yardage from the single wing formation with Chapman and Bottari doing most of the work.

College football Hall of Fame member Vic Markov *(above left)* was part of the intense Huskies defense that made Washington a feared competitor in the mid-1930s. Bill Ingram left Cal and the coaching chores there to 'Stub' Allison *(above)* who produced the Thunder Team, and crushed Washington State's Cougars in 1937—a feat which is explicated in the 1937 Cal program cartoon shown *at right*.

Schwartz, for example, later went on to become a pass-catching star with the New York Yankees in the old All-America Football Conference (the pro league which spawned the San Francisco 49ers and Cleveland Browns) yet Cal threw probably no more than a dozen passes his way all year.

'Andy Smith's original Wonder Team used to kick and wait for the breaks,' Jack James wrote in the *San Francisco Examiner*. 'This outfit, its late successor, didn't even wait for 'em. Rather, the boys went out and created 'em, which is after all, the epitome of sound business practice for a "Businesslike Team."'

With the Pacific Coast Conference title went the Rose Bowl bid. The western team still had the option of choosing its own opponent and California favored Pitt, which had another strong team. Pittsburgh declined and the Bears went to their second choice, unbeaten Alabama. The Crimson Tide still had Frank Thomas as their coach—Bear Bryant was now an assistant—but he didn't have a Dixie Howell or Don Hutson.

Alabama had won 19 in a row including nine that season, but the Bears simply wore them down. Their two touchdown drives were entirely on the ground; in fact, all but 16 of California's 208 total yards were gained running the football.

The play that might have broken Alabama was made by Schwartz. The reports of the game said that on a 55-yard punt by Chapman in the second quarter, Schwartz roared downfield, picked up a blocker, threw him at the punt return man to create a fumble and then recovered the ball himself.

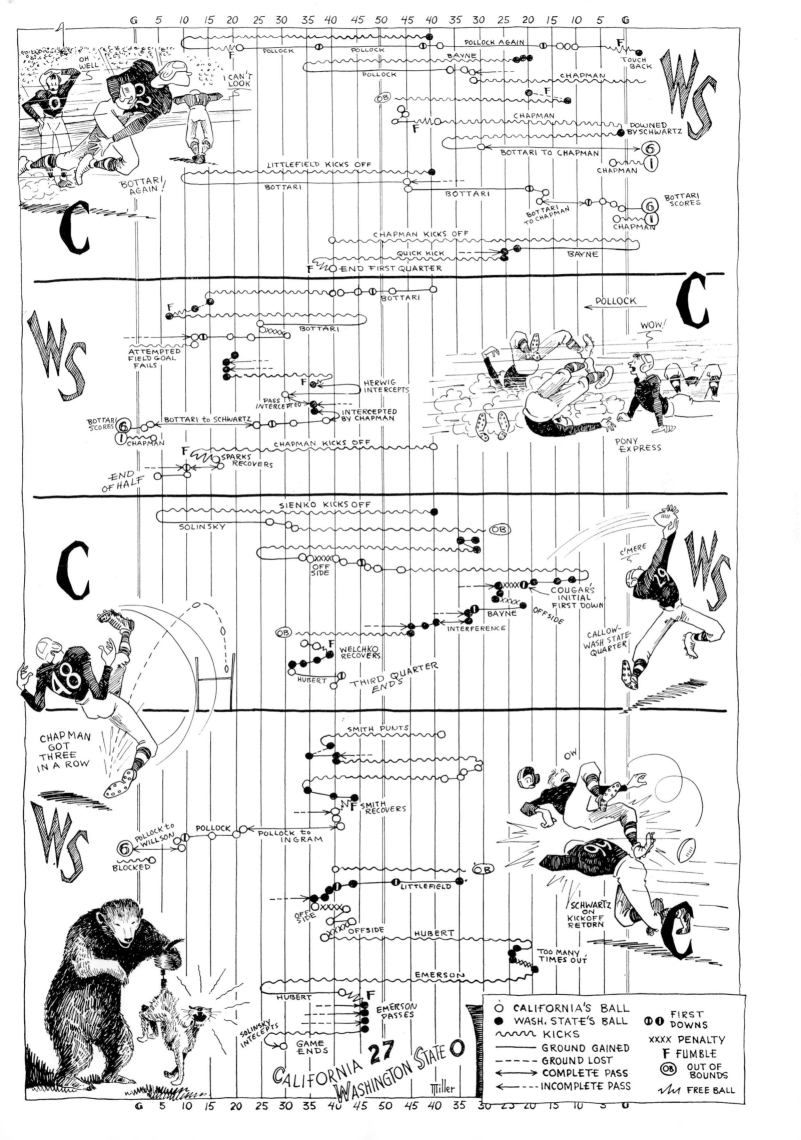

'I wasn't THAT strong,' Schwartz recalled many years later. 'I ran right through the blocker, knocked him back into the receiver who dropped the ball. It might have looked that way up in the stands, but if I had stopped to grab the blocker, the other guy would have been on his way downfield.

'It kind of spoils a good story, doesn't it?'

Regardless, the fumble recovery at the 'Bama 39-yard line set up Cal's first touchdown, Bottari carrying it in from the four. In the third quarter 'Vallejo Vic' scored again after a 53-yard drive and California won the game 13–0.

The unbeaten Bears were named national champion in some polls, but the 'official' rankings by Associated Press had them Number Two behind Pittsburgh, which also finished undefeated with one tie.

The following year California had only five starters returning— but one was Bottari, and Allison had the foresight to give his reserves a lot of playing time. The Bears had another fine year, finishing 10–1 and sharing the PCC title. Their lone loss was to Howard Jones' USC team, 13–7; the Trojans, meanwhile, lost to Washington 7–6 and the Huskies in turn were beaten by the Bears 14–7. If the current selection procedure had been in effect, Cal would have gone to the Rose Bowl; it wasn't and the Pasadena selectors chose USC and its 8–2 record.

Not that it was a bad pick. Jones, after compiling an amazing 84–11–3 record in his first nine years as Trojan coach—including three Rose Bowl victories in four years—had fallen on hard times. In the following four seasons Southern California's record was 17–19–6; in that stretch the Trojans beat Stanford only once, and California and Notre Dame not at all. All those horses that

'Vallejo Vic' Bottari, shown *at left* cranking up for a pass, and Bears teammate Sam Chapman *(opposite)* were the explosive heart of the opportunistic 1938 Thunder Team which beat 'Bama in the Rose Bowl 13–0, won the Big Game 13–0, had only one tie—to Phelan's Huskies—and no losses. Cal's quarterback Mushy Pollock is shown *below* being tackled by Trojan Lyman Russell in 1936. Cal won 13–7.

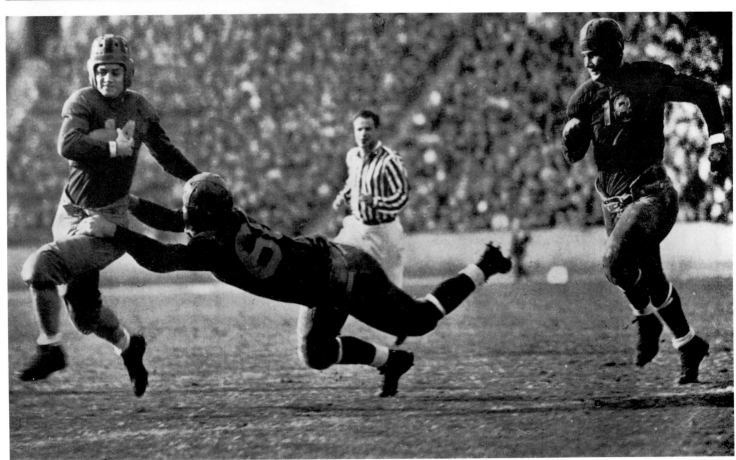

Babe Hollingberry had once talked about at USC had somehow escaped the corral.

But Howard Jones was too good a coach to stay down for long. He had not changed his style, and now he was getting some players again who could win with it—people like two-time All-American guard Harry Smith and and two fine backs in Grenville Lansdell and Parks Ambrose 'Amby' Schindler (USC halfbacks do seem to have the most romantic names, don't they?).

'He (Jones) liked a highly-contested game; he didn't like runaways,' Amby Schindler recalled later. 'That is to say, he liked to win by seeing that his techniques prevailed, and that his methods were superior. He didn't believe in gambling, he was basically conservative, but not to the point where he wasn't mentally ahead of things. I consider him a genius.'

Duke was chosen as the Trojans' opponent for that 1 January 1939 Rose Bowl. The Blue Devils, with a great pair of backs in George McAfee (later a great professional star with the Chicago Bears) and Eric Tipton and their 'Seven Iron Dukes' in the line, was unbeaten, untied and unscored upon and had beaten a great Pittsburgh team in Jock Sutherland's last game as Pitt coach. But it was not the All-Americans that decided this game. This Rose Bowl belonged to an unknown assistant coach and a fourth-string tailback.

Duke, living up to its reputation as a great defensive team, was leading the game 3–0 with slightly over two minutes remaining and the ball in the Trojans' possession at their own 34-yard line. That was when Joe Wilensky, an assistant freshman coach who was manning the phones to the press box, took matters into his own hands. The regular assistant coaches upstairs, who had been sending down plays, already had left their station to work their way down to the field but Jones didn't know that. Wilensky yelled to the empty scouting booth, 'I've got it, I'll tell them.' He then told the coaches on the USC bench, 'They said put in Nave and have him throw the ball to Krueger.'

Wilensky might not have lived to see another football season if it hadn't worked, but it did. Doyle Nave (another of those movie-hero names) was a fourth-stringer who had played exactly 28 and one-half minutes all season. He just couldn't run very well, and of course at that time tailbacks (who functioned much as the quarterback does now, handling the ball on almost every play) were runners first. However, he was an outstanding passer and had worked on that with end Al Krueger, another reserve.

Nave immediately passed to Krueger for 13 yards; he passed again to Krueger for nine more; he threw a flat pass to Krueger, but this one lost two yards. It was third down at the Duke 14 yard line, with less than a minute to play. Krueger went deep into the end zone and Nave put the ball right in his hands. With 41 seconds left in the game, USC had a touchdown and a 7–3 win in a game that, in an *Esquire Magazine* poll several years later, was deemed the most exciting bowl game of all time.

With both Landsell, who would make All-American, and Schindler returning for the 1939 season, the Trojans were again the Rose Bowl favorites. But even though they went unbeaten, the road to Pasadena was no easier this time.

The season opened inauspiciously enough for the Trojans with a 7–7 tie with Oregon. The next five were easy enough—four of them were shutouts—and then Notre Dame fell 20–12. Then came Washington. It was not one of Jimmy Phelan's better teams—the Huskies finishing 4–5 that year—but it battled Southern California to the wire. It took a safety followed immediately by a long touchdown pass in the final minute to give the Trojans a disputed 9–7 victory.

UCLA was next—and surprise!—the Bruins were also unbeaten. Bill Spaulding had stepped aside following the 1938

season and in his capacity as athletic director, brought in former great Cal center Babe Horrell as head coach. He was blessed with two great backs in All-American Kenny Washington and a junior named Jackie Robinson. Every sports fan remembers Robinson as the first black player in organized baseball; not so many recall that he was a great all-round athlete at UCLA who led the nation in punt returns both as a senior and a junior.

They were an explosive combination. Washington gained 164 yards rushing against Montana, 142 against Washington, 141 against California; Robinson ran for 148 on just 10 carries against Washington State. Washington not only rushed for 812 yards—and consider that for comparison, only one man in PCC history, Morley Drury of USC in 1927, had ever rushed for 1000 yards in a single season—but he also was an effective passer, throwing for seven touchdowns. At season's end UCLA was ranked seventh in the nation in the Associated Press poll; USC was third—marking the first time the PCC had had two teams in the final top ten.

But the Bruins were having a strange season. They beat Texas Christian 6–2 to open the year. In the third game they tied Stanford, which only won one game all year 14–14; in the seventh game they fought a scoreless draw with Santa Clara 0–0; the next week they were tied again 13–13 by Oregon State. So, although they were undefeated, they went into the final game against Southern California with three ties.

They came out of the game with four.

UCLA had its first chance to go to the Rose Bowl—at the expense of cross-town rival Southern California, whom the Bruins had never beaten. There were 103,000 people jammed into the

Coach Babe Horrell (at left) led UCLA to a share of the conference title in 1939; great UCLA back Kenny Washington rushed for 850 yards that year, and his backfield partner Jackie Robinson (above) led the league in punt returns for both 1939 and 1940. Fourth-stringer Doyle Nave tossed the ball, and reserve Al Krueger caught it (at right) for USC's 7–3 win over Duke in the 1939 Rose Bowl.

Coliseum that day but if they were looking for points they went home disappointed. The Trojans threatened early, but were turned back. Finally, late in the game UCLA finally put together a drive, marching 76 yards to a first down on the USC four-yard line. But the Bruins—ignoring their outstanding 6-foot-5-inch end, Woody Strode (who later appeared in many motion pictures)—ran four straight plays and four straight times the Trojans stopped them.

The game ended 0–0, UCLA settled for a share of the Pacific Coast Conference title and Howard Jones went to the Rose Bowl for the fifth and last time.

The opponent was Tennessee, which was in the midst of a dynasty under the great coach, General Robert Neyland. The Volunteers had won ten straight games in 1938, then shut out Oklahoma in the Orange Bowl; in 1939 they again went 10–0 and came into the Rose Bowl not only unbeaten but—just as Duke had been the previous year—unscored upon. And they were to go unbeaten again in the 1940 regular season before losing to Boston College in the Sugar Bowl.

It was a typical Neyland team, small but extremely fast, strong defensively and boasting a good kicking game. In Bob Suffridge, a 185-pound guard, they had a leader who is still generally recognized as one of the greatest linemen of all time. However, Tennessee had some key injuries in the Rose Bowl game, notably

two-time All-American halfback George Cafego, who had finished fourth in the Heisman Trophy balloting that year.

The Trojans were just too big and too deep. Amby Schindler did the most damage for USC, replacing All-American Grenny Landsell in the second quarter and running for most of the yardage on Southern California's first touchdown drive; he himself scored from three yards out. Later he returned to the game and guided an 85-yard march which took the ball to the Tennessee one yard line. At that point, he told the Trojan huddle 'We're in the Rose Bowl, let's give these people something to talk about.'

That something was a pass to Al Krueger, the unheralded sub who had caught the winning pass from Doyle Nave in the previous year's Rose Bowl and now was a star who had made the All-Coast team in that 1939 season. He caught the one yard toss from Schindler and the Trojans had a 13–0 win and the school's sixth straight Rose Bowl victory.

Nave, incidentally, played briefly in that game against Tennessee, but this time was not a factor.

That was Howard Jones' last hurrah. The Trojans managed only three wins—although one of them was over UCLA—and two ties in nine games in 1940 and on 27 July 1941, at the age of 56, one of the great football coaches in history died. Jones had lived long enough, however, to see a season that changed the collegiate game—completely and forever.

The Wow Boys and the T-Formation

The 1940 football season promised to be a dismal one for Stanford.

After all, the Indians were coming off their worst season in history, a 1–7–1 record and had lost the 1939 Big Game to California for the fourth straight year by an embarrassing 32–14 score that would have been even worse had not a sophomore named Frankie Albert generated two fourth-quarter touchdowns. Tiny Thornhill, who was 10–21–5 and had had only one winning season (barely, at 4–3–2 in 1937) in the four years since the Vow Boys had graduated, was under heavy fire; Stanford's first win of the season, an Albert-led 14–3 upset of Dartmouth in the final game, couldn't save his job.

A search for a new coach who could turn the program around and put the Indians back on top was begun. But when the name of Clark Shaughnessy came up, Stanford people thought at first that somebody was pulling their collective leg. After all, Shaughnessy had just finished a 2–6 season at University of Chicago and had lost to Michigan by 85–0, to Illinois by 66–0, to Ohio State by 61–0 and to Harvard by the same score, to West Virginia by 47–0.... Well, you get the idea.

And yet, football people kept telling the Stanford officials, 'You should hire this guy.' When they did, they completely revolutionized college football.

Clark D Shaughnessy was another of those coaches who lived football. He neither smoked nor drank—although he reportedly was stopped for drunk driving on his way home one night because he actually was diagramming plays on the breath-fogged inside of his windshield with one hand and steering with the other. He led a spartan life, retiring early and arising even earlier—often waking his assistants well before dawn because he'd had an idea for a new play.

'I remember the first (team) meeting,' star halfback Pete Kmetovic recalled. 'Shaughnessy was quite different from Thornhill, more like a professor lecturing up there. Thornhill was very loose, not really very well-organized compared to Shaughnessy.

'He ran the whole show, and he was very formal—everybody called him coach. The people that played a lot worshipped him, although I guess those who didn't play much weren't so sure.'

At the same time that Shaughnessy was suffering through the death throes of collegiate football at Chicago, he also was working with George Halas of the National Football League's Chicago Bears, renovating the old T-formation. When Stanford, finally convinced that Shaughnessy was no joke, hired him to replace Thornhill, he brought that formation to Palo Alto and brought Bears quarterback Bernie Masterson along to help teach it in spring practice.

'Gentlemen,' he told his players at their first meeting, as he began to draw diagrams on the blackboard, 'I'm going to teach you a new formation. If you master it, it will take you to the Rose Bowl.'

The T-formation was not, however, precisely new. It had first been used by Walter Camp at Yale and A A Stagg at Chicago around the turn of the century. But when Pop Warner came along with his single and double wings at Carlisle, the intricate T-formation was all but forgotten.

A sportswriter once complimented Shaugnessy on 'inventing' the formation. 'Young man,' the coach said, 'I appreciate the compliment, but I must admit that I played the T under Doc Williams at Minnesota in 1911. I've just added a few little extras.'

Indeed he had. The formation as Shaughnessy taught it was based on quickness and deception instead of the raw power and sustained blocking of the then-popular single wing. A very few schools were using the T then, but within one year 50 percent of the college teams in the nation had adopted it; within two years it was 90 percent.

Yet, there were moments of doubt at first. 'We installed it in the spring,' Kmetovic remembered. 'We weren't very optimistic because we had a tough time the year before. We all accepted it—I don't remember anybody saying it wouldn't work or anything like that. The only time I remember us having great doubts was when we scrimmaged just before the (season-opening) USF game and we had a tough time beating the freshmen, 7–0.'

Others were even less confident. Shaughnessy himself almost scrapped it after a particularly poor spring practice scrimmage. And Pop Warner—perhaps the most innovative football coach of all time—was quoted thusly before the 1940 season: 'If Stanford wins a single game with that crazy formation, you can throw all

Clark Shaughnessy (at right) and George Halas improved the old disused T-formation, and Shaughnessy brought it to Stanford when he started coaching there in 1940. It revolutionized football—just the thing for a truly dedicated football coach such as Shaughnessy.

Above: Stanford's 'Wow Boys' practice the T-formation for their tough 1941 Rose Bowl opponent, Nebraska. The Indians won 21–13, as the 'T' enabled their quick backfield to 'walk through walls'—ie, their opponent's defensive line. Stanford's backfield was (above, left to right, at rear) Hugh Gallarneau, Norm Standlee, Frankie Al-bert (also below right) and Pete Kmetovic. Indian linemen Vic Lindskog (at right) and Chuck Taylor (below left) learned Clark Shaughnessy's hole-opening 'brush blocking'—in which the opposition was literally brushed aside—which gave linemen mobility and maximum utility, but made uninitiated runners a little timorous.

the football I ever knew into the Pacific Ocean. What Clark is doing is positively ridiculous.'

No prophet, he.

Actually, Shaugnessy had walked into a perfect situation. Not only did he have a team that could do nothing but improve, but as Kmetovic said, 'I think the formation happened to click with the personnel at the time. He made some good moves, and we had ideal players for the T.

Frankie Albert and Kmetovic had alternated the previous year—Don Liebendorfer, the Indians' publicist and chronicler, described them as 'two somewhat inept tailbacks.' But Albert, the little lefthander who became the San Francisco 49ers' first quarterback and later their coach, was perfectly suited to the T—a capable passer, master ball-handler and first and best of the bootleg T quarterbacks. Kmetovic, at 175 pounds and with fine speed, was the breakaway runner needed for one halfback and Hugh Gallarneau, a slashing 200-pound runner who had boxed in Chicago because his high school didn't have football, was perfect at the other halfback. Norm 'Big Chief' Standlee was the perfect T fullback—a 225-pound bruiser who could block and run inside. All four, incidentally went on to successful pro careers.

Shaughnessy also took two single wing blocking backs, a sophomore named Chuck Taylor and a junior college transfer named Vic Lindskog, and moved them to the line. Taylor (later a Rose Bowl coach and then athletic director at Stanford) is in the National Football Hall of Fame; Lindskog, who at first rebelled at the move but finally relented, became one of the great centers in pro football. And Stanford already had a standout tackle in Bruno Banducci—yet another who made his mark as a pro with the 49ers.

The pieces were in place.

Understand that although the T was a wide-open offense, it was not the aerial circus seen nowadays. In the mid-1930s the rules had been changed to open up the passing game, but consider the reporter who, before the 1939 Stanford-California

game, said that one of the Indians' bright spots had been the passing of a sophomore named Frankie Albert; he had thrown for 258 yards that season! That's about an average afternoon for most quarterbacks now.

In 1940 the Indians—soon to be dubbed 'The Wow Boys'—threw only about nine passes per game. In fact, Washington State and its great but unheralded quarterback Billy Sewell led the nation that year in pass completions—with 99.

What Shaughnessy's Stanford team relied on was again quick-hitting plays and (against a strong USF team in the 1940 season opener), stood directly behind the center and set Pete Kmetovic in motion,' Albert once recalled. 'USF didn't know what to do. They had never seen a man under the center, or a man in motion. I just kind of flipped the ball to Kmetovic; that's all I had to do and he went 40 yards.'

Utah had played Santa Clara in the opener of a doubleheader at Kezar Stadium that day. Albert recalled Utah's Mac Speedie, later a professional end with Cleveland, coming back onto the field after his game to watch the Stanford game, taking one look and running back to his locker room shouting, 'Hey, you guys come out here. There's this crazy formation and these guys are running all over the place. I can't find the football.'

Bill Leiser, one of the fine sportswriters and long-time sports editor of the *San Francisco Chronicle*, wrote after that game: 'T football is different. Why, some of those Stanford kids running away from the play actually had defenders chasing them harder than other defenders were chasing the ball-carrier. George Malley, the USF coach, looked like a man who had seen a ghost.'

Nobody knew what to expect or what to do about it. Stanford was the underdog in every one of its firs six games—and just kept on winning.

'For the first four games,' Kmetovic said, 'we got a different defense against us each time. Mostly people used a six man-line. But we didn't really pay much attention; I never really worried about the defenses, I just worried about scoring touchdowns.'

That the Wow Boys did with great regularity. They beat USF 27–0 in that opener, then polished off Oregon. They barely got past Santa Clara 7–6—but the Broncos went on to finish the season ranked 12th in the nation. Washington State fell, and Stanford then ended USC's 17-game unbeaten string with a 21–7 victory with Albert throwing 61 yards to Kmetovic for one touchdown and returning an intercepted pass for another. The next week it was UCLA.

What turned out to be the Indians' most important victory came in the seventh game. Washington was to lose only two games all year, to Number One ranked Minnesota in the opener and to Stanford. The Huskies led 10–0 late in the third quarter and had the ball at the Stanford 29 yard line, second down and just one yard to go for a first down. Three successive plays; the first one lost half a yard, the second got that back—but no more—and the third was stopped dead for no gain. Stanford took over the ball and three plays later Albert and the explosive Kmetovic hooked up on a 56-yard touchdown pass that turned the tide. Soon after that Albert intercepted a Husky pass to set up a touchdown by Hugh Gallarneau and give Stanford the lead. Kmetovic finished it off with a 43 yard interception return that made the final score 20–10.

Washington always felt that had its star fullback Walt Harrison not been injured and forced out of the game when the Huskies had a 10–0 lead, they would have won—but they forget that Stanford's own fine fullback Norm Standlee was hurt early in that game and did not return.

Be that as it may, the Indians then beat Oregon State and came to the last hurdle of the regular season, California.

The Stanford Wow Boys *(above)* affirmed the importance of the modern T-formation in their 1941 Rose Bowl win. No longer was blocking a matter of destoying your man: runners discovered the wide open spaces—the game took on a supple, tactical and sleight-of-hand aspect—and the quarterback directed the on-field action.

The Bears were just 4–4 going into that game (they would finish the season with a 4–6 record), but were playing better than that. Their three losses in the PCC were by a total of 10 points and they had upset USC. The other loss was in the opener to powerful Michigan and its great runner Tom Harmon. Harmon, who won the Heisman Trophy that year, had an incredible game—in more ways than one; he scored four touchdowns, three of them from more than 50 yards out including a 94-yard return of the opening

kickoff; and on one of his long scoring runs, a devoted California fan named H J 'Bud' Brennan leaped out of the stands and tried to tackle Harmon at the goal line.

As had all the Bears that day—he missed.

California gave the Indians all they could handle in that Big Game, but two bad center snaps on punts were very costly to the Bears. After the second of them, Albert competely fooled everybody with a bootleg and, ball tucked on his hip, waltzed un-molested into the end zone to give Stanford a 13–0 lead.

That was just enough. Late in the third quarter Carl Hobert intercepted an Albert pass and ran it back to the Indian one-yard line but Stanford stopped the Bears on four straight plays and that was the game. Cal mounted another drive later, but by the

time it reached the end zone there were just 15 seconds left in the game and Stanford had a 13–7 win, a 9–0 record, the Number Two ranking in the nation and a Rose Bowl invitation.

The Indians wanted Number One Minnesota as the opponent but the Big Nine (not yet the Big Ten—Michigan State had not yet joined) banned post-season play at that time. Nebraska—ranked seventh and with only a loss to Minnesota marring its record—was asked instead.

At Pasadena the Indians were their usual explosive, deceptive selves. The Associated Press called them 'Magicians of the gridiron.'

'Twice Nebraska forged ahead,' the A P reported, 'and each time Stanford, with Frankie Albert, Hugh Gallarneau, Pete Kmetovic and

Norm Standlee (although Standlee was hurt in the first half and missed the rest of the game), battering and befuddling the Huskers, came from behind, then roared on to a decisive triumph.'

'Little Kmetovic,' as the players called him, ran 29 yards to set up the first Stanford touchdown, by Gallarneau; Albert had a 40-yard touchdown pass to Gallarneau and Kmetovic then provided the play of the day—some say the play of the year or the decade. Nebraska had just put on a great goal-line stand, stopping Stanford four times inside the one-yard line but the Huskers then were forced to punt from their own end zone.

Kmetovic caught it at the Nebraska 40 and returned it 'with the most sensational touchdown run of the game,' the AP reported. He ran first to the left, wheeled and headed to the right. The

Oregon State's Beavers gnawed the Duke Blue Devils' pitchforks to kindling, beating them 20–16 in the 1942 Rose Bowl. Alonzo 'Lon' Stiner *(above)* had a knack for putting fire under his teams' tails, including staged arguments and well-timed property damage.

downfield blocking that followed was a sight to behold. Huskers were strewn like cornstalks over the turf. Francis (Nebraska fullback Mike Francis) was somersaulted by one block (by Dick Palmer) and was injured, and there was Kmetovic squatting on the ball across the goal stripe.' There literally was not a Nebraska player on his feet when Pete scored.

The final score was 21–13 and Stanford had completed one of the greatest turnarounds in football history, from a 1–7–1 record to 10–0 and a Rose Bowl victory. Clark Shaughnessy was named National Coach of the Year, Albert was a unanimous All-American choice and the Indians placed eight players on the first two All-Coast teams.

But there was something even more important about that game, something that had far-reaching consequences and thus was merited so much space here. 'That was the game that sold the T-formation—the modern T style of offense—to school and college football,' Shaughnessy said later. 'Prior to this game the system had been regarded as too intricate and too complicated....The performance by the Stanford boys in their first year with this system proved it could be worked. Then everybody accepted it. That's why I contend this was one of the most important games of modern football.'

The 1941 season was an anti-climax, and not only for Stanford. Many of the Wow Boys returned, including Albert and Kmetovic in the backfield, but even Magic doesn't last forever; there were injuries, and several players were suspended for taking favors from alumni. The Indians won their first two, but Oregon State—which went on to win the PCC title—ended their unbeaten string with a 10–0 victory in the third game when Kmetovic was hurt on a late tackle. They also lost to Washington State 14–13 and finally were shut out by California 16–0; the

Bears, who had only a 3–5 record coming into the game, threw Albert for 62 yards in losses and blocked three punts (one led to a safety and another was turned into a touchdown by All-American tackle Bob Reinhard).

Just days later the Japanese bombed Pearl Harbor, the United States was in World War II to stay, and football again was shunted aside. Shaughnessy—predicting correctly that many of the West Coast schools, including Stanford, would give up football for the duration—resigned a week later to become coach and athletic director at Maryland.

That the next few years would be unsettled ones for the college game became apparent almost immediately. Oregon State, guided by the outstanding and underrated Lon Stiner, had finally won a Rose Bowl bid and was scheduled to meet Duke—but they had no place to play. The week after Pearl Harbor, military officials told California Governor Cuthbert Olsen to shut down Santa Anita race track and cancel the East-West Shrine and Rose Bowl games, fearing that large gatherings of people on the Pacific Coast would be too inviting a target for air raids. Percy Locey, Oregon State's dynamic athletic director, tried to get the edict changed but when the army threatened to send in troops if necessary to stop the game, he formulated another plan.

If he, Locey, would assume responsibility for organizing the game (he told Duke coach Wallace Wade), could they play in Duke's home stadium in Durham, NC? Done, said Wade—who then had the difficult task of convincing his players.

The Duke team had voted unanimously to accept a Rose Bowl bid—when it meant a trip to Los Angeles. But stay home and put in another month's practice? That wasn't so popular; the vote was 25–2 against until Wade finally agreed to give the players a long Christmas holiday.

Duke was ranked Number Two in the nation behind Minnesota. Texas also was in the Rose Bowl picture, incidentally, and when Duke was chosen the Longhorns felt slighted and took it out on their final opponent, Oregon, by a 71–7 score.

The Blue Devils were 9–0, had scored 311 points, had an All-American tailback in Steve Lach and were heavy favorites to win in Wade's sixth trip to the Rose Bowl (it was his fifth as a coach). But the oddsmakers reckoned without Lon Stiner.

Stiner had been named coach of the Beavers in 1933 and he was to hold the job through the 1948 season, compiling a 74–49–17 record. When he took over, Oregon State still was playing teams like Ashland Normal and Willamette in addition to its PCC schedule, but he surprised people immediately by compiling a first-year record of 6–2–2—including a 0–0 tie with Howard Jones' fine USC team, which was 10–1–1 and lost only to Stanford that year.

Stiner had a great knack for getting his teams fired up—whether by his emotional pre-game pep talks or by other ploys. Once, after delivering his pre-game fight talk, he went on to lead his team onto the field—and discovered that the dressing room door had inadvertently been locked. Shouting, 'They can't keep us off the field, boys,' the former All-American tackle at Nebraska threw his 230 pounds against the door, smashing it off its hinges; the Beavers poured onto the field and proceeded once again to take it out on the other team.

'Lon was a hard-nosed coach,' Quentin Greenough, the fine center on that Rose Bowl team, once said. 'He was a real character, but he didn't fool around when it came to practicing football.'

Stiner's best team may have been in 1939, but unfortunately for the Beavers their 9–1–1 record included a loss to USC and a tie with UCLA—who wound up playing each other for the Rose Bowl bid. The following year Oregon State fell to 5–3–1, and before the 1941 season the team was picked to finish last in the

PCC. 'Our situation is terrible,' Stiner said, and the Beavers proceeded to prove it by losing to USC in the opener. They barely beat Washington 9–6 and ended Stanford's win streak with that 10–0 victory, but then fell to Washington State 7–0.

However, they gave up only seven points in their final five games; won all of them and went to Pasadena—sorry, to Durham, North Carolina—with a 7–2 record. Even at that, they didn't figure to be much of a test for Duke, but while the Blue Devils were enjoying Christmas at home, Stiner was working his players hard. And if that didn't get them ready, he had another ploy.

He talked one of the highway patrolmen who was escorting the Oregon State team to the stadium for the game into staging an argument. He called the patrolman every name he could think of, then stormed angrily back onto the bus. 'It worked,' he said later. 'The boys were ready to walk on hot coals and eat broken glass.'

They didn't have to do quite that much. Beaver halfback Don Durdan, a great all-around athlete who also played on championship basketball and baseball teams at Oregon State, scored the first touchdown and passed for the second. Duke came back to tie it at 14–14, but two minutes later Bob Dethman passed 70 yards to Gene Gray for a score. Duke then drove to the OSC nine yard line, but suffered its fourth pass interception of the game (the Devils also fumbled three times) and although Durdan subsequently was tackled in the end zone for a safety, Oregon State won 20–16.

As expected, the war was having its effect; many players were now in the service or in some cases, at other schools for military training. In the 1942 season UCLA, with Babe Horrell still at the helm and led by Bob Waterfield—who went on to become a great professional quarterback with the Los Angeles Rams (and incidentally, the husband of sultry movie star Jane Russell)—beat USC for the first time ever, 14–7 and narrowly won the PCC title with its 7–3 record.

The Bruins' Rose Bowl opponent was Georgia, coached by Wally Butts and featuring a wide-open attack led by Heisman Trophy winner Frankie Sinkwich and sophomore Charlie Trippi—another future Hall of Famer. The Bulldogs were 10–1 and had scored 367 points, but had lost to Auburn, the only other T-formation team it had faced before meeting UCLA.

Sinkwich, the first man ever to gain more than 2000 yards rushing and passing in a single season, had two sprained ankles but played long enough in the Rose Bowl to score the only touchdown; Trippi rushed for 130 yards and passed for 96 more and was named the game's MVP. The game was scoreless until the fourth quarter, but after UCLA's third great goal-line stand of the game, this one aided by Sinkwich's fumble at the three-yard line, Waterfield had to punt from his own end zone and it was blocked for a safety. The next time UCLA got the ball Waterfield threw an interception which was run back to the Bruins' 25 yard line and Sinkwich finally scored from the two.

The following season, 1943, all of the PCC teams except USC, UCLA, California and Washington dropped football temporarily. Southern California went 7–2—both losses coming late in the season to service teams; Washington won all four games in an abbreviated season with the only collegiate opponent being Whitman College. Because of war-enforced travel restrictions and so many teams being in a state of flux, the Huskies and Trojans met in the first non-intersectional Rose Bowl since World War I.

The Huskies had not played since October, and USC had little trouble. Quarterback Jim Hardy threw three touchdown passes and Norm Verry, the fine Trojan guard who had missed all season with injuries, returned to play what coach Jeff Cravath called 'the greatest defensive game at guard the bowl ever saw.' Southern California won 29–0.

Heisman Trophy winner Frank Sinkwich *(top)* made the scoring difference in Georgia's 9–0 win over UCLA in the 1943 Rose Bowl. Sinkwich was the first man ever to gain more than 2000 yards rushing and passing in a single season. Jeff Cravath *(above)* continued the USC dynasty, which he inherited from Howard Jones.

The following year the Trojans went unbeaten, including two wins over California and a win and a tie in two games with UCLA, and beat a freshmen-laden but previously unbeaten Tennessee team in the Rose Bowl 25–0. Hardy threw two more touchdown passes and scored one himself, prompting Cravath, never short of superlatives, to call him 'the greatest T-formation quarterback I have ever seen in action.'

In 1945 all of the conference schools resumed football except Stanford, which took it up again a year later. A new era was dawning—and for a while at least, it was a pretty bleak one for the Pacific Coast Conference.

The New Rose Bowl

With the end of World War II in sight, all of the schools in the Pacific Coast Conference resumed football in 1945—except Stanford, which came back the following year. A new Rose Bowl contract with the Big Nine was in the works—but every silver lining, they say, has a cloud: this one had several.

For one thing, the three oldest coaches in the PCC, in terms of service, left before that 1945 season—the venerable Babe Hollingbery at Washington State, Stub Allison at California and Babe Horrell at UCLA. For another, the Rose Bowl pact which began with the 1 January 1947 game proved to be an unmitigated disaster for the Pacific Coast schools (at least on the field) for a good many years—the Western representative won only one of the first 13 games from the Big Nine (soon to become the Big Ten).

And finally it was just generally a difficult time, with the country recovering from war. By 1946 the nation had more pressing concerns than college football and in addition, many of the players were returned veterans three or four years older than the average collegian, who had had their fill of strict regimentation from their sergeants and didn't want it from their coaches too.

Jim 'Truck' Cullom, a fine tackle at California at that time and later an assistant coach there, summed it up nicely. He had been a freshman in 1946 under Frank Wickhorst, who had been ousted after one year and an almost open rebellion by his players.

'You had 40 guys who had just come back from getting their butts shot at,' Cullom said, 'and they didn't want to be disciplined. Waldorf (Pappy Waldorf, who replaced Wickhorst in '47) said he learned a lot coaching (at Northwestern) in 1946, and as a result he treated us as mature men instead of college students.

'I think anybody who was successful in 1946 was either a genius or damned lucky.'

The new coaches might have been both—or neither—but they had mixed success. Phil Sarboe replaced Hollingbery, who had left in a salary dispute after 17 years at Pullman; Sarboe had only one winning season in the five he coached at Washington State—but that one season was his first, 1945, when the Cougars went 6–2–1. Those were all conference games, incidentally, including two each with Oregon, Oregon State and Idaho but the only California school they played was Cal (a 7–7 tie) and Southern California got the Rose Bowl bid on the basis of a 5–1 conference mark.

Bert LaBrucherie meanwhile succeeded Horrell at UCLA, went 5–4 in 1945 and the next year had the Bruins in the Rose Bowl.

At Berkeley, Allison had been under pressure even before the war. Following his great teams of 1937–38, Stub had not had a winning season; in 1944 the Bears got off to a 3–0–1 start, the tie being with Rose Bowl-bound USC—and then lost their last six games by a composite score of 136–21. Allison resigned and Lawrence 'Buck' Shaw took over. Shaw is in the National Football Hall of Fame as a coach but he barely created a stir at Cal; his 1945 team went 4–5–1 and following that season he left to become the first coach of the San Francisco 49ers in the brand new pro league—the All-American Football Conference.

The return to normalcy—more or less—didn't change some things, of course: in 1945 Southern California won another title and went to another Rose Bowl, their third in a row under Jeff Cravath.

It was not the Trojans' best team. They had their 16-game unbeaten string ended in the fourth game of the year when a little back named Marv Tommervik, later a Rose Bowl and East-West Shrine game official, ran for three touchdowns including a 67-yard dash, and passed for two more as the San Diego Navy team embarrassed USC 33–6. They also lost to Washington 13–7 and to St Mary's 26–0—although in fairness, the Gaels, who then played big-time football, did wind up that season ranked seventh in the nation. Southern Cal finished the regular season with its second win of the year over UCLA and a 5–1 record in the PCC (7–3) overall and met Alabama in the Rose Bowl.

It was hardly worth the drive out to Pasadena for the Trojans. The Crimson Tide had finished the season with a 9–0 record, was ranked Number Two in the nation behind the great Army team of Doc Blanchard and Glenn Davis and still was coached by pass-minded Frank Thomas—who, you may recall had unleashed the Dixie Howell-Don Hutson combination on Stanford's Wow Boys in the 1935 Rose Bowl. And in 1945 he had another great passer, Harry Gilmer.

But this time it wasn't passing that beat the Trojans. Gilmer threw just 12 times, completing only four; however, he ran for 116 yards as Alabama handed USC just a plain, old-fashioned horsewhipping. The final score was 34–14 and it wasn't that close—the Tide led 27–0 in the second quarter. Southern California gained just six yards rushing and 41 yards total in the entire game.

'The ushers,' wrote Ned Cronin of the *Los Angeles Daily News*, 'were having trouble finding places in the stands for the guys wearing white jerseys and red helmets who were constantly being thrown up there by the Alabamans.'

In 1943, all of the PCC teams except Washington, Cal, USC and UCLA dropped football until 1945—the end of World War II. In 1947, the PCC signed a new Rose Bowl pact, and the Pasadena stadium *(at right)* kept its gates open to Pacific Coast football.

That was USC's first Rose Bowl loss after eight wins, and the last Rose Bowl game involving an 'outside' team; the following year the Pacific Coast and Big Nine Conferences signed a contract guaranteeing (with certain reservations) that their two champions would meet in Pasadena on New Year's Day. But if the PCC thought that was going to make things any easier, it was in for a rude disappointment.

The conference was whole again in 1946: Stanford resumed football that year under Marchie Schwartz, a former Clark Shaughnessy assistant who had been named head coach in 1942. The Indians had lost their first three games that year but, led by an All-American guard named Chuck Taylor—Stanford fans would hear a lot more of that name—they won six of their last seven and were in Rose Bowl contention. Schwartz also produced a winning record in 1946 (6–3–1) but the championship remained in Los Angeles that year.

It just moved across town.

Babe Horrell had had UCLA on a football roller coaster; his two best years—a 6–0–4 record and tie for the PCC title in 1939 and a 7–3 record and a Rose Bowl bid in 1943—had been immediately followed by respective marks of 1–9 and 1–8. Bert La-Brucherie replaced him in 1945; he finished 5–4 that season, but the following year it all came together.

The core of that team—which won 10 straight games during the regular season—was a group of veterans back from the service: end Burr Baldwin, a unanimous All-American and one of

In 1946, UCLA had an outstanding team—including Burr Baldwin, Don Paul, Ernie Case and Tom Fears—that won 10 straight games only to crumble 45–10 in the Rose Bowl to Illinois. The coaching staff of this team was *(above, left to right)* AJ 'Sturzy' Sturzenegger, William 'Dutch' Fehring, head coach Bert LaBrucherie, Shelby Calhoun and Ned Mathews. Lynn Osbert 'Pappy' Waldorf *(opposite)* took three straight Cal Berkeley teams to the Rose Bowl—in 1949, '50 and '51. From 1947 to 1951, he led Cal to a regular season record of 38–1–1, and had an overall record at Berkeley (1947-56) of 62-32-4.

just seven Bruins who has ever had his number retired; tackle Don Malmberg; center Don Paul, a future pro star; and quarterback Ernie Case—all of them All-Coast selections. The other end was Tom Fears, who became a National Football League great; Bill Chambers, who played tackle along with Malmberg, also was an all-conference selection; Cal Rossi, although he broke his leg in mid-season; and fine runners Gene Rowland and Ernie Johnson. They outscored their regular-season opponents by 313 points to 72 and only USC and California made a game of it— the Bruins winning those two games by identical 13–6 scores. LaBrucherie was named Coach of the Year.

But Illinois also had an outstanding team. As the champion of the Big Nine (Michigan State had not yet joined the league), the Illini became that league's first Rose Bowl representative since Ohio State had lost to the Cal Wonder Team 28–0 in 1921. The Illini were coached by one of the all-time greats, the inspirational Ray Eliot, but they had started slowly, losing to National Champion Notre Dame and to Indiana in their first four games. At that point even, there was a petition circulated among the student body to fire Eliot, but then the team caught fire and finished fifth in the nation—one spot behind UCLA.

Illinois also was led by service returnees—notably All-Americans Buddy Young and Alex Agase. The pint-sized Young, who ironically almost went to UCLA instead of returning to Illinois when he got out of the service, was one of the most elusive backs ever to play the game. Agase was a three-time All-American; first at Illinois; then at Purdue, where he was in training during the war; and finally again at Illinois. In addition, his brother Lou was a fine tackle; Young had great backfield help in quarterback Perry Moss and halfback Julie Rykovich, and the defensive line was anchored by Les Bingaman, the 300-pound giant who later starred for the Detroit Lions.

UCLA took an early 7–6 lead in the Rose Bowl game and then the roof fell in. Young and Rykovich each ran for 103 yards and were named co-MVPs of the game and Illinois breezed to a 45–14 victory despite a 103-yard kickoff return by a 144-pound substitute UCLA halfback named Al Hoisch. Following the game the Illini rather unkindly referred to the Bruins as 'weaker than the weakest Big Nine team.'

It was a dismal start to this new relationship and things weren't going to get any better for a long time.

It did not look—in 1946—as if California would have to worry about the whys and wherefores of the Rose Bowl for a long time, either. Frank Wickhorst had been an assistant coach at Berkeley for 15 years and it seemed natural enough to give him the head job when Buck Shaw moved to the 49ers. But wherever the fault lay, Wickhorst's short tenure was a disaster; the Bears finished with a 2–7 record—their worst in 64 years in football. When Cal lost to Stanford in the Big Game 25–6, some of the Bear fans finally vented their frustration by tearing up seats in the Memorial Stadium rooting section. The team insisted it would not play in 1947 unless it was under a different coach—all in all, a dark situation.

Brutus Hamilton, a great track coach and one of the finest gentlemen in intercollegiate sports, was doubling as athletic director at that time—he has been heavily criticized for his performance in that job, but he certainly knew his coaches. He hired Pete Newell, who led the Bears to the 1959 NCAA basketball championship, and he hired Pappy Waldorf.

Lynn O Waldorf had been an All-American tackle at Syracuse, and then had worked his way through the ranks on several college staffs to become a successful head coach at Northwestern, where he was named Coach of the Year in 1935. Perhaps he'd done all there was to do at Northwestern; perhaps he liked what he had seen of the Bay Area when he coached in the Shrine East-West game. But whatever the reason, he was convinced by Hamilton to move to Berkeley.

Waldorf, the 'Wise Walrus of Strawberry Canyon,' was a colorful character. He was never without a cigar—he even took it into the showers with him and, some swear, came out with it still lit. He may have known more limericks than any man alive, many of them not reprintable in a family text. He was in fact a man of myriad interests—among them bird-watching and Civil War military strategy.

He had a perpetual twinkle in his eye, a deep, jolly voice and an admirable girth; he once told his players they were a good group, and the irrepressible Jim Cullom responded, 'You're a pretty good group yourself, Pappy.' He would have made a terrific Santa Claus—and for the Bears, that's exactly what he turned out to be.

In the next four years, California's regular-season record was 38 wins, one loss, one tie. Waldorf immediately turned what had

been the worst team in the school's history into what may have been the best.

Character or not, Pappy was one of the most highly-respected men in the profession. When he left California after the 1956 season and was scouting for the 49ers, Bud Wilkinson—the great Oklahoma coach—said: 'You know, we don't allow pro scouts on our campus—except when Waldorf comes to town. Then I go meet the train.'

'Pappy was brilliant in handling players,' recalled Cullom, who played for Waldorf, was a student assistant and then (following a stint in Korea during which he was wounded) was Pappy's freshman coach. 'He never set down a hard, fast set of rules, but he was one of the few people I ever met who could be inconsistent but fair in every case, if that's possible. By that I mean he took every incident, every individual on their own basis. If he caught you drunk the night before a game, for instance, that would have been bad; if he caught you drunk in the middle of March, it was okay—not that that necessarily ever happened.

'He was exactly what he called himself, the chairman of the board. He hired a great staff—Wes Fry, Eggs Manske, Nibs Price, Bob Tessier (who died tragically two days after the Big Game in 1950)—all good teachers and tacticians. His staff did most of the coaching and he gave a lot of credit to them, I think justifiably. But he was a helluva chairman.

· 'He was extremely, painstakingly detailed. The first coaching meeting I attended lasted two hours, and when it was all over we had the center-quarterback exchange down. He listened to all his assistants, considered what they had offered, then said, "This is the way we're going to do it."

'I never had any idea that we were learning that much detail, except we went through 10 games (in 1948), won them all—then came back after two weeks off to practice for the Rose Bowl and, hell, they started all over with the stance.'

Waldorf wasted no time asserting himself in the PCC. From a 2–7 record in 1946, the Bears ran up a 9–1 mark in 1947: surely one of the great turnarounds in football history. The only loss was to USC 39–14, and that came about largely because of California's own mistakes; since the Trojans did not lose until the final game at the regular season (to Notre Dame) and went on to the Rose Bowl and a Number Eight national ranking, it made for a pretty respectable year.

Pappy also found out what the traditional Big Game with Stanford was all about in that, his first season. The Indians had lost their star running back Lloyd Merriman before the season even began, when he passed up his final year of eligibility to sign a pro baseball contract with the Cincinnati Reds—and they proceeded to go winless, the worst season in Stanford history. Oddsmakers rated California a 10–1 or four-touchdown favorite in the Big Game.

But these games are never easy. Cal led most of the way but Stanford, led by George Quist (who was returning to action from a broken ankle) hung in gamely. Finally a fourth-quarter fumble by the Bears' great fullback Jackie Jensen set up a touchdown pass from Don Campbell to Bob Anderson and an 18–14 lead, and when Quist intercepted a pass moments later and returned it to the Bears' 16-yard line, it looked like a miracle was at hand.

Cal's defense stiffened, however, and the Bears took over at their own 20 with less than three minutes to play and 80 yards to go. It didn't take long. Paul Keckley, who had sat out the entire game with an injury, pleaded with Waldorf to send him into the game and Pappy finally relented. On second down Jensen passed to Keckley at the Cal 35, and he raced the remaining 65 yards—an 80-yard play in all. Truck Cullom kicked his third conversion of the day and Cal had a 21–18 win in what some consider the most exciting Big Game of all time. Waldorf was graceful in victory—'Stanford outplayed us, they deserved to win the game,' he said—but it was California that took home the Axe.

The loss to Southern California kept Cal out of the Rose Bowl—the Trojans finished 6–0 in the conference while California and Oregon were each 5–1. That may have been a blessing in disguise.

USC had won seven of its first eight games—the exception being a second-game tie with Rice, 7–7. The Trojans had two All-American selections in end Paul Cleary and tackle John Ferraro, but in truth they lacked their usual offensive punch and it was the defense that made the early part of the schedule easy. Jim Powers would be a capable quarterback but he was just a sophomore, and Don Doll was a fine all-around back but he led the Trojans in rushing that year with just 246 yards in nine games, and he made his mark in the pros as a defensive back. The defense, meanwhile, gave up only 27 points in the first eight games—14 of them to California—and had five shutouts.

But Southern Cal was forced to play the Numbers One and Two teams in the nation in the final two games, and class told; the Trojans lost to top-ranked Notre Dame 38–7 and then was totally dismantled 49–0 by Michigan and its great back Bob Chappius—who accounted for 279 yards total offense (or 146 yards more than the entire USC team gained all day).

That was the end of USC domination for awhile. For the next three years it was all Golden Bears.

The Berkeley coaching staff responsible for three straight trips to the Rose Bowl was *(above left to right)* Ed 'Eggs' Manske, Wes Fry, Zeb Cutihy, Pappy Waldorf, Bob Tessier and Nibs Price. From 1948 into and including 1951, Cal was the PCC power. While three trips to the

In 1948 Waldorf's team was favored from the start and it didn't disappoint. Jensen gained 7.3 yards every time he ran the ball and rushed for 1080 yards to become the first 1000-yard rusher in the PCC since USC's Morley Drury in 1927, and only the second ever; the Bears averaged 30 points a game and had only two close matches—one a 13–7 win over USC. The other? By now it was getting to be habit.

Stanford had rebounded slightly from its terrible 1947 season but the Indians still were just 4–5 coming into the Big Game. It was another dogfight; Stanford was stopped once at the Cal two-yard line and on another occasion a quick whistle on a fumble recovery may have cost the Indians a touchdown. But Jensen ran wild—170 yards on 19 carries and another 35-yard touchdown run called back by penalty—and Cullom not only kicked Cal's conversion, he also blocked Stanford's. The Bears won 7–6 in what was, despite all the dramatic finishes of past Big Games, the first one-point decision in the game's history.

tures later showed clearly that he had fumbled before crossing the goal—but he was given the TD anyway.

In 1949 California put together its second straight undefeated regular season, and only USC lost to the Bears by less than two touchdowns (16–10). Stanford had a 4–1 conference record going into the final game and had an outside chance at the Rose Bowl if it could beat the Bears, but immediately after the Indians had scored to take a 14–12 lead, Cal's Jim Monachino broke loose for 84 yards to the Stanford four; Jack Swaner scored from there and the rout was on—it ended 33–14.

The Bears were ranked third in the nation but the Rose Bowl against Ohio State was destined to be just another New Year's Day disappointment. The game was tied when, with two minutes left in the game, Bear quarterback Bob Celeri couldn't handle a bad center snap on a punt attempt. He scrambled around and finally tried to kick the ball left-footed, on the run, but it went out of bounds at the California 13-yard line. The Bears held there but Jimmy Hague kicked a 30-yard field goal to give the Buckeyes—who had outplayed Cal throughout and certainly deserved the victory—a 17–14 win. (Stanford, incidentally, also played on New Year's Day, with considerably more success; the Indians beat Hawaii, 74–20.)

The 1950 season saw the first major change in PCC alignment—not counting the war years, of course; Montana, which had become a member in 1924 and had won only nine conference games in 24 seasons of play, finally saw the handwriting on the wall and dropped out of the league following the 1949 season. But, nine teams or ten—nobody was likely to slow up California.

The Bears again were undefeated going into the final game against Stanford, boasting a 33-game regular season win streak and featuring what Stanford coach Marchie Schwartz called 'the best backfield in the country.' He had some justification: the Bear running backs that year were Jim Monachino, who had gained 190 yards against Stanford the previous year and in 1950 had 604 yards and a 4.8-yards-per-carry average; Pete Schabarum, 511 yards and a 4.6 average; and the great 'Johnny O,' John Olszewski, who ran for 867 yards, and 6.6 yards every time he touched the ball. Stanford, however, had a fine passing game—a harbinger of things to come for many years—with quarterback Gary Kerkorian, and Cal was playing without injured Carl Van Heuit, an All-American that year whom Waldorf called 'the best safety in college football.' The game ended in a 7–7 tie, with both touchdowns—a 31-yard run by Schabarum and a nine-yard pass from Kerkorian to Boyd Benson—set up by fumbles. Stanford might have won had it not been for Les Richter, California's All-American linebacker, who intercepted a pass at the Cal two-yard line to stop one drive and sacked Kerkorian at the Bear 15 to halt another one.

So it was back to Pasadena for the Bears: one more Rose Bowl; one more disappointment. The opponent was Michigan, which had started the season with three losses and a tie in its first six games but had earned the bowl bid on the final day when Northwestern upset Illinois and the Wolverines, despite gaining only 27 yards all day, beat Ohio State 9–3 in a full-scale blizzard. The favored Bears took the early lead again, on a rare pass play—quarterback Jim Marinos had thrown only 49 times in 10 regular season games—from Marinos to Bob Cummings for 39 yards in the second quarter. But Cal missed a scoring chance at the end of the first half, when Waldorf disdained the field goal and ran on fourth down from the Wolverine's four-yard line and a 73-yard run by Schabarum was called back by a penalty. Michigan then dominated the fourth period, taking a 7–6 lead on a long drive capped by Don Dufek's first of two touchdowns and

Rose Bowl were unproductive, it wasn't Cal's fault; the PCC won only one Rose Bowl game (USC over Wisconsin 7–0 in 1953) from 1947 to 1960, when Washington would break the spell—and the Pacific Coast would again exercise national collegiate football power.

Number One Michigan would have been the Rose Bowl opponent for the undefeated and fourth-ranked Bears but the Big Nine had a no-repeat Rose Bowl rule at the time and Northwestern, Waldorf's old team which was ranked seventh in the nation, got the call—and a 20–14 win. Neither team threw the ball much—the Wildcats completed only one of four passes in the game—but it was still wide open. Frank Aschenbrenner raced 73 yards for a Northwestern touchdown—the longest TD run from scrimmage in Rose Bowl history. Jensen went 67 yards for Cal, the third longest ever and Ed Tunnicliff sprinted 43 yards for the winning score with two minutes and 58 seconds left in the game.

However, it was two very questionable calls that cost the Bears the game. One came on the first play of Northwestern's final 88 yard drive to the winning touchdown, when Tunnicliff fumbled at a fast whistle and left the Wildcats in possession of the ball. Earlier, Art Murakowski scored on a short plunge into the line and pic-

then locked up the 14–6 victory after the Bears, with nothing to lose in the closing minutes, disdained the punt on fourth-and-12 from their own 13 yard line and failed to make the first down.

That was Waldorf's last Rose Bowl although he continued to turn out good teams for awhile—the Bears were 8–2 in 1951, including a 20–7 win over Rose Bowl-bound Stanford, and 7–3 in 1952. But Pappy had made his mark on the Pacific Coast Conference, and he did it with good old-fashioned football—a powerful running game and hard-nosed defense.

California had a number of great players in that period. Guard Rod Franz was the first three-time All-American ever from the West Coast, in 1947–48–49. Tackle Jim Turner was a two-time All-American (48–49), as was Richter (50–51). Guard Forrest Klein, Monachino and Van Heuit all made at least one national team, as did Celeri, the colorful quarterback whose value lay far more in his signal-calling and daring field generalship than in his spotty passing. And there was Jon Baker, who later was an All-Pro linebacker. 'You can't talk about that group without mentioning Baker,' Jim Cullom said. 'He was totally without grace, totally without form and the best damned football player around.'

But Waldorf's teams were most famous for their running backs. They were legion: Billy Main, Monachino, Schabarum, Jack Swaner; Frank Brunk, who ran a kickoff back 100 yards for a touchdown to help beat USC 16–10 in 1949; Charlie Sarver, who only played about half a season because of injuries, but whom Waldorf called 'the best small back I've seen since Cotton Warburton'; and the best of all—Jackie Jensen and Johnny Olszewski.

Jensen was a great athlete, the 'Golden Boy'—a nickname inspired as much, perhaps, by his blond hair and good looks as by his athletic prowess. But athletic skill he had. Even though he left

Pete Schabarum was known as 'the One Man Gang,' and 'Mr Elastic,' due to his speed and elusiveness as a Cal halfback. In action *(above)*, during Cal's 35–0 crushing of UCLA in 1950, we see him extend a leg for yardage even as he's going down; and again, lunging as he's going down *(below)*. Even though he left after his Junior year, Jackie Jensen *(at right)* set a Cal career yardage record.

school after his junior year to sign a pro baseball contract, he ran for 1703 career yards (then a California record and still fifth on the Bears' all-time list). On the field he did everything. Old-time fans remember his 80-yard pass to Keckley that won the 1947 Big Game; fewer of them recall that in 1948, with Cal leading by a point in the fourth quarter, and the Bears in a fourth down and 29 yards to go situation, Jackie went back into punt formation— and then ran right up the middle for 31 yards; and fewer still are aware that Jensen still shares the Cal record for pass interceptions in a single season, with seven. In 1948 he was an All-American and finished fourth in the Heisman Trophy balloting behind Doak Walker, Charlie Justice and Chuck Bednarik—all among the all-time greats of the sport. Had he returned for his senior year he might very well have been the first West Coast player to win that coveted award, but instead he married Olympic diver Zoe Ann Olsen and signed with the Oakland Oaks of the Pacific Coast League, managed by Casey Stengel, for what was then an un-heard-of bonus—$25,000. It worked out pretty well; he went on to stardom in the American League with the Boston Red Sox.

Olszewski was another story. Like Jensen he was big enough— 195 pounds—and extremely fast and powerful, but stories about his off-field exploits (some true, some not) may have detracted from the fact that he was an amazing runner with a football under his arm. 'He puts the greatest pressure on a defense that I've ever seen,' was the way that Bear backfield coach Wes Fry described Johnny O. 'He has more power, both as a runner and blocker, than Jackie Jensen.'

In 1951 Olszewski rushed for 269 yards in 20 carries against Washington State—at the time the second-greatest single-game performance in league history, and his career total of 2504 yards was a PCC record, breaking the mark set just the previous year by Washington's great Hugh McElhenny. He led Cal in rushing for

Johnny Olzewski *(right)* set a league career total record of 2504 yards and a single-game record of 269 yards in 20 carries (in 1951). He is shown *above and below* in action during the 1950 Cal-UCLA game, in which season he had 1008 yards rushing. He led Cal in rushing for three straight years and set the school record for 23

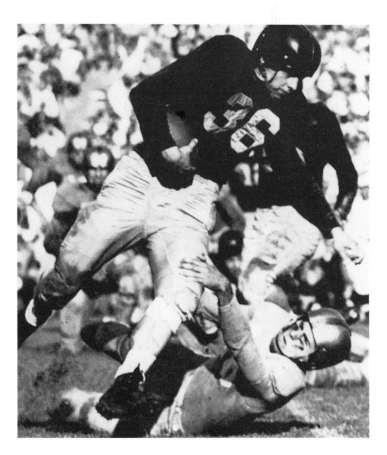

three straight seasons and held the school career record for 23 years. As a sophomore in 1950 he had 1008 yards, losing the PCC rushing crown to McElhenny, who had 1107. In 1951 Olszewski suffered a controversial knee injury in the opening seconds of the USC game—Cal people insisted Pat Cannamela, the Trojans' All-American linebacker, twisted Johnny O's knee intentionally; he missed that game, three others and much of a fifth game and the Bears, who had been undefeated and ranked Number One in the nation through the first four games, lost to USC and also fell to UCLA while he was out of action. He still finished the season with 651 yards on just 89 carries, and in 1952 he added another 845 yards; needing 118 yards against Stanford in his final game to break the conference record, he gained 122.

Of course, it wasn't just Waldorf and the Golden Bears who stood out in that era. Two of the finest players in the history of the conference were almost—but not quite—enough to shift the balance of power to the Northwest.

The University of Oregon had finished fourth in the PCC with a 6–3 record in 1935, under Prink Callison; from that time until 1947 the Ducks never had a record that was better than .500 nor a finish that was higher than fifth. Then in 1947, Jim Aiken took the head coaching job.

He also got a very lucky break. George Bell, a highly-regarded running back, transferred in from a Southern California junior college and he brought his friend with him—a quarterback named Norm Van Brocklin. And it was Van Brocklin, of course, who turned out to be the All-American and Hall of Famer and later a great professional passer.

Aiken had his problems as a coach. The Ducks went to the Cotton Bowl following the 1948 season and lost to Southern Methodist—which had Heisman Trophy winner Doak Walker and a sophomore named Kyle Rote. The final score was only 21–13 but a headline in the Eugene, *Oregon Register-Guard* said, 'Too Much Party, Not Enough Football Blamed for Duck Defeat.' Dan Garza, an All-PCC end that year, said later, 'We didn't have the coaching experience to know how to handle a post-season game. We went down there two weeks early and there was so much going on. There just wasn't time to get involved in football. Then there was the dissension; players were hollering at players, coaches were arguing with players. Then Coach Aiken decided to change our defense from the one we'd been playing all year. There were just a lot of things like that.'

The Ducks felt they should have been in the Rose Bowl—'We knew we were the best football team on the Coast,' Garza insisted. In 1947 Oregon had finished 7–3 and in 1948 the only loss was to Number One-ranked Michigan and the Ducks finished the regular season 9–1, ranked ninth in the nation (only the second time the PCC had two teams in the top ten—Cal was fourth). They had not played California, and figuring correctly that the unbeaten Bears—with whom they shared the PCC title—would get the Rose Bowl bid, the Ducks challenged Cal to a post-season 'title playoff.' California officials refused. Cal won the Rose Bowl vote by the slimmest of margins (6–4) and the league then granted Oregon a special dispensation to play in another bowl—the only such exception ever made until the rule was changed in the mid-1970s to allow member schools to play in bowl games other than the Rose Bowl.

Van Brocklin was the reason for the Ducks' success. He not only threw the ball well—passing attacks were far less sophisticated and quarterbacks threw far less often then—but he was an outstanding field general, confident, strong leader and one of the few QBs of the time who called his own plays. Many years later, when he was coaching the Minnesota Vikings in the NFL he said, 'As far as I'm concerned, the coach might just as well go fishing

At right: **Norm Van Brocklin quarterbacked the Oregon Ducks to a 1948 record of 9–2, and went on to a great pro career. He said that, when passing, he paid most attention to defenders. One of Van Brocklin's supporting cast was a young halfback named John McKay (shown in later years *above*), who led the team in scoring.**

on the day of the game. It's the quarterback's game. By Sunday it's too late to teach them anything.'

He also had an outstanding supporting cast at Oregon—a fine center in Brad Ecklund, two good ends in Garza and Dick Wilkins and great running backs in Jake Leicht (who had been an All-American in 1945 and was still around in 1947), Bell, Woodley Lewis and a substitute halfback who nevertheless led the team in scoring named John McKay. Wilkins later contributed something else to Oregon athletics—his son Mac, a world record holder and Olympic champ in the discus. Lewis went on to pro stardom and still holds the Duck records for longest kickoff (102 yards) and punt returns (92), and McKay of course turned the Pacific Coast on its ear a few years later as the Southern California coach.

Aiken lasted only two more years after those players left, finishing 4–6 and 1–9. But he did do Oregon one other great favor: when he left, the Ducks hired Len Casanova.

There was another great player in the PCC in that period, maybe the greatest of all—'The King,' Washington's Hugh McElhenny. He didn't have the supporting cast that some others had—with the exception of 1950—and that probably cost him some recognition at the time. But 'Hurryin' Hugh,' who had been a fine high hurdler at Compton Junior College, was one of the most explosive runners in the history of the game. As a sophomore in 1949 against Minnesota, he had a 97-yard kickoff return and *averaged* nearly 15 yards per carry from scrimmage; in 1950 he had five touchdowns, including an 84-yard run, 296 yards rushing against traditional rival Washington State, and a 91-yard touchdown run against Kansas State; in 1951 he returned a kickoff 100 yards against USC, and was on the receiv-

U of Washington Huskies coach Howie Odell *(above)* was often astounded by the actions of his star player, halfback 'Hurryin' Hugh' McElhenny (number 32 *at right*), who led the PCC in yards rushing in both 1950 (1107 yards) and 1951 (936 yards).

ing end of a 77-yard touchdown pass against Illinois…. Well, the list goes on.

'He'd do some totally incredible thing,' Husky coach Howie Odell said of McElhenny, 'and you think, OK, that's it, I'll never see the likes of that again. Then, damn, he does something even more incredible.'

A frustrated opponent was even more succinct: 'He's like trying to grab an armful of eels.'

McElhenny led the PCC in rushing in both 1950—with 1107 yards and a brilliant 6.2 yards per carry average—and in 1951 with 936 yards and a 5.5 average. In 1950 the Huskies also had a fine quarterback, Don Heinrich, who completed what was then an incredible 60.6 percent of his passes for 1846 yards, with 14 touchdown passes and only nine interceptions. Heinrich led the nation in passing and Washington, which had won only five games total in Odell's previous two years, lost only to Illinois and, by 14–7, to ultimate champion California. Both McElhenny, who is in the College Hall of Fame and went on to a great pro career with the 49ers, and Heinrich, who also was a fine professional player, made some All-American teams, but neither was a consensus choice.

It figured to be another good year for the Huskies in 1951 but Heinrich sat out the entire season—he did come back to lead the nation in passing again in 1952—and McElhenny couldn't do it alone; Washington won only one conference game and finished 3–6–1 overall. By the time Heinrich returned in 1952, McElhenny was gone, and although the Huskies did win seven games, they lost badly to USC and UCLA and were not a serious title contender. The next season Odell was gone and Washington didn't have another successful season until 1959.

Meanwhile, there were some other coaching changes going on in the Pacific Coast Conference that brought more immediate results.

Stanford, USC and UCLA

There were several coaching changes in the Pacific Coast Conference around the end of the 1940s, and three of them in particular had an immediate and dramatic impact on the league.

Following the 1950 season Marchie Schwartz—who was generally popular but had been under fire from a small but vocal group of Stanford alums—first accepted a new five-year contract, then changed his mind and quit. The Indians interviewed almost every big-name coach in the nation but they needn't have bothered; the final choice was Chuck Taylor, their former All-American guard on the Vow Boys team, who at the tender age of 31 became the first alumnus to coach Stanford since Jimmy Lanagan had left following the 1908 season.

Taylor never had been a head coach. Following graduation he served as a naval officer in World War II and then played a year with the Miami Seahawks in the old All-American Football Conference. From 1947–49 he coached the Stanford freshmen—and just about anybody else, it seemed, that needed coaching; at various times the obliging Taylor was asked to 'just help out' by coaching wrestling and Rugby—neither of which, he freely admitted, he knew anything about—and running the intramural program. He then served a year as the San Francisco 49ers line coach before moving into Stanford's head coaching job.

It was a good choice, despite his inexperience. The popular redhead had some knowledge of the Indians, having guided such players as Gary Kerkorian, Dick Horn and Bill McColl during the stretch in which he coached the freshmen to a 14–0–1 mark, and he was well-known and well-liked on the campus. He immediately hired an outstanding staff—including, incidentally, Joe Ruetz, who was a former head coach at St Mary's and later became athletic director at Stanford.

Not much was expected of the Indians in 1951; they had finished with a 5–3–2 record in Schwartz's last year and although there was some talent on hand—notably the passing combination of quarterback Kerkorian and ends McColl and sophomore Sam Morley—there was precious little depth. Stanford was expected to finish somewhere around the middle of the pack in the PCC.

California and USC were expected to be the big noises in the league that year. Pappy Waldorf's Bears had after all won 35 straight regular-season games going into the season and had, among other standouts, the great Johnny Olszewski returning at fullback; Southern California had a down year the previous season—but new coach Jess Hill had a load of talent, including brilliant tailback Frank Gifford.

Cal won its first four games and was ranked Number One in the nation at that point. But Olszewski suffered a controversial injury on the first play of the fifth game, against USC; and the Bears, after taking a 14–0 lead, lost that game to the Trojans 21–14; they also lost to UCLA 21–7, while 'Johnny O' was out of action.

Taylor, meanwhile, went along predicting victory every week; that might have been contrary to the unwritten rules of the football coaches' union, but it also happened to be damned accurate. His Indians won their first two, then began to draw national notice in the third game when they beat Michigan 23–13 at Ann Arbor.

That also marked the first appearance of Bob Mathias, who as a schoolboy in 1948 had stunned the sports world with his dramatic victory in the Olympic Games decathlon at London—a victory he repeated, incidentally, in 1952. Mathias hadn't played football at Stanford prior to 1951, preferring to concentrate on track—despite his obvious size and speed, nobody expected too much of him. He didn't play in the first two games and in fact didn't even make the traveling squad for the opener. But the Indians, as noted, were not deep and injuries gave Mathias his chance; against Michigan, he simply returned kickoffs—but the following week regular fullback Bob Meyers was hurt and Mathias stepped in and scored two touchdowns in a 21–7 win over UCLA. A week later he scored two more as Stanford beat Santa Clara.

That made the Indians 5-0 going into their first crucial game, against Washington—the Huskies had lost two games, but they had Hugh McElhenny. Although Stanford clearly outplayed Washington (the Indians had a big statistical edge and had two touchdowns called back), McElhenny ripped off a 69 yard touchdown run to tie it 7–7 in the third quarter, and it took a long drive and Ron Cook's scoring plunge in the fourth quarter to pull out a 14–7 victory.

The game with Southern California was the clincher—two teams with identical 7–0 records and the Rose Bowl at stake. It turned out to be everything promised.

After three quarters it was tied 7–7 but the fireworks were just beginning. The Trojans took a 14–7 lead early in the fourth quarter, but Mathias raced 96 yards for a touchdown with the ensuing kickoff. The extra point was missed and when Southern California recovered a Stanford fumble in the Indians' end zone, it appeared as if the bubble had burst.

Chuck Taylor (at right) became, at age 31, the youngest national Coach of the Year ever, in 1951. First year coach Taylor took his underdog Indians to the top of the season.

But Stanford was, as Trojan coach Jess Hill said afterward, 'a team of opportunists.' USC also missed its extra point, keeping its lead at 20–13 and with five minutes to go, Kerkorian passed 30 yards to Morley to set up a touchdown plunge by Mathias—his second score of the game, and it was tied again. The Trojans weren't willing to settle for a draw, however, and came out throwing—which proved to be a big mistake. Linebacker Skip Crist intercepted, returning the ball 31 yards to the USC 11 yard line, and halfback Harry Hugasian ultimately scored in the closing minutes for a 27–20 win. There had been 33 points scored in the wild fourth quarter; Stanford had a victory and a trip to the Rose Bowl, but for USC the season was over—the Trojans then dropped their final two games to UCLA and Notre Dame.

The Indians of course also wanted an unbeaten season. They went into the Big Game with a 9–0 mark, the conference title locked up and ranked third in the nation, and Pappy Waldorf called Stanford 'as strong as any team we've had to face in my five years at Cal, including the Rose Bowls.' But the Bears were no slouches either—7–2 and ranked 19th in the country—and they had Olszewski healthy. California dominated the game and won easily, 20–7.

That didn't keep the Indians out of the Rose Bowl—perhaps unfortunately for them. Illinois had an 8–0–1 record coming in and ranked fourth in the nation (Stanford had fallen to eighth after the loss to Cal); the Illini trailed 7–6 in the third quarter and Stanford was moving toward what looked like another sure score, but Stan Wallace intercepted a Kerkorian pass from midfield and returned it all the way to the Indians' 12 yard line. Don Tate, who had 150 of Illinois' 371 rushing yards in the game, ran it in for 13–7 and Stanford just collapsed. The final score was 40–7.

Gary Kerkorian, quarterback for Chuck Taylor's Stanford team, shows his stuff *above left.* **Frank Gifford says that he always got butterflies when playing for big audiences; as a USC tailback** *(below right),* **he got lots of butterflies. Giff ran wild behind Jess Hill's Single Wing offense. Stanford Indians Bob Mathias** *(above)* **and All-American Bill McColl** *(above right)* **never surrendered.**

That game inspired the famous story by Los Angeles sportswriter Dick Hyland, a former Stanford halfback himself, that 'too many milkshakes at the training table' had cost the Indians the game; it may have been written in jest, but as time passed it began to be taken seriously.

McColl, who went on to stardom with the Chicago Bears and then had a successful medical career, was a consensus All-American, and Kerkorian also made a number of All-American teams. The low-keyed Taylor was named national Coach of the Year—at 31 the youngest man ever accorded that honor.

That was Taylor's only Rose Bowl—the Indians won the first four the next year, then faded to 5–5—but when Chuck gave up coaching to become an assistant athletic director following the 1957 season, he had a respectable 40–29–2 record and the respect of his players and peers.

'Chuck Taylor was a great coach, one of the finest I've ever met,' John Brodie, who was a star quarterback under Taylor a few years later and went on to NFL stardom with the 49ers, once said. 'He also was a fine man; I've heard you can separate the two, but I've never seen it done.

'Don't think Chuck wasn't tough, but he was fair and that's what made him such a great guy. You could respect him as a person. He knew the purpose football held, and he wanted the guys to go out there and have fun because he knew that if they

were enthusiastic about playing the game they were going to play a helluva lot better than if they weren't.'

Stanford's crushing Rose Bowl loss to Illinois was the sixth straight to the Big Ten since the contract between the two conferences had been inaugurated, and many sportswriters and fans were calling for an end to the relationship when the pact expired after the 1953 game. Prescott Sullivan wrote that 'Big Ten football is too much for our boys.' But as Bill Leiser, the highly-respected sports editor of the *San Francisco Chronicle*, pointed out, 'You don't call a halt because you lose six in a row—you just go out and try to win the next one.'

And lo and behold, that's just what Southern California did!

Jeff Cravath had guided the Trojans to four Rose Bowls in five years from 1943–47, but USC fans were spoiled—after all, Howard Jones and Cravath had won or shared 12 PCC championships in 21 seasons from 1927–47. Cravath then lost to California for three straight years, albeit by close scores and to great teams. And when his talented but extremely young team finished the 1950 season with a 2–5–2 record and was blasted by cross-town rival UCLA 39–0, the handwriting was on the wall; even a season-ending 9–7 upset of Notre Dame wasn't enough to save his job.

The Trojans, just as did Stanford, went after a lot of big-name coaches and, like Stanford, finally chose an alumnus from their own backyard. Jess Hill had been a fine athlete at Southern California—fullback on the 1929 Rose Bowl winner, a 25-foot long jumper, baseball outfielder who was good enough to play four years with the New York Yankees. His coaching experience, however, was limited to Corona High School, Riverside and Long Beach Junior Colleges and some time with the USC freshmen.

Hill, like Taylor, was an instant success. The first thing he did was to install the single wing offense: 'I know more about the single wing and other things being equal, a team can operate more effectively off a single wing with variations,' he said. Those 'variations,' incidentally, included occasional T-formation plays.

The second thing Hill did was make Frank Gifford his tailback.

Cravath had played Gifford primarily on defense but Frank, who was to go on to stardom with the New York Giants of the NFL and in the broadcast booth on Monday Night Football, could do everything—run, pass, punt, placekick, catch passes and play defense. He still is considered one of the finest all-around backs the West has ever produced.

He led the 1951 Trojans in rushing with 841 yards (only 95 behind PCC leader Hugh McElhenny), in total offense and in scoring. (Incidentally, USC also had a statistical rarity that year; one man, Dean Schneider, led the Trojans in both passing and receiving.) Although it was an incredible year for individual stars on the West Coast—McElhenny, Stanford's Bill McColl, Ollie Matson at University of San Francisco—Gifford was named to some All-American teams and was the main reason the Trojans finished with a 7–3 record.

The next year, Gifford was gone to the pros but Hill had another All-American tailback, Jim Sears, and one of the finest defensive teams in the nation—allowing only 177.5 yards per game and only 47 points all season. The Trojans romped through their first eight games, outscoring the opposition 233–25 and getting only one mild scare, a 10–0 win over California, and they went into the UCLA game unbeaten and untied.

So, however, did the Bruins. UCLA also was a single-wing team, also had an All-American tailback in Paul Cameron and also boasted a fine defense. The Bruins led the game 12–7 and were driving relentlessly toward another touchdown at the USC 18-yard line, when the Trojan defense pulled off the play that made the season. Cameron, under heavy pressure, threw a bad

pass and All-American guard Elmer Willhoite intercepted it and took off for the opposite goal line; Cameron finally hauled him down but not until Willhoite had run nearly the length of the field to the Bruins' eight yard line. Sears passed to Al Carmichael for a touchdown on the next play and USC had pulled out a 14–12 victory.

A 9–0 loss to third-ranked Notre Dame on a frozen field in South Bend, Indiana—during which the Trojans fumbled three times, threw five interceptions and failed to score from the Irish one-yard line—cost USC its unbeaten season and a chance for a Number One ranking, but it had no bearing on the Rose Bowl selection. Southern California faced Wisconsin and its great fullback, Alan 'The Horse' Ameche, on 1 January 1953. Another lopsided loss in this, the final game under the existing PCC-Big Ten agreement, could have spelled an end to the series but the Trojans not only made a respectable showing—they won the game.

Ameche gained 133 yards on 28 carries but the Trojan defense, led by George Timberlake, Charley Ane and Marv Goux—later a USC assistant coach for more than 20 years and perhaps the most loyal Trojan of all time—kept Ameche and the Badgers out of the end zone. Southern California meanwhile lost both its All-Americans early; Sears to a broken leg and Willhoite when he was ejected for throwing a fist on defense. Sears was replaced by Rudy Bukich, not as versatile as Sears but a fine passer (although he spent most of his USC career as a sub, Bukich was to go on and play 15 years in the NFL, leading the league in passing in 1965 while quarterbacking the Chicago Bears), and he was the player of the game in that Rose Bowl—

Above: Jim Sears (dark helmet) gains some yards before having the ball tucked a little too firmly into his breadbasket by helpful Stanford players (white helmets) in the USC/Stanford 7–7 tie game of 1950. At right: Outstanding USC halfbacks Sears (right) and Al Carmichael (left) celebrate following the 14–12 Trojan win over UCLA in 1952, which allowed USC's 7–0 Rose Bowl trump of Wisconsin.

throwing a 22 yard touchdown pass to Al Carmichael in the third quarter. When the inspired Trojan defense turned back a last-ditch Wisconsin drive with 24 seconds left in the game, Southern Cal had a 7–0 victory and the Pacific Coast Conference—Finally!—had a Rose Bowl win over the Big Ten.

Following that game the Big Ten agreed to renew the pact for three more years; had the PCC but known what lay ahead—six more losses in a row—it might not have been so quick to accept.

USC was not short of challengers in that season. In addition to UCLA and Washington—which finished 7–3 behind Don Heinrich—defending champion Stanford started fast, winning the first four including another upset of Michigan, and California had another strong team. But the Indians faded fast; star quarterback Bobby Garrett suffered a shoulder separation during a 54–7 rout by USC and Stanford finished with a 5–5 record. Cal was 7–3 including a 26–0 final win over the Indians notable for two things—Johnny Olszewski, with 122 yards in the game, broke Hugh McElhenny's one-year-old PCC career rushing record; and Ray Willsey, who later became coach of the Golden Bears, made a surprise debut as quarterback. Willsey, a defensive back, was pressed into service when regular QB Bill Mais was hurt and proceeded to pass for one touchdown, run one yard for another and race 55 yards to set up a third score.

The Rose Bowl victory made Hill the first man to both play on and coach winning teams in the Rose Bowl. Like Taylor he stayed in the job only six years before moving up to the athletic director's chair, but he never had a losing season and compiled a 35–17–1 record overall.

Taylor and Hill both had turned their programs around dramatically but their success was somewhat fleeting; the truly dominant coach of that period was Henry 'Red' Sanders.

Bert LaBrucherie had coached UCLA's Bruins for just four years when Sanders succeeded him in 1949; LaBrucherie's final season had been his worst, a 3–7 record and losses to every PCC team except Idaho and Washington State (the Bruins did not play Montana). In 21 years in the league, UCLA had just two seasons in which it lost less than two games—1939 (6–0–4) and 1946 (10–1). Then Sanders took over.

In his nine years at the helm, Sanders' Bruins never lost more than three games in a single season; his overall record was 66–19–1 and from 1952–55, UCLA was 34–5; won three PCC titles and one national championship; and never was ranked lower than sixth in the country.

A couple of years before his sudden and shocking death in 1958, Sanders was voted in a newspaper poll as Los Angeles' Most Valuable Citizen, winning by a landslide over people such as the Mayor and famous comedians Bob Hope and Harold Lloyd. At the time, Sanders pretty well expressed his philosophy: 'In my opinion, winning coaches get twice as much credit, and losing coaches ten times as much blame, as they really deserve. Any coach who stays at a school long enough is bound eventually to have thin material, injuries or bad breaks. It doesn't matter how smart you are, no coach can think a player out of fumbling during a game or make him run any faster than God intended. An average coach with vastly superior personnel will defeat the best coach with poor personnel 95 out of 100 times. I don't think any coach can provide more than 15 percent of the net results.'

But Sanders made the most of that 15 percent. He had a great ability to evaluate potential, and he made a number of position moves that were surprising at the time but turned out splendidly. He was sharp-tongued on the practice field but he also knew when to joke with his players. He could spot talent and he could make that talent produce.

'Character building?' he once said. 'Sure, I'm for character all right—but first we've got to get a number of big, strong, phenomenal animals that can run fast.'

He did. Like Hill, Sanders installed the single wing offense and concentrated on building a rock-ribbed defense. His first three seasons were spent rebuilding although the Bruins finished those years with very respectable records—6–3, 6–3 and 5–3–1. By 1952 Sanders had all the pieces.

Paul Cameron, the Bruins' brilliant tailback, was hurt a good part of that season; although he still led the team in total offense and made All-Coast for the second of three times. But the defense, led by All-American linebacker Donn Moomaw and back Bill Stits, was exceptional; UCLA allowed only 94 yards per game rushing among the national leaders, and when the other team was forced into throwing the ball the Bruins responded with 34 interceptions, eight of them—returned for a record 235 yards—by Stits. The narrow loss to USC cost them the conference title but an 8–1 record and the placing of 10 men on the first All-Conference team spoke eloquently of things to come.

In 1953 Cameron was healthy, and what a year he had! Sanders called Cameron 'the finest all-purpose single wing tailback I ever coached,' and who could argue? He set seven school records that year (and wound up his career with 12) and literally led the team in every single statistical category except receiving—

Above: **Jess Hill coached USC football for six years, compiling a 35–17–1 record, including one win and one loss in the Rose Bowls of 1953 and 1955, respectively. Tailback Paul Cameron *(at left)* made All-American and All-Coast *(three times)* in his UCLA career. Henry 'Red' Sanders *(below)* coached UCLA to the Rose Bowl twice.**

rushing, passing, scoring, punting, punt returns, kickoff returns and interceptions. Small wonder that he was a unanimous All-American choice and finished third in the Heisman Trophy voting behind Johnny Lattner of Notre Dame and Paul Giel of Minnesota. That was the first time, incidentally, that a Pacific Coast player had cracked the top three; Stanford's Frankie Albert and Cal's Jackie Jensen each had finished fourth, and in 1952 the Bruins had a peculiar 'split vote' in which Moomaw finished fourth and Cameron sixth.

There was little subtlety in Sanders' offense, and little need for it. The Bruins' most devastating play was a simple power sweep by Cameron behind a wall of blockers that included fullback Jim Davenport, quarterback (blocking back) Terry Debay, tackles Jack Ellena and Chuck Doud and guard Jim Salsbury. Davenport, Ellena and Salsbury all were juniors, and all were to be All-Americans the following year.

UCLA lost to Stanford in 1953 21–20 but sailed through the rest of its regular-season games by the lopsided margin of 184 points to 27 and finally clinched the title with a 13–0 win over Southern California. Stanford, meanwhile, had lost to USC 23–20 on a last-minute field goal, and had non-conference losses to Illinois and the College of the Pacific. Nevertheless, had the Indians beaten California and Southern Cal beaten UCLA, Stanford would have been in the Rose Bowl.

Stanford was led by Bobby Garrett, who not only led the nation in passing and was a consensus All-American but, under the new one-platoon rules, played a full 60 minutes in five different games and also led the country with nine interceptions. California's quarterback was Paul Larson, who led the nation in total offense that year and the following season set what was then an NCAA completion percentage mark of 64.1. In that crucial 1953 Big Game, Larson completed 13-of-22 for 179 yards, Garrett 12-of-27 for 131 yards; each kicked three conversions; each intercepted two passes, Garrett returning one of them 56 yards for a touchdown.

Stanford had a 21–7 lead in the fourth quarter, but Larson completed four passes and then ran 18 yards himself for the score that made it 21–14 and a wild defensive series set up the tying score—Matt Hazeltine, the Bears' All-American center, intercepted a pass, immediately fumbled it back to the Indians, and then one play later recovered a fumble to give Cal the ball again and set up the touchdown. Shortly thereafter Larson returned an intercepted pass to the Stanford 22 but on fourth down at the 17, somebody on the sideline threw out a kicking tee for the field goal attempt; it was ruled coaching from the sidelines, which then was against the rules, and Cal was penalized 15 yards—out of field goal range. The Bears got the ball back one last time but Larson missed a last-play field goal and it ended in a 21–21 tie.

The drama of the finish and the Indians' disappointment were lessened only slightly when they learned that UCLA had won its game—and would have clinched the Rose Bowl bid anyway.

The Bruins faced Michigan State (making its first Rose Bowl appearance). Clarence 'Biggie' Munn had built a powerhouse at East Lansing; his teams, which relied more on speed and quickness than on size, were 53–9–2 from 1947–53. Cameron was magnificent in the Rose Bowl game, passing for two touchdowns and running for another but after UCLA took a 14–0 lead, Ellis Duckett blocked a Cameron punt for a touchdown and Leroy Bolden and Billy Wells, the Spartans' fine little backs, each scored a touchdown to give Michigan State the lead. When Cameron brought UCLA back to within a point, Wells returned a punt 62 yards for the TD that locked up a 28–20 Michigan State win.

Tommy Prothro, who had played for Duke in the 1942 Rose Bowl and would coach Oregon State to two Rose Bowls later,

was an assistant coach at UCLA then, and he called Michigan State 'the best team I've ever seen, either as a player or coach.'

He had not yet seen the 1954 UCLA Bruins.

There were some outstanding players in the PCC that year, All-American quarterback George Shaw led the nation in total offense and paced Oregon to a 6–4 record, its first winning season since 1948; Cal's Paul Larson also made some All-American teams as he set a national completion percentage mark, and his batterymate Jim Hanifan—later a player and coach in the NFL—led the nation in receiving with 44 catches, seven of them for TDs; Stanford's hard-working Bill Tarr led the league in rushing, and two future greats—Stanford quarterback John Brodie and USC tailback Jon Arnett—already were making their marks as sophomores. But there was no team like UCLA.

Cameron was gone, but Sanders came up with a fine replacement in Primo Villanueva—and behind him on the long bench was an explosive JC transfer named Sam 'First Down' Brown. Davenport was back at fullback and the underrated Terry Debay at blocking back (underrated outside of Westwood, that is; he was named the team's MVP that year, despite the presence of All-Americans Davenport, Ellena and Salsbury in the lineup). In front of them was an absolutely awesome line—Ellena, a consensus All-American at tackle, Sam Boghosian and Salsbury at guard, Bob Long and Rommie Loudd at end, and players like guards Hardiman Cureton and Jim Brown, who both (along with Loudd) made some All-Americans the next year, providing depth.

Not surprisingly, with that kind of talent, the Bruins went unbeaten. They scored 367 points in nine games—and allowed 40. They gave up only 189.8 yards per game and led the nation in rushing defense, allowing just 73 yards per game and only 35 first downs on the ground all year. They had just two close games—12–7 over Maryland (which wound up that season ranked eighth in the nation) in the third game and 21–20 over surprising Washington (which won just two games all season), the next week. But enough of that nonsense: UCLA then closed out the season by beating Stanford 72–0, Oregon State 61–0, California 27–6, Oregon 41–0 and USC 34–0. When it was all over the Bruins

Donn Moomaw *(at left)* is considered one of the greatest linebackers in UCLA history. Moomaw was an All-American in 1950 and 1952. Speedy USC back Jon Arnett *(above)* suffered in the payoff scandal of 1956, but went on to play in the pros. Hardiman Cureton *(below)* was a UCLA All-American guard in 1955, and played a vital role on the Number One-ranked UCLA team of that year.

were 9–0, ranked Number One in the nation by *United Press* and Number Two by the Associated Press: all dressed up in their championship finery—and with absolutely no place to go.

Under the no-repeat rule which the Big Ten had observed since the beginning of their Rose Bowl pact (and which the PCC had recently adopted) UCLA was ineligible for the Rose Bowl because the Bruins had been there the previous year. USC, with an 8–3 record including back-to-back season-ending losses to UCLA and fourth-ranked Notre Dame, got the nod. The opponent was Ohio State, ranked either first or second, depending on which poll you believed, and coached by Woody Hayes—making his first Rose Bowl appearance. Despite an 88-yard punt return through the rain and mud by the romantically-named Trojan tailback, Aramis Dandoy, the Buckeyes made short work of Southern California, 20–7. Hayes, who even that early in his career was a cantankerous sort, carefully ignored the fact that the PCC's best team was not there and that the mud had badly hampered USC's speed and passing and told reporters afterwards, 'There are four, possibly five Big Ten teams that could beat your Trojans.... Big Ten teams are better in the Rose Bowl because they are raised on tougher competition.' That would come back to haunt him years later, but at the moment all it meant was another Rose Bowl loss for the Pacific Coast, the eighth in nine years.

UCLA lost an assistant coach for the 1955 season—Tommy Prothro became the head coach at Oregon State and immediately transformed a team that had had five straight losing years into a contender. Otherwise, it was hard to see much difference in the Bruins. With Sam Brown and transfer Ronnie Knox at tailback; Davenport still at fullback; and Loudd, Cureton, Jim Brown and all-conference center Steve Palmer up front, they led the PCC in both scoring offense (299 points) and scoring defense (74), lost only to third-ranked Maryland 7–0 in 10 regular-season games, were ranked fourth nationally and went to the Rose Bowl, again to face Michigan State.

The Spartans now were coached by Duffy Daugherty and led by quarterback Earl Morrall and halfback Clarence Peaks. With the score tied late in the game, a series of penalties forced Knox to punt out of his own end zone and Jim Kaiser, who because of a leg injury had not practiced kicking for two months, booted a 41-yard field goal with seven seconds remaining to give Michigan State a 17–14 win.

Ronnie Knox's father Harvey had been a thorn in the side of several coaches, including Pappy Waldorf at Cal and Sanders. Ronnie was a great athlete, especially as a passer, who had first attended California; by the spring of his sophomore year he had left Berkeley because Harvey claimed that Waldorf had not revised the pass offense to his, Harvey's, liking. In 1955 Ronnie—hardly the most popular man on the squad thanks to his father's continual interference—was struggling, but Sanders had a long talk with him, got him out of his shell and he performed brilliantly over the latter part of the season.

The elder Knox 'covered' the Rose Bowl game for the *Los Angeles Herald-Examiner*, and the headline over his story the next day was an indication of the man's tunnel vision: 'Sanders Blew It—Harvey'. His complaint? Ronnie hadn't been allowed to play enough in the second quarter—and never mind that the Bruins' other tailback, Sam Brown, had led the PCC in rushing that year.

But that was simply Knox's bluster. He may have done far more damage when, piqued at California after he had transferred Ronnie to UCLA, Harvey claimed to Mel Durslag of the *Herald-Examiner* that the Bears had broken rules and made illegal payments to his son.

It was the first cloud. In the next three years, the Pacific Coast Conference was in for a real storm.

The End of the PCC

The storm broke in the late spring of 1956, and although it took two years before the breakup became official, the Pacific Coast Conference was on its last legs.

UCLA was, so to speak, the eye of the hurricane—although Washington actually was penalized first, being handed two years probation, and other schools later. But it was the Bruins who were hit the hardest, and it was the Bruins who raised the biggest commotion.

The PCC, then guided by stern Commissioner Victor O Schmidt, found UCLA guilty of a number of rules violations, primarily in areas of recruiting and illegal payments to players, and fined the school the equivalent of $95,100—a $15,000 flat fine plus loss of any benefits from the Rose Bowl (which all PCC schools shared in, no matter which team participated) for three years. Even more galling to the Bruins, they were declared ineligible for conference or NCAA titles for three years—not only in football but in *all* sports.

Finally, every single UCLA football player, varsity or freshman, from the 1955 teams was declared ineligible unless he could *prove* he hadn't been getting paid—and that included, incidentally, the Bruins' passing star, Ronnie Knox, whose father Harvey, had fired one of the early shots with his charges against California. The repercussions on that ruling were nationwide: Red Smith the *New York Herald-Tribune*'s famous sports columnist, wrote, 'Evidently the flighty notion about the presumption of innocence hasn't managed to scale the Rockies.'

There seemed to be no question that violations had taken place—and not only at UCLA. The sniping and in-fighting among the conference schools was absolutely vicious. It reached a ludicrous point a few weeks into the 1958 season. George Dickerson, who had been named UCLA head coach when Red Sanders died suddenly earlier that year, jumped on a midweek flight to Berkeley, stormed into the California athletic offices unannounced and proceeded to rage at the Bear coaches. Dickerson, who obviously had some problems, was relieved of his job soon afterward and Bill Barnes finished out the season as 'acting coach.'

Nevertheless, the penalties, especially those imposed on UCLA, had been very severe and the Bruins (not entirely without justification) were incensed. 'They took the core and sinew of my team,' Red Sanders said at the time. 'I'll probably have enough players to field a ball club, but the humane society will take a dim view of it.' Vic Schmidt was hanged in effigy in front of the *Los Angeles Times* building. Southern California sportswriters and columnists to a man flayed the PCC presidents and faculty

representatives for the penalty. Edwin C Pauley, a member of the University of California Board of Regents (which also governed UCLA), and Cyril Nigg, president of the UCLA Alumni Association, both went on record as approving the school's withdrawal from the PCC if the penalties were not rescinded and the league's code liberalized.

Rube Samuelsen, the canny veteran Pasadena sports editor, summed up neatly what a lot of people were feeling about then: 'The whole roof hasn't fallen in yet, men,' he wrote, 'but give it time, give it time.'

In January of 1957 the PCC did loosen its rules, adopting a grant-in-aid policy which by today's standards seems ridiculously mild, but which then was too liberal for many. All it did was exacerbate the situation.

'The Pacific Coast Conference is going professional,' an editorial in the *Stanford Daily* said, 'and Stanford is the only school that seems to be worried about it.' In its meeting last week the conference opened the door to unlimited financial aid by adopting its grant-in-aid for subsistence. The pressure from (President) Fred Fagg of USC and (Chancellor) Raymond Allen of UCLA and the worry of dropping nine out of 10 (Note: actually it was 10 of 11) bowl games to the Big Ten have been too much for the rest of the schools.' The editorial also quoted Stanford President J E Wallace Sterling as saying the change in PCC policy would force Stanford 'to re-examine the nature of its participation in intercollegiate athletics' if the new code was not changed.

In June of 1957—a bit ironically, considering UCLA's loud protests of the original PCC rules—the University of California Board of Regents decreed that Cal and UCLA must hew to stricter scholastic and athletic aid policies than those passed a few months before by the PCC. The two schools, the Regents said, must fulfill the 1957 PCC schedule but thereafter were free to schedule games outside the conference as they wished—even if it meant leaving the conference. University President Clark Kerr said, 'The PCC either must institute a major change in policy over the course of the next several years, or some new alignment of schools will develop.'

The Regents also developed a plan of their own. 'To the best of our ability,' said Cal athletic director Greg Engelhard, 'we will try to sell the Regents' five-point program to the conference. If we are not successful, then we will probably withdraw.'

Len Casanova, *(at right)* head coach at the University of Oregon, and Tommy Prothro, at Oregon State, helped the dying PCC to save face during the payments scandal of the late 1950s. The Ducks' close 1958 Rose Bowl game with Ohio State helped especially.

The Regents' plan called for (1) a grade point average of 2.0 (a C average) to be eligible; (2) tuition grants-in-aid to be limited to the basis of need; (3) wage rates no higher for athletes than non-athletes, and athletes must actually work the time they are paid for; (4) each institution to be responsible for enforcement—which of course took a lot of power away from Commissioner Schmidt; and (5) the scheduling of games to be subject only to the free choice of each institution, consistent with the first four points.

In November of 1957 the PCC presidents approved the plan, but they did not have the final say. A month later, at its winter meeting, the Pacific Coast Conference voted it down. Almost immediately, California and UCLA announced they would withdraw from the league on 30 June 1959. Southern California said it would leave the PCC 'sometime after' 30 June 1958. Stanford decided, after some soul-searching, to remain in the conference, but President Sterling said: 'I do not know whether the conference can survive. Of its nine members, one has been something less than a full-fledged member (presumably referring to Idaho); three have announced their withdrawal; and one has recommended that the conference dissolve itself.'

Sterling was dead right. Although, like the phoenix it was to rise from its own ashes, the Pacific Coast Conference as an entity was dead.

While all this was going on in the meeting rooms, the PCC still was playing football. Tommy Prothro, an assistant coach at UCLA, had taken over the head job at Oregon State in 1955 and immediately turned the program around—the Beavers, who had won only 13 games in the previous five years, finished with a 6–3 record—second in the PCC behind powerful UCLA. Then in 1956–57, it was Prothro's Beavers—with an assist from Len Casanova at Oregon—who kept the crumbling conference from looking totally foolish.

Oregon State lost the conference opener to USC in 1956 but its only other blemish in PCC play was a 14–14 tie with Oregon in the regular-season finale. Southern California, in Jess Hill's final year, finished with an 8–2 record but both losses were within the league—to Stanford and Oregon. UCLA, with another fine team despite Sanders' cries of anguish and despite the absence of Knox, who played in the Canadian League that year, finished 7–3 but lost to Oregon State 21–7 and to USC. The Bruins, of course, were ineligible for the title anyway, as was Washington (which was 5–5 that year) but had UCLA finished first, it would have been one more minor embarrassment to the league.

Stanford also had great hopes in 1956. Chuck Taylor's Indians had finished 6–3–1 the year before and two of the losses had been to the Rose Bowl teams UCLA and Michigan State. Included among the wins was a 6–0 conquest of Ohio State in which the Stanford defense, led by the great Paul Wiggin, held Howard 'Hopalong' Cassady, the Buckeyes' Heisman Trophy-winning halfback, to 26 yards. And the 1956 Indians had two All-Americans returning—Wiggin at tackle and quarterback John Brodie—both of whom would go on to professional stardom.

But it was a disappointing season for Stanford, which finished 4–6. The Indians had lost to Oregon State and UCLA back-to-back, each by one point, and had been routed by Washington and yet, going into the final game against California, they still had a slim chance for the Rose Bowl bid. Brodie gave them terrific firepower—he led the nation in passing that year and was a consensus All-American in a season that also produced quarterbacks Paul Hornung at Notre Dame, Milt Plum at Penn State, Sonny Jurgensen at Duke and Len Dawson at Purdue.

But unfortunately for Stanford, California had emotion on its side that day. The Bears had slipped to 2–7–1 in 1955 and had a 2–7 record at that point in 1956, and Pappy Waldorf had been under fire, albeit not seriously. On the Tuesday before the Big Game, Waldorf announced that after 10 seasons at Berkeley he was resigning. 'I wanted to end all speculation,' he said, 'and above all I didn't want the boys to feel they were playing this one for me.' And of course that was exactly what the Bears did. 'We're all boiling,' fumed outspoken center Frank Mattarocci, 'and we're going out and tear Stanford apart.'

They did for awhile, at least. California scored the first three times it had the ball and led 20–6; at that point perhaps the adrenaline wore off, and the Bears then had to hold on for dear life to win 20–18. Lou Valli rushed for 209 yards for Stanford and Brodie, although just 9-for-18 passing, broke Don Heinrich's PCC completion record. For California, a sophomore quarterback named Joe Kapp—who had begun the season as a third-stringer and gotten into the lineup when the first two QBs were injured early in the year—ran for 106 yards, including a 29-yarder to the Stanford one-yard line to set up a touchdown.

Coincidentally, there were three players on the field that day—Kapp, Wiggin and Cal end Mike White—who later became head coaches at their alma maters.

Oregon State's Rose Bowl opponent was Iowa, a team that the Beavers had lost to by a single point, 14–13, early in the season. The two were a contrast in styles. The Beavers, who were the first non-California team in the Rose Bowl in 15 years, played the single wing, featuring a powerful, deep line—led by All-American tackle John Witte—and a running game built around steady Joe Francis and explosive Paul Lowe at tailback and speedy Earnel Durden at wingback. Iowa was coached by Forest Evashevski, like Prothro a former blocking back in the single wing—*Prothro* at Duke and *Evashevski* on the Tommy Harmon teams at Michigan; a fact the egotistical Evy rarely let anybody forget. He had had a short (two years) but successful tenure at Washington State in the early 1950s before moving to Iowa; with the Hawkeyes, he had uncovered a fine quarterback in Ken Ploen and installed an exciting winged-T offense that had earned them the Number Three ranking in the nation.

The game was not close. Ploen ran 49 yards and Collins Hagler nine yards for first-quarter touchdowns and a 14–0 lead. Hagler later raced 66 yards for another score and Ploen passed for a TD. Iowa won 35–19.

The following year was a shambles in the all-but-defunct PCC. By now, California and USC had joined UCLA and Washington on probation—making them all ineligible for the Rose Bowl. Small wonder that the season was a series of upsets, with no team losing less than two conference games; it developed into a four-team race and again, fortunately for the sake of what little credibility the league had left, three of the schools were among those still eligible for a title.

Jim Sutherland's Washington State team, led by quarterback Bobby Newman (the nation's total offense leader that year) and ends Bill Steiger (an All-American) and Don Ellingsen (the PCC receiving leader) made a race of it for awhile but lost to Oregon, Oregon State and UCLA within four weeks. Stanford—in Chuck Taylor's final season as coach—lost an early heartbreaker to Washington State. The Indians led 18–7 late in the game before falling 21–18. Stanford also lost to Oregon by one point, but still was in the race until a 24–14 loss to Oregon State in the next-to-last game. UCLA, although ineligible itself, made its presence felt by knocking over Oregon State and Washington State.

In fact, about the only schools that weren't a factor were two of those on probation, Cal and USC (and of course Idaho—which played only three conference games). California, in its first year under new coach Pete Elliott, won only one game (against Southern California) while the Trojans, also with a new coach in Don Clark, also finished 1–9, beating only Washington.

When it was all sorted out the standings read like this: Oregon State was 8–2, Oregon 7–4 and each was 6–2 in the PCC; UCLA (8–2 overall) was 5–2, Washington State (6–4) was 5–3 and Stanford (also 6–4) was 4–3. Since Oregon State had been to the Rose Bowl the previous year, Oregon was awarded the bid.

Lucky Ducks! All they had to do was face Ohio State, ranked either Number One or Number Two in the nation—depending on which poll you believed.

Len Casanova had coached at his alma mater, Santa Clara—and taken the Broncos to an Orange Bowl—and briefly at Pittsburgh. When his daughter's illness dictated a move back to the West Coast, Cas had taken over the reins at Oregon in 1951 after Jim Aiken's 1950 team had gone 1–9. There was very little talent on hand at first, with the exception of a freshman named George Shaw, who that year set an NCAA record by intercepting 13 passes. The Ducks went 2–8 that year, 2–7–1 in 1952 and 4–5–1 in 1953. Then, in 1954 quarterback Shaw led the nation in total offense and was the Number One pro draft pick (by the Baltimore Colts) following that season, and he and guard Jack Patera (later a pro player and NFL coach) paced Oregon to a 6–4 record, with the only conference losses coming to Number One-ranked UCLA, Rose Bowl-bound USC and Stanford.

In the next 12 years, before he retired from coaching to become Oregon athletic director, the popular Casanova had eight winning seasons and took the Ducks to three bowl games.

The Ducks' 1957 season was a strange one. 'The Rose Bowl team was not my best team, ability-wise,' Casanova said later. 'But it was a close-knit group with good leadership. We had four team captains; the voting for captain was so close, we picked 'em all.'

The Ducks barely beat Idaho 9–6 in the opener and lost a non-conference game to Pittsburgh a week later, 6–3. But they got it together to upset UCLA 21–0, and beat San Jose State 26–0. The fifth game against Washington State was a turning point; the Cougars cut Oregon's lead to 14–13 late in the game and according to one story, Eddie Stevens was supposed to come into the game to kick the conversion. But Newman waved him off, saying 'I'll kick it'—in that era of limited substitution, every team had more than one placekicker. Newman's kick hit the upright and bounced away, costing WSU a tie and giving Oregon what might have been the key win in its Rose Bowl drive.

Oregon had a dramatic win over Stanford, finally pulling it out 27–26, but didn't lose again until the final regular-season game, a 10–7 setback at the hands of co-champion Oregon State.

The Ducks had not been to a Rose Bowl since 1 January 1920, and now this game was termed by one Los Angeles writer as 'the biggest mismatch in Rose Bowl history.' Not everyone went that far, but few people gave Oregon much of a chance.

Not that the Ducks were hopeless. They had the best defense in the PCC, one that had allowed opponents just 81 points in 10 games—including just seven to USC (16–7) and none to UCLA (21–0) (only the fourth shutout of a Red Sanders team in nine years). They had an outstanding backfield in quarterback Jack Crabtree, halfback Jim Shanley and fullback Jack Morris—who had gained 212 yards in the Rose Bowl-clinching win over Southern Cal—and an excellent end in Ron Stover. 'It wasn't that

Having not been to a Rose Bowl in 38 years, when Oregon faced Ohio State, everyone thought it would be 'Duck soup' for the Buckeyes. Oregon lost, but barely, and even eastern sportswriters felt that Oregon had outplayed Ohio State. The coaching staff of that 1958 Oregon Rose Bowl team is pictured *at left, from left to right*—Bill Hammer, Jerry Frei, head coach Len Casanova, John McKay (yes, *that* John McKay) and Jack Roche. *Above:* The 1958 Rose Bowl Ducks.

they (Ohio State) were overrated,' Crabtree said after the Rose Bowl game, 'it was just that we weren't given enough credit.'

It was a typical Woody Hayes Ohio State team—three yards and a cloud of dust. The Buckeye offense was no mystery; they had run for 2681 yards that year and had passed for just 445. Oregon shut down Ohio State's attack, outgained the Buckeyes and were unfortunate to lose 10–7 on a Don Sutherin field goal early in the fourth quarter. Crabtree was named player of the game. Even many of the Eastern writers felt the Ducks should have won, and it was a tremendous boost for the faltering Pacific Coast Conference.

'Thanks a lot,' Casanova told the assembled press after the game. 'You Los Angeles sportswriters helped us a lot. A team can't be derided by everybody and not be mad.'

But Oregon's performance, as gratifying as it may have been to the West Coasters, wasn't nearly enough to save the league. On 2 June 1958, there was a report that Stanford and Washington had been invited to join a 'Big Five' with Southern California, UCLA and California. Stanford denied it, but there was no doubt that the PCC was dead.

The last team to represent the Pacific Coast Conference in the Rose Bowl—or anywhere else, for that matter—was the 1958 California Bears, who performed one of the greatest turnarounds in college football history. In 1957 they won one game—and that

was over USC, another team that won only once; in 1958 Cal, with the same coach—Pete Elliott—and virtually the same cast, finished 7–3 in the regular season and went to the Rose Bowl.

In fact, it was the Bears' year. Three months after their Rose Bowl appearance, Pete Newell's Cal basketball team won the NCAA championship in Louisville.

That football team was an unlikely collection. One guard, Don Piestrup (later a quite successful orchestra leader), wore thick glasses off the field and probably never weighed much more than 175 pounds; one tackle, Pat Newell—Pete's nephew—stood 6 feet, 2 inches and came out of one particularly hard game weighing 169 pounds. It wasn't that the team was devoid of individual talent, but it was indicative that when the season was over the Bears placed only two men on the All-Conference team.

Co-captains quarterback Joe Kapp and halfback Jack Hart were the core of the Bears. Hart was not very big and not exceptionally fast but he was a fine all-around player, a tough runner and the target of most of the few passes that Kapp threw out of Elliott's Split-T formation.

Kapp, however, made that team. He was a fine all-around athlete who had been recruited by UCLA as a basketball player and played varsity basketball at Cal as a sophomore and junior (the Rose Bowl kept him from being a part of the NCAA championship team). But more than that, he was one of the most intense competitors the game has ever known. Kapp was a wild character off the field, and stories were many: Kapp and Hart paying late-night visits to players they felt weren't giving 100 percent, Kapp running a teammate helmet-first into the stadium wall because the other player wasn't listening to the coach. ... They may just have been stories, but Joe was the sort of player and the sort of man that made them believable.

Joe Kapp *(shown above)* quarterbacked for the last PCC team to play the Rose Bowl—Cal, which met defeat to the tune of 38-12 under the cleats of ill-mannered Forest Evashevski's Iowa team in 1959. The 'Academic Association of Western Universities' replaced the PCC that same year. *At right* is the program jacket for that 1959 game.

And he carried a team as few others could—physically and emotionally. His passing wasn't pretty, but he did complete a very respectable 64–of–114 (32 of them to Hart) and he certainly proved later he could throw the football by setting passing records in the Canadian League and then quarterbacking the Minnesota Vikings to the Super Bowl. But he also led the PCC in rushing with 616 yards—no common feat for a quarterback.

California lost its first two games: a 24–20 thriller to the College of the Pacific and its great runner Dick Bass, and a 32–12 rout by Michigan State. The pressure on Elliott, which had started with the terrible 1957 season, was growing. Surprisingly, however, that might have been the turning point; the Bears played well in the second half against Michigan State, then proceeded to win seven of the next eight games. Another key came in a mid-year game against Oregon; the Ducks finished a disappointing 4–6 that year but they were the defending co-champions and they finished 1958 ranked Number Two in the nation in defense. Cal won 23–6, with one of the touchdowns coming when Kapp missed a handoff to Hart—then followed him through the hole that had opened in the line and ran 94 yards for a touchdown.

It came down to the final game with Stanford, and the Rose Bowl bid that year was determined by a rule that had just been put into the books—the two-point conversion. Previously a point-after-touchdown—whether by kick, run or pass—counted one point; beginning in 1958 a kick still was one point but a successful pass or run counted two points. California won the Big Game by demonstrating that now two touchdowns could beat two touchdowns and a field goal.

Stanford had a new coach, 'Cactus Jack' Curtice, who had been brought in from Utah with a reputation for wide-open offense. His Utes, with Lee Grosscup at quarterback, had led the nation in passing in 1957. Stanford led the PCC in passing in 1958 (and would lead the nation the following year) but still won only two games all season. Nevertheless, the Indians gave California all it could handle.

The Bears scored first and Grover Garvin ran in the conversion for 8–0. Stanford got a touchdown of its own and, in an effort to tie, quarterback Dick Norman passed to the great Chris Burford; it bounced off Burford and into the hands of another Stanford receiver, Irv Nikolai, but officials ruled him out of bounds—a very controversial call. Skip Face's field goal gave the Indians a 9–8 halftime lead but in the third quarter Hart scored his second touchdown of the game, and Kapp passed to Wayne Crow for another two-pointer.

Late in the game Stanford drove 78 yards for a touchdown but decided to go for two points and the win rather than settle for a tie. Face swept right but Cal fullback Bill Patton met him with a crushing tackle at the one-yard line, and several other Bears finished the job. California had won 16–15. That gave the Bears a 6–1 conference record to 6–2 for Washington State (which also had a 7–3 record overall); in addition, Cal had whipped the Cougars 34–14 during the season.

But in the Rose Bowl the Bears were just plain outmanned. Evashevski had a team at Iowa that might have been the best in the nation—a 38–28 loss to Ohio State and a tie with Air Force notwithstandng. (In fact, they were voted Number One by the Football Writers Association after the Rose Bowl.) The Hawkeyes led the nation in offense; quarterback Randy Duncan topped the country in pass percentage and yards passing, and was second in total offense; and there was a tremendous set of running backs in Willie Fleming, Bob Jeter, Bob Jauch and John Nocera.

Iowa also had a fine tackle named Mac Lewis who weighed 300 pounds. Evashevski was his usual gracious self before the game. 'You know that 180-pound tackle Cal is so proud of?' he asked, referring to Pat Newell. 'We're going to build a freeway right over him.'

They nearly did. Iowa gained 516 yards; Jeter had 194 yards in just nine carries —81 of them on one third-period run (then a Rose Bowl record) that really broke the game open. Even Kapp and Hart couldn't turn the tide; Iowa won 38–12.

'Randy Duncan,' said Cal assistant (and later Oregon State head coach and athletic director) Dee Andros, 'was a good quarterback on a great team; Joe Kapp was a great quarterback on an average team.'

And that was the end of the Pacific Coast Conference. In March of 1959, a 'Big Four' was formed, and it was immediately announced that they would represent the Pacific Coast in the Rose Bowl. Four months later Stanford joined USC, UCLA, California and Washington to make it a Big Five and already there was talk about also bringing in Oregon, Oregon State and Washington State—although it was three more full years before any of them actually joined.

The new conference was handed the unwieldy title of Academic Association of Western Universities. Pacific Coast football was back in business, and there were some big changes looming on the horizon.

Rising from the Ashes

Within three years after the collapse of the Pacific Coast Conference and the emergence of the AAWU, three things happened that brought rapid success and credibility to the new league.

For one thing, Southern California hired John McKay—an assistant coach who had been there less than a year—to turn its program around, and for the next 16 years his Trojans were the power of the Pacific Coast. For another, the Rose Bowl series, which the Big Ten had dominated to an embarrassing degree, took a dramatic turnabout. And finally the Heisman Trophy, emblematic of the best in intercollegiate football, at last began to find its way West with great regularity.

The Rose Bowl Committee had aligned itself with the new AAWU immediately, and since the contract with the Big Ten had ended the new conference was given the right to choose its opponents. The five West Coast teams preferred to stay with the Big Ten, but the Big Ten wasn't so sure; a new Rose Bowl pact was defeated on a split vote of 5–5 but because it was that close, the league allowed its members to negotiate individually if they so chose.

They so chose.

McKay's first two years at USC were the only two losing seasons he had there, but Jim Owens' Washington Huskies took up the banner. Owens had taken over at Washington in 1957, and the situation he inherited was a nasty one. There had long been problems with alumni and boosters shading the recruiting rules, and Washington had been the first school hit with probation when the PCC purge began. Hugh McElhenny, the great running back of the early 1950s, said many years later, 'I actually took a pay cut when I went from Washington to the (San Francisco) 49ers as a rookie—and that's the truth.'

Darrell Royal had been hired to turn things around in Seattle but he stayed just one year before moving on to greatness at Texas. His replacement was Owens, just 30 years old, a former star end for Bud Wilkinson at Oklahoma and later an assistant under Bear Bryant. When Washington went shopping for a coach, Bryant told them, 'There is no more promising coach available than Owens. He'll build you a winner.'

That didn't happen right way. Owens' teams went 3–6–1 in 1957, 3–7 in 1958 and the Huskies still weren't considered a threat when the 1959 season began. But Jumbo Jim had studied what worked for other coaches, added his own touches, gathered a motley collection of recruiting also-rans and built them into a solid team centered around quarterback Bob Schloredt, a one-eyed converted fullback. In 1959 Washington lost just one game all year, 22–15 to USC. The Trojans finished 8–2—losing to UCLA and Notre Dame in the final two games—and Washington received the Rose Bowl bid.

The opponent was Wisconsin, which had finished one spot above the Huskies (ranked sixth and seventh) in the national rankings. The Badgers were favored by some 10 points but they were never in the game. Led by Schloredt and halfback George Fleming (who were named co-players of the game), Washington scored 17 points in the first quarter and wound up on the right end of a 44–8 final score.

That was only the second victory for the Pacific Coast in 14 Rose Bowl tries against the Big Ten since their contract had begun in 1947. Nobody knew it at the time but the Big Ten's New Year's Day domination was coming to an end.

The 1959 season also produced a second successive turnaround at California—this one not quite so pleasant for Bear fans—and one of the most exciting Big Games in the long history of that rivalry. Pete Elliott's Bears had gone 1–9 in his first year (1957) and 7–3 with a Rose Bowl bid the following season. Now Cal slipped back again, winning only two games and following that season, Elliott resigned and was replaced by Marv Levy.

In the final game that year, the Bears met another Jack Curtice Stanford team that threw the ball often and extremely well—the Indians led the nation in passing and quarterback Dick Norman was the individual national leader—but didn't do anything else well enough to win many games. The final record was 3–7, with losses to all four conference opponents.

Absolutely nothing was at stake in the Cal-Stanford game except Bay Area bragging rights. Norman was incredible; time after time he found his great receivers All-American Chris Burford and Ben Robinson wide open, and time after time he hit them. Norman completed 34 of 39 passes for 401 yards, an NCAA single-game record at the time—but as had been the case all season, the Indians just couldn't get into the end zone. They scored only 17 points. California, passing far less often but nearly as effectively—Wayne Crow, a converted halfback, completed his first eight passes—scored 20. But Stanford was always knocking at the door; in the closing minutes Norman mounted yet another drive and during a time out at midfield he had the foresight to get a kicking tee and stick it in his belt. Then, with the final seconds ticking away and Stanford at the Cal 10-yard line, Norman went

'Jumbo' Jim Owens *(at right)* **coached his Washington Huskies to a 44–8 victory over Wisconsin in the 1960 Rose Bowl, serving notice that the East's football dominance was soon ending. The payola scandal was wafting away, and there were sunny skies in the West.**

back to pass once more, couldn't find a receiver, tried to run and was hauled down before he could get out of bounds. The Indians, with no time outs left, tried to line up quickly for what would have been an easy field-goal try by Skip Face, but the gun sounded before the ball could be snapped.

Washington had been overlooked before the 1959 season, but nobody was taking the Huskies lightly in 1960. Schloredt, who had made some All-American teams the previous year, was back and although he was overshadowed by UCLA tailback Bill Kilmer—who led the nation in total offense—Schloredt had another fine year. 'Bob was a really fine athlete,' Owens told author John D McCallum years later, 'and he could do just about everything on the football field well. There wasn't a harder tackler on the team, and I could have used him as a linebacker had I needed him there. He was big and strong, and although he wasn't unusually fast he was a very good runner. He improved his passing terrifically, and he was a very fine kicker.... I was particularly impressed with his knack for coming up with the big play that saved the day. Bob was not afraid to take a chance. Our players respected him for it; they believed in him.'

Behind Schloredt was a crew of good running backs, including the explosive Fleming, sophomore Charlie Mitchell and tough Don McKeta; and a big group of fast, lean and rangy linemen led by All-American center Roy McKasson, guard Chuck Allen and tackle Kurt Gegner. The only other winning team in the five-school AAWU was UCLA, but both of the Bruins' losses that year came in conference games with Washington and USC.

Navy (and Heisman Trophy winner Joe Bellino) handed the Huskies their only loss of the year, 15–14 in the third game; there were three air-tight finishes in a row in mid-season but Washington won all of them—10–8 over UCLA (a game in which Schloredt broke his collarbone and was sidelined for the rest of the regular season), 30–29 against Oregon State and 7–6 over Oregon. Then, in the final three regular-season games the Huskies gave up only 14 points, and they were ready for a second consecutive Rose Bowl appearance.

The opponent this time was Minnesota, ranked Number One in the nation in both polls. The Gophers' acceptance of the Rose Bowl bid had been a major boost to the continuing success of the game, and even though Schloredt was back in action and the Huskies were getting full credit this time Minnesota still was a seven-point favorite. The Gophers were not fast and not clever, but they had an outstanding line led by All-American guard Tom Brown (the Heisman runnerup that year, almost unheard of for a lineman) and center Greg Larson; big backs and a fine all-purpose quarterback in Sandy Stephens.

Schloredt was dazzling. He averaged 12 yards a carry on the ground, ran in one touchdown, punted for a 41-yard average, played well on defense and although he threw only six passes, one of his two completions was for the last touchdown. For the second year in a row he guided the Huskies to a quick 17-point lead, with the two scores he accounted for plus a 47-yard field goal by Fleming. There would be no rout this year; Owens went conservative in the second half and turned it over to the defense. Although Minnesota dominated after intermission, it could score only once. Washington won 17–7.

Owens coached at Washington through the 1974 season and although the 'Purple Gang' of 1959–60 was the high point of those years with two Rose Bowl wins, he also took the Huskies to the Rose Bowl following the 1963 season. When he finally hung it up it was with a 99–82–6 record—more wins than any other coach in Husky history.

The 1961 season was not a particularly significant one in AAWU annals. Of the five teams, three—USC, Cal and Stan-

For a 'one-eyed converted fullback,' Bob Schloredt (opposite) was a heckuva quarterback, commanding the Huskies to two Rose Bowl victories—in 1960 and 1961. He had a great coach in Jim Owens, and assisting him on the field were such as Don McKeta (above).

ford—had losing records, and Washington barely missed it with a 5–4–1 mark. UCLA, under coach Bill Barnes and led by tailback Bob Smith and wingback Kermit Alexander, lost to Washington but finished 7–4 overall, won the league title and faced Minnesota in the Rose Bowl.

The Gophers were not the powerhouse of the previous year although Sandy Stephens was back at quarterback. Ohio State had won the Big Ten title and was invited by the Rose Bowl Committee, but—much to the chagrin of Woody Hayes, the Buckeye players and thousands of students who nearly rioted in Columbus, Ohio—the faculty committee turned down the invitation by a narrow margin. The runnerup Gophers were invited instead, and had no trouble beating the Bruins 21–3.

But there would be no long dry spell for the Pacific Coast this time. Enter John McKay.

When Jess Hill moved up to athletic director at Southern California following the 1956 season, he hired Don Clark as head football coach. The Trojans, who were 8–2 in Hill's final season, went 1–9 in 1957 and 4–5–1 in 1958. Then, in the last of Clark's three years, they improved to 8–2.

But there were other factors besides the record involved. For one thing, Clark had never beaten either UCLA (although they did tie in 1958) or Notre Dame—the two biggest games in any Trojan season. For another, he coached (or at least countenanced) a rough and tough type of game—a little too rough and tough. Two of Southern Cal's stars in that period were twins Mike and Marlin McKeever, and Mike was the epitome of roughhouse football. The most famous incident in which the Trojan guard was involved was against California in 1959, when he landed on Bear halfback Steve Bates, who was well out of bounds, with his elbow in Bates' face, breaking Bates' jaw and

This photo of 1961 Rose Bowl Game action shows Don McKeta (*at left*) carrying the ball through the Minnesota line during Washington's 17–7 victory over the Minnesota Gophers.

USC coach Don Clark *(above)* was very close with his players, and brought the team from 1–9 in 1957 to 8–2 in 1959, resigning perhaps in response to the Mick McKeever/Steve Bates incident at the Trojans-Bears game in 1959. John McKay *(opposite)* replaced Clark, and brought home four national championships and nine conference titles.

causing so much damage that his face virtually had to be reconstructed. Mike McKeever was thrown out of the game, not for that, ironically, but later—for elbowing Cal quarterback Pete Olsen well after he had thrown a pass downfield. (In fact Mike was thrown out of several games, including one against Stanford and—believe it or not—three in a row against California, including their freshman game. Had McKeever not been injured and unable to play against the Bears as a senior, he might have set a record that would never be broken.)

Clark naturally enough defended McKeever, but Elliott called it 'one of the most flagrant violations I have ever seen in football.' An editorial in *Sports Illustrated* magazine said, 'This seemingly calculated mayhem, according to USC's way of thinking, is all a part of the game.... When a boy misconstrues aggressiveness as modified manslaughter, the game is better off without him. Mike McKeever seems unclear on the point, possibly because Don Clark, a genuinely fine coach, has never taken the time to drive the point home.' *Los Angeles Times* writer Jim Murray said of the McKeever-Bates incident, 'It was like watching Richard Widmark hitting a cripple in a gangster movie.'

That incident may have had something to do with Clark's resignation. Whether it actually did or not, upon Clark's recommendation, McKay was brought in to replace him. McKay had been assistant coach at Oregon before joining the USC coaching staff, and he'd been at USC just nine months previous to Clark's leaving. Yet, when USC offered him Clark's job, it was one of the wisest moves the Trojans ever made.

McKay—in addition to being one of the funniest football coaches ever—was one of the best. His strategy was simple enough: Get a lot of big and talented linemen and one great running back and keep giving him the football. In his autobiography, *McKay: A Coach's Story,* John wrote: 'Every team in the nation knows that when they play us they better keep all 22 eyes on the tailback.' But of course that was an oversimplification—'Great runners are not born; great runners are made,' McKay said later. But born or made, the 'student body right, student body left' formula worked well enough to earn him four national championships, nine conference titles and an overall record of 127 wins, 40 losses and eight ties—a remarkable .749 winning percentage.

In that period, Southern California not only had six All-American running backs—two of them Heisman Trophy winners—but 12 offensive linemen (including two tight ends) who also made at least one first-team All-American. One of them, tackle Ron Yary, won the Outland Trophy as the nation's best lineman in 1967.

And from 1964 on, every starting tailback but two carried the ball at least 200 times during the season, and usually far more often. When something works, go with it.

'Before my time in college football,' Mike Garrett, the 1965 Heisman winner, recalled, 'I don't think anyone ran 25 to 30 times and McKay started that with me.... I learned to relax between plays. If you watch *every* USC tailback who carries the ball a lot, you will see they move like Jim Brown—very slow and relaxed between plays to reserve their strength.'

Garrett carried the ball 267 times that year for a national-best 1440 yards, but USC opponents hadn't seen anything yet. In 1968 O J Simpson carried it 383 times, gaining 1880 yards. McKay summed up his philosophy neatly when asked that year if he wasn't afraid that Simpson would get tired carrying the ball so often.

'Why?' McKay shot back. 'It isn't heavy.'

It took McKay a couple of years to rebuild, but by 1962 there was no stopping him. He had a capable tailback in Willie Brown, and for once the Trojans not only had one outstanding quarterback, they had two—Pete Beathard and Bill Nelsen—and a consensus All-American in Hal Bedsole. Bedsole was a tall, lanky end who didn't do much besides catch the ball, but did that very well; his 33 catches went for an amazing 827 yards (a 25.1 yards-per-catch average) and an even more amazing 11 touchdowns. Southern California won 10 straight regular-season games (few of them even close), capped by wins over UCLA and Notre Dame. The Trojans were named the Number One team in the nation in both polls, and prepared to meet Wisconsin in the Rose Bowl.

That 1962 season was an eventful one for the Pacific Coast. In addition to Southern Cal's national title, it saw the AAWU expanded to six teams with the addition of Washington State (which played just two conference games, splitting them), and the first Heisman Trophy ever awarded to a West Coast player. Interestingly enough, it was not an AAWU player that won it but Terry Baker, of Oregon State—which did not re-enter the league until 1964.

Baker was an incredible athlete. In high school he had been an A student and had quarterbacked his football team to two state titles, pitched the baseball team to a state crown and led the basketball team to two city championships. He was recruited in all three sports and went to Oregon State on a basketball scholarship. As a sophomore he played tailback in the single wing and in his first start rolled up a school record 284 yards in total offense. In 1961, his junior year, coach Tommy Prothro switched to the T and installed Terry at quarterback. As a senior he led the nation in total offense, carried the Beavers to an 8–2 record (and a

Above: **In a scene from the early 1960s, Washington Huskies coach Jim Owens *(left)* shakes hands with Oregon State's great Tommy Prothro *(right)*. Tommy Prothro's great quarterback was Terry Baker *(at right)*—the first West Coast player to be awarded the Heisman Trophy. Baker won most of the major national awards available.**

Liberty Bowl victory), won virtually every major college award in the nation including the Heisman, and was named *Sports Illustrated*'s Sportsman of the Year. After a dramatic, come-from-behind 20–17 win over Oregon in the regular-season football finale, it was Baker who his teammates carried off the field. 'In all my years in football,' said Prothro, 'I have never seen the players do that to one of their own.'

In the Liberty Bowl, the lone touchdown in a 6–0 Oregon State win was by Baker—on a 99-yard run. After that, he went back to the basketball team and helped the Beavers make the NCAA Final Four. Oh, and incidentally, he also was an honors student majoring in engineering.

His winning of the Heisman started a trend; in the following eight seasons, four more Pacific Coast players also won it.

There was another all-time great in the West that year, Washington State end Hugh Campbell. Campbell was one of those receivers who was too small, too slow and couldn't do anything except somehow get free and catch the football. He set what were then NCAA career records with 176 catches and 2452 yards; overlooked by the NFL, he went to Canada and set a variety of receiving records there.

Washington State, incidentally, played in one of the strangest games of all time in that 1962 season. The Cougars were tied with Iowa 14–14 but were driving toward a winning score. On third down, quarterback Dave Mathieson passed incomplete and, with three seconds remaining and the ball at the Hawkeye 25-yard line, the WSU field goal team ran on the field with a strong aiding wind behind them. But hold it! The officials were giving the ball to Iowa.

Cougar coach Jim Sutherland ran nearly to midfield complaining, but the referee chased him off. In the press box Iowa sports publicist Eric Wilson held his head and said, 'This is unbelievable, they've *lost* a down,' and his statistics crew confirmed it. Iowa then completed a long pass but time ran out; the officials were informed of the error, but by then they and the Iowa team had left the field and the tie stood.

With all these wonderful goings-on, the only thing the Pacific Coast needed now to cap the 1962 season was a Rose Bowl win. The AAWU-Big Ten Rose Bowl pact had now been formally renewed, and Wisconsin came out to face the mighty Trojans. What followed was one of the wildest games in the long history of that Pasadena classic.

Beathard threw four touchdown passes, two of them to Bedsole, and Southern Cal took a 42–14 lead early in the fourth quarter. Surely the game was over. Then suddenly, Badger quarterback Ron VanderKelen got hot. He threw three touchdown passes of his own in that fourth quarter, and that, combined with a safety, brought Wisconsin to within five points. USC held on for a 42–37 victory—but had the game lasted another five minutes it might have been a different story. For the game, VanderKelen wound up throwing 48 passes, completing 33 of them for 401 yards; 11 Rose Bowl records were broken—and you can bet none of them were on defense.

USC finished with a 7–3 record in 1963, but lost 22–7 to Washington; the Huskies were 6–4 overall and lost to UCLA, but had a 4–1 AAWU record and the win over Southern Cal (3–1)—and as a result went to the Rose Bowl. Washington had a good running game behind fullback Junior Coffey (who had led the AAWU in rushing in 1962) and a solid defense led by Rick Redman, but in the Rose Bowl the offense never got untracked and the Huskies fell to third-ranked Illinois 17–7. (That Illini team, incidentally, was coached by Pete Elliott, who five years before had been on the other side of the field—as the coach of the Cal team that lost to Iowa.)

Oregon and Oregon State joined the AAWU for the 1964 season—bringing the league to eight teams—and both brought successful programs. In the five years the two were out of the conference, Tommy Prothro had had only one losing season and in 1962 had a 9–2 record, a Liberty Bowl champion and a Heisman Trophy winner at Oregon State. At Eugene, Len Casanova had gone 8–2 in 1959, 7–3–1—including a 41–12 loss to Penn State in the Liberty Bowl—in 1960, 4–6 in 1961, 6–3–1 in 1962 and then 8–3 in 1963—including a 21–14 win over Southern Methodist in the Sun Bowl.

With their return to the conference, the race became a real dogfight. Oregon finished 7–2–1 overall but both losses and the tie were within the league, and the Ducks were not a factor. USC, behind Mike Garrett and quarterback Craig Fertig, went 7–3 against a tough schedule; one of the losses was to Number Nine Ohio State and the Trojans upset third-ranked Notre Dame 20–17 in the season finale. Southern Cal was ranked 10th in the nation in both polls, but one of the losses was again to Washington, and again it cost the Trojans the undisputed AAWU title and a Rose Bowl bid. The Huskies, with another fine defense anchored by All-American linebacker Rick Redman (the colleges had gone to a complete platoon system that year) finished with a 5–2 conference record and 6–4 overall.

Oregon State finished 8–2 overall, 3–1 in the conference (the same as Southern California, whom the Beavers did not meet) and were eighth nationally in both polls. The Beavers, in the last of Prothro's 10 years as head coach, were voted into the Rose Bowl.

California was not a factor in those seasons, but the Bears had a player worth mentioning—quarterback Craig Morton. As a high school star the six foot, four-inch, 205-pound Morton had been a good enough runner to be used as a kick returner, but a knee injury before his sophomore year sidelined him for half that season—and severely limited his mobility through his college and long pro career. In his varsity debut, he entered the game in the second quarter for a 'brief appearance'—and wound up setting a school record with 283 yards total offense, nearly pulling off an upset over Penn State. From that moment he never again sat on the bench and, despite playing in pain for his whole career, Morton set a flock of conference records by completing 355 of 641 passes for 4501 yards and 36 touchdowns. In 1964 he completed 185 of 308—a 60 percent completion mark—for 2121 yards and had only nine passes intercepted; he made some All-American teams (despite the fact that Heisman Trophy winner John Huarte of Notre Dame, record-setting Jerry Rhome of Tulsa and a guy from Alabama named Joe Namath were around that year), and was seventh in the Heisman voting—a truly remarkable accomplishment for a player whose team finished with a 3–7 record.

The Oregon State team that went to the Rose Bowl that year was not a particularly outstanding one. In fact, the Beavers placed only two players on the 22-man all-conference team: tackle Rich Koeper and defensive back Dan Espalin. Fourth-

The University of Washington Huskies went to the Rose Bowl in 1964 on a 4–1 AAWU record, and their able defense was led by guard Rick Redman *(opposite)*, who tried to make sure that AAWU-leading fullback Junior Coffee would not score in vain, but alas, the Illini kenneled the Huskies 17–7. *Above:* The Washington Husky logo.

ranked Michigan, coached by Pete Elliott's brother Bump, came West and demolished Oregon State in the Rose Bowl, 34–7.

But that was the end of that nonsense. Over the next 20 years the Big Ten—which had, remember, once been described by a West Coast writer as 'too much for our boys'—won only four Rose Bowl games.

The team to begin the Pacific Coast surge was fittingly enough, UCLA— which had been demolished 20 years earlier in the first game under the contract with the Big Ten. It was another tight race; USC had Garrett back for his senior year and finished 7–2–1 including a loss to Number Nine Notre Dame, to finish ranked 10th in the nation. Washington State's 'Cardiac Kids' under Bert Clark had an incredible season and finished 7–3, but were only 2–1 in the conference.

But UCLA had two new ingredients that season: Tommy Prothro had been lured back to Westwood as the head coach, and he installed a sophomore named Gary Beban at quarterback. 'He's not that great of a passer,' somebody once said of Beban, 'and he's not that fast. What he does best is win.'

Behind Beban and Mel Farr, a fine running back who averaged nearly seven yards a carry that season, the Bruins ran off a 7–2–1 regular-season record and beat USC 20–16 in a thriller to win the conference title and the Rose Bowl bid. But the opponent there was Michigan State, which not only was ranked Number One nationally by United Press International (Number Two by the Associated Press) but had beaten UCLA early in the season by a 13–3 score that could have been worse. However this was not the same Bruin team. Beban scored twice on one-yard runs in the second quarter, Kurt Zimmerman kicked the important conversions, and the UCLA defense, led by player of the game Bob

Below: The Rose Bowl of 1964 saw the Washington Huskies (in gold helmets) fall to a low-ranked Illinois team because the Huskies offense just couldn't break loose.

Above and left: **Mike Garrett, USC tailback and 1965 Heisman Trophy winner, shows his All-American style. The year 1965 brought still other news to college football—as coaches sought to 'outfox' each other—making it truly jargonesque with code words like** *scrambling quarterback, sprintout pass, I-formation* **and** *shotgun defense.*

Stiles, stopped the Spartans until the fourth quarter. Michigan State scored twice then, but could convert neither score, and the fourth-ranked Bruins had a 14–12 upset.

Southern California had to settle for a 'consolation prize' in that 1965 season—a Heisman Trophy for Mike Garrett. Garrett had led the AAWU in rushing for three straight years, and the nation in his senior season (when he carried 267 times for a conference record 1440 yards). For his career he rushed, caught passes and returned kicks for 4876 yards; his 3221 career yards rushing was an NCAA record, breaking a 14-year-old mark set by Ollie Matson of San Francisco.

Garrett was a fine baseball player in high school—he later was offered a $65,000 bonus by the Pittsburgh Pirates—as well as a standout quarterback. He chose USC, and his performance as a

freshman in dummy drills convinced McKay that here was the workhorse tailback he was looking for to make his offensive theory work.

Mike was nicknamed 'Duck' because of the way he walked, but put him on the football field and he became one of the finest open-field runners of all time. When he later played in the pros with Kansas City, one of his offensive linemen said, 'The way he runs, you feel you should get up and throw another block, because he might be coming back your way.' But Garrett also was a fine receiver, a fierce blocker (he knocked himself cold twice in practice before a Notre Dame game) and a great team player. When he was awarded the Heisman Trophy, he donated it to the school's impressive trophy case—and he himself paid to have a plaque with the names of all his teammates attached to it.

The one thing that had eluded Garrett throughout his college career was a Rose Bowl, even though in those three years he had led the Trojans to a record of 21–8–1. But in the next nine years, the Trojans went to the Rose Bowl an amazing seven times.

The John McKay era was under a full head of steam.

A Trojan Dynasty

When John McKay's Southern California team sneaked into the Rose Bowl following the 1966 season, even the most diehard Trojan fans couldn't have suspected what was to come over the next decade.

It is entirely possible that that USC team was underrated; after all, it did have the strongest defense in the league, anchored by All-Americans Nate Shaw and Adrian Young, a great offensive tackle in Ron Yary and—the key to any Trojan team—a capable tailback in sprinter Rod Sherman. And although the record was 7–4, the losses all were to Top Ten teams, and three of them were very close: 14–7 to Number Five UCLA, 10–7 to Number Nine Miami and 14–13 to Number Seven Purdue in the Rose Bowl.

There were several factors, however, that kept the Trojans from getting the recognition they deserved. For one, they had not been to the Rose Bowl for three years—even though they lost out twice on conference votes, and then in 1965 when UCLA had come from behind in the final three minutes to win 20–16 despite a courageous 210-yard rushing performance by USC's great Mike Garrett.

For another thing, Southern California wound up that 1966 season with two straight losses; the one to UCLA could be countenanced, but that was followed by a 51–0 thrashing by Notre Dame. Never mind that the Fighting Irish wound up the season ranked Number One in the nation in both polls—it was the worst defeat in Southern California history, and it came at the hands of an old and bitter rival.

McKay, in his autobiography, called that game 'the worst occurrence of my life—far worse than anything that ever happened off a football field. USC has been playing football for 85 years, and I directed the worst defeat in Trojan history. As I stood there in the fourth quarter, I heard the public address announcer remind the crowd of that fact 14 times.

'... It took a year—until we beat Notre Dame in 1967—before I could go to sleep without thinking of that game. But it still sticks in my mind and will for a long time. After that we didn't lose to Notre Dame again for six straight years. I guarantee we'll never lose to anyone 51–0 again, if I have to run 87 quarterback sneaks.'

The Trojans' other major problem was having to share Los Angeles with UCLA. Gary Beban quarterbacked the Bruins to another great year—a 9–1 record and a Number Five national ranking. Coach Tommy Prothro's team had run up some impressive victories—57–14 over Pitt; 31–12 over Syracuse, with great running backs Floyd Little and Larry Csonka; 49–11 over Penn State; 38–13 over the Air Force Academy. The Bruins lost only

to Washington, in a 16–3 upset—but that cost them a second straight trip to the Rose Bowl. Despite their win over USC, they finished with a 3–1 conference record (to 4–1 for the Trojans), and in addition UCLA had gone to Pasadena the previous year.

So Southern California got the bid, and almost a victory. With Purdue leading, 14–7, and less than three minutes remaining, the Trojans' aptly-named quarterback Troy Winslow found Sherman with a 19-yard touchdown pass. But when Winslow tried to pass for the two-point conversion that would have won it, the Boilermakers' George Catavolos intercepted to save the Purdue victory.

The only serious challenge to the Trojans and Bruins that year (and for two years thereafter) came from Oregon State. Dee Andros, a former Oklahoma lineman and one-time assistant at California, had succeeded Prothro when Tommy moved to UCLA. While McKay ran his tailback left and right, Andros ran his fullback right up the middle. In 1965–66, Pete Pifer carried 464 times for 2183 yards; in 1967–68 240-pound Bill 'Earthquake' Enyart carried 492 times for 2155 yards. They weren't very fast and they weren't nifty, but the Beaver fullbacks were always dependable—in his two seasons, with almost 500 carries, Enyart was thrown for the amazing total of just eight yards in losses.

The Beavers were just 5–5 in Andros' first season, 1965, but in 1966 they went 7–3 overall and 3–1 in the conference, sharing the AAWU title but missing any chance for the Rose Bowl in a 21–0 early-season loss to USC. In 1967 they were 7–2–1 and tied UCLA, and in 1968 they were 7–3 and lost in the league only to the champion Trojans 17–13.

Another team that was supposed to make a title run that year was Washington State. Coach Bert Clark's 'Cardiac Kids' had had an amazing season the previous year; the record was a respectable 7–3, but the way they did it was what kept the fans screaming. A touchdown in the fourth quarter beat Iowa 7–0 in the opener; they edged Minnesota (which the week before had tied USC) by coming from behind 14–13 on two conversions by defensive back Willie Gaskins, who had never kicked one before; later in the season they beat Indiana 8–7 by scoring a touchdown and a two-point conversion on the final play of the game—moments after an apparent game-saving Hoosier interception in the end zone had been nullified by an offsides penalty; they beat Oregon State 10–8; and they lost to Arizona State 7–6 when a two-point conversion try in the fourth quarter failed.

In the photo *at right*, John McKay looks like a man who 'knew all along' what would become of his Trojan teams—tremendous success.

Above: **O J Simpson tries to fly over the Indiana defenders in the 1968 Rose Bowl. Orenthal James 'Orange Juice' Simpson gained 128 yards and scored both of USC's touchdowns in this 14–3 Trojan victory. His speed was featured in McKay's '23-Blast' play. If Ron Yary** *(left)* **looks feisty—well, he was an Outland Trophy-winning of-fensive tackle and one of McKay's (mighty tough) best.**

It was an incredible year, and Cougar fans were talking Rose Bowl in 1966. But WSU wasn't done with the bizarre just yet. In the opening game of the season, the Cougars totally dominated California in every department—except the score. The Bears could do nothing offensively, but got a long punt return from Jerry Bradley, three interceptions—one for a touchdown—from a six-foot-seven sophomore defensive back named Wayne Stewart and finally a record-shattering 108-yard return of a missed field goal by swift defensive back Don Guest (who 10 years later would represent the United States on the Rugby field against France and Canada). Cal won 21–6; Washington State never recovered, finishing the season 3–7, and didn't have another winning year until 1972.

All of these, however, were sideshows. The center ring of AAWU football was in Los Angeles—and it was going to stay there for awhile.

McKay's teams ran up an incredible record in that nine-year stretch. Beginning with the 1966 season and running through 1974, the Trojans not only went to seven Rose Bowls and won four of them, they compiled an overall record of 79 wins against just 17 losses and six ties—and that included the two 'bad' years when they had back-to-back 6–4–1 records in 1970–71. In the Associated Press national poll, they were ranked first twice, second, third, fourth and eighth; the United Press International coaches' poll gave them three Number Ones, a second, a fourth and a seventh. In the six seasons from 1967 to 1974, excluding the 1970–71 down years, Southern California lost exactly one conference game—and that was to Oregon State, 3–0 in a Cor-vallis mudbath in 1967.

The 1967 season saw the Trojans finish Number One in the nation in both polls, but it may have been their most challenging year. USC breezed through the first nine games with only the loss to Oregon State, in which the muddy field successfully neutralized the incomparable Trojan tailback O J Simpson. In-cluded in the victories were a 24–7 win over Notre Dame (which wound up the season ranked fourth nationally); in that one Simpson had 38 carries, 150 yards and three touchdowns, and USC came from a 7–0 halftime deficit. McKay could sleep again.

Southern California went into the final regular-season game against UCLA ranked third in the nation. But the Bruins were undefeated and ranked Number One! They had a 16–16 tie with Oregon State (which, incidentally, wound up that season with a 7–2–1 record and ranked seventh in the country), and had beaten both Tennessee and Penn State, who would end the season rated Number Two and Number Ten respectively.

This was perhaps the best of all the games in this traditional intra-city rivalry—with not only the AAWU title and the Rose Bowl bid at stake, but the national championship as well. It was everything a football fan could hope for—and more.

Gary Beban, the Bruin quarterback who was on his way to the Heisman Trophy, played with badly bruised ribs but still completed 16 of 24 passes for 301 yards and two touchdowns. Simpson, his chief competition for the Heisman, ran for two touchdowns—it was his incredible 64-yard scamper, in which he cut back to escape a seemingly inescapable roadblock and then outran the defense, that ultimately decided the game. USC won 21–20.

After that, the Rose Bowl was almost anticlimactic. The Trojans, who began the game with five starters on the bench injured and lost two more during the game, got 128 yards and two short touchdown runs from Simpson and beat Indiana 14–3.

The loss to USC, and a meaningless season-ending defeat by Syracuse, dropped the Bruins to 10th in the final polls, but it did nothing to diminish Beban's glory. Beban probably should have won the Heisman as a sophomore—then (even though he had his worst statistical year as a junior in 1966), his all-around brilliance in leading UCLA to its 9–1 record made many people believe he should have won that year, but he finished fourth to winner Steve Spurrier. Now, as a senior he did win it—and sure enough, there were just as many who said no he didn't deserve it this year: OJ Simpson did.

It was a close race—Beban had 1968 points in the voting, Simpson 1722. Beban's brilliance as a sophomore and junior undoubtedly swung it, since Simpson had just come to USC in that 1967 season as a transfer from City College of San Francisco. 'The Heisman wasn't a one-year performance,' Beban said later. 'I don't think anyone in the country in 1967 played better than OJ Simpson. But I don't think anyone in the country had a better year than I did in 1965, when Mike Garrett won the Heisman. So to me, the Heisman reflected three years of always being in the chips, and making UCLA a power in football again.'

Beban and Simpson were very different, but they had some things in common besides skill on a football field. Both were from the San Francisco Bay Area, and both had failed to make the Northern California squad for an annual high school all-star game against Southern California. Beban had been a single wing tailback under coach Joe Marvin at Sequoia High School in Redwood City, and nobody knew if he could make the switch to quarterback—nobody except Beban, Marvin and the UCLA recruiters. Simpson had played on an undistinguished team at Galileo High School in San Francisco and as a senior was rated probably the third-best back in the City. It was not until he scored 54 touchdowns in two seasons at City College that he gained national notice.

Now, in the space of two seasons both were All-Americans and Heisman Trophy winners.

The gracious Simpson insisted at the time he wasn't disappointed when Beban won the trophy in 1967, but later he admitted that he had been at Mike Garrett's home on New Year's after the Rose Bowl, and had seen Garrett's Heisman. 'It hit me kind of hard,' O J said. 'For the first time, I was aware how close I had come to winning it—and how badly I wanted it.'

Gary Beban *(opposite)* was UCLA's star quarterback and Heisman Trophy threat from 1965-67. He finally won the award in 1967, in competition with O J Simpson, who had to wait until 1968 to get his Heisman. The Heisman Trophy *(above)* is named for John W Heisman, football genius and Shakespearean actor of the 1890s-1920s.

It wouldn't be long before he had it.

Although they had some narrow squeaks, the Trojans won their first nine games in 1968 before a tie with Notre Dame ended the regular season. Needless to say, they represented the Pacific-8 Conference—the name had been changed officially before the 1968 season—in the Rose Bowl against national champion Ohio State, led by quarterback Rex Kern. The Trojans took a 10–0 lead and got a characteristically spectacular performance from Simpson—171 yards, including an 80-yard touchdown run. But they also had an uncharacteristic five turnovers and finally lost to the Buckeyes, 27–16. Consolation was on the way; in December Simpson, to the surprise of absolutely nobody, got his Heisman Trophy.

It is unlikely that there's ever been a more exciting running back than O J Simpson. His statistics tell part of the story: as a junior he led the nation in rushing with 1415 yards on 266 carries (and another 128 yards which do not count in NCAA statistics—in the Rose Bowl), scored three touchdowns in the win over Notre Dame, clinched the Rose Bowl bid with his spectacular 64-yard touchdown run against UCLA and scored both TDs in the Rose Bowl; as a senior he again led the nation in rushing with 1709 yards on 355 carries (both national records—again not including the Rose Bowl, where he gained 171 yards more). He scored 36 touchdowns in two seasons. In 17 of his 21 games he gained more than 100 yards; five times, including four in his senior year, it was more than 200. He averaged 32 carries a game; as McKay said, 'It's a good thing he doesn't belong to a union.'

But that wasn't all of it. O J was big—six feet, two inches, 210 pounds—and fast enough to run a 9.3 100-yard dash and be part of a USC 4x100 relay team that set a world record. In addi-

tion, he had an incredible ability to 'see' the field, find a hole in the defense and then, when the hole closed up, to make a startling change of direction and run away from would-be tacklers. Like many great backs, he might be stopped with two or three or five yards for several plays in succession. Then, in the words of John McKay, 'Whoosh! Touchdown!'

'Simpson accelerates like a jackrabbit,' McKay said, 'but his speed is deceptive because he seems to glide. He doesn't seem to be going fast until you try to tackle him.'

When OJ was named the Heisman Trophy winner by the largest margin ever (he had 2853 points to 1103 for runnerup Leroy Keyes of Purdue), Minnesota coach Murray Warmath, who'd lost to the Trojans in the 1968 opener, summed it up nicely: 'They all say OJ is the greatest,' Warmath said, 'but he's been misrepresented. He's better than that.'

Orenthal James Simpson had come from a shaky start. As a child he had rickets and wore braces. Later he was leader of a street gang, and he had some minor problems and near-misses at Galileo High. 'He's a great guy,' Joe Bell, a high school teammate and later a fine running back himself at CCSF and Washington State, said of OJ, 'but he wasn't any angel. If circumstances had been just slightly tilted, instead of a football star he could have been Public Enemy Number One.'

Instead, of course, he not only became one of the great runners in college and pro football history, but has gone on to success as an actor and TV announcer and is one of the genuinely classy people in the sport.

The loss of an OJ Simpson would have to decimate any team, right? Not the Trojans. In 1969 McKay simply unleashed another All-American tailback, Clarence Davis—a JC transfer who had been a guard in high school. Davis did everything well, including block, catch passes and return kickoffs. McKay felt his endurance was not up to that of Garrett or Simpson—but Davis still carried

O J Simpson *(at right)* had guts, talent and real sportsmanship. He won the Heisman in 1968 with 2853 points, the highest scoring ever. Both he and UCLA's Gary Beban showed their mettle in the grueling 1967 USC/UCLA 21–20 shootout. Beban played brilliantly with bruised ribs, O J with a broken foot *(above); note* McKay to O J's *left.*

the ball 297 times for 1351 yards. With the 'Wild Bunch,' a powerful defense led by All-American linemen Jimmy Gunn and Al Cowlings (Simpson's teammate from Gailileo High and CCSF), allowing only 10 points a game, the Trojans blasted their way to another unbeaten season—marred only by a tie with Notre Dame—a Number Three national ranking and yes another Rose Bowl, the record fourth in a row for Southern California.

Michigan was the foe, and although the Wolverines played well on defense, their offense was no match for Gunn, Cowling and the Wild Bunch. A 13-yard touchdown pass from Jimmy Jones to Bob Chandler was the margin in a 10–3 Trojan victory. That was incidentally the first of many Rose Bowls for Michigan coach Bo Schembechler—and the first of five losses in a row in Pasadena before he finally won one. Schembechler didn't see this one, however; he suffered a heart attack and missed the game.

The Trojans' next two years were noteworthy only because, for a change, they didn't go to the Rose Bowl. The 1970 season was a strange one. USC tied Number One-ranked Nebraska 21–21, and beat Number Two-ranked Notre Dame 38–28. They scored 343 points, including 156 in the first four games against Alabama, Nebraska, Iowa and Oregon State. But they lost four of their last seven games, gave up 233 points for the year and finished 6–4–1. The following season they had the same record—for Southern California fans, a disappointing one—although they again beat Notre Dame.

But if that was a low point, 1972 was the pinnacle. There were five All-Americans that year—tight end Charles Young, offensive tackle Pete Adams, fullback Sam Cunningham, defensive tackle

John Grant and linebacker Richard Wood (a sophomore who was to become USC's first three-time All-American)—and there were four others who would win national honors the following season, including the great receiver Lynn Swann. Tailback Anthony Davis (no relation to Clarence) was only a sophomore and would have to wait two years to be an All-American, but he gained 5.8 yards every time he touched the ball; 1191 yards in all.

The Trojans won 12 games in a row; they never trailed in the second half of any game; they beat two-time defending champion Stanford 30–21 and that was the only game they won by *less* than three touchdowns. They walloped Notre Dame 45–23 as Davis scored six touchdowns and had 368 yards—99 rushing, 51 receiving and 218 on kickoff returns including 97 and 96-yard returns for touchdowns.

McKay considered it his best club; 'I've never seen any team that could beat them,' he said.

At halftime of the Rose Bowl they were tied with Ohio State 7–7; the final score was 42–17. Davis ran for 157 yards, and Cunningham, known primarily for his blocking, set a modern Rose Bowl record with four touchdowns, all on short blasts into—or leaps over—the line. There is a story that, as USC lined up just prior to Cunningham's last score, quarterback Mike Rae—who had thrown for 229 yards in the game—looked across at the Ohio State defense, smiled and said, 'Here he comes again.'

The next two years were nearly as good. In 1973 the Trojans won nine games against a murderous schedule—the two losses

Jimmy Jones *(above)*, the 1970–71 Trojan quarterback, said he chose USC over 111 other schools which vied for his abilities because he 'had always wanted to go to the Rose Bowl'—and he got to win one, 10–3 over Michigan in 1970. USC receiver Lynn Swann (number 22) is shown *at below right* en route to a 92-yard punt-return TD in USC's 1972 51–6 route of Michigan State. Anthony Davis *(above right)* scores a TD against Ohio in USC's 1973 42–17 Rose Bowl romp.

were to Notre Dame, and to Ohio State in the Rose Bowl (those two teams finished one and two in the nation), and there was a tie with third-ranked Oklahoma. At halftime of the Rose Bowl USC had a 14–14 tie, but in a reversal of the previous year's game, the Buckeyes—behind quarterback Cornelius Greene, Heisman Trophy winner Archie Griffin and fullback Pete Johnson (who scored three TDs)—exploded for a 42–21 victory.

The following year USC lost the opener to Arkansas, but went through the rest of the year with 10 wins and only a 15–15 tie with California marring the record. Davis led the conference in rushing for the second time in three years and twice ran back kickoffs 100 yards for touchdowns against Arkansas and Notre Dame—which was getting a little tired of Anthony Davis, thank you.

However, Davis was injured and had to sit out the Rose Bowl, and it turned out to be one of the best games in the long history of the Pasadena Classic. For the third straight year the opponent was Woody Hayes' Ohio State Buckeyes—the Big Ten had dropped its no-repeat rule a few years earlier—and it was a battle

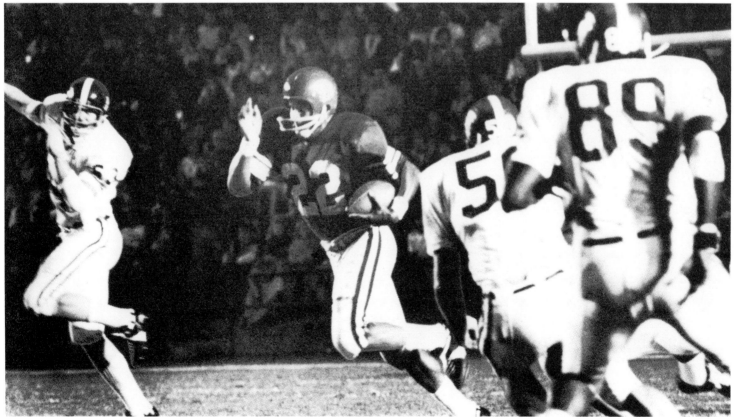

for Number One. The Buckeyes were ranked third in both polls; the Trojans were Number Two in the Associated Press poll behind Oklahoma, but first in the UPI ratings—since the coaches' board would not pick a team that was on probation, as Oklahoma was.

Trojan quarterback Pat Haden had had a spotty year but he rose to the occasion, throwing for 181 yards and two touchdowns. Nevertheless Ohio State led 7–3 after three quarters and 17–10 in the closing minutes, before Haden passed to clever receiver Johnny McKay (the coach's son) for a touchdown, and then to Shelton Diggs, who made a miraculous catch for the two-point conversion that gave Southern California an 18–17 victory.

It was John McKay's fifth Rose Bowl victory—and his last. The Trojans opened the 1975 season with seven straight wins, including a 24–17 win over Notre Dame. But following that game McKay announced he was leaving Southern California for the pros, and the deflated Trojans lost their final four games before putting it together one last time to give John a going-away present—a 20–0 win over Texas A&M in the Liberty Bowl.

Only one team had been able to disturb McKay's equanimity, or what seemed like his permanent tenancy in the Rose Bowl. That was Stanford, under John Ralston.

McKay and Ralston were not the friendliest of coaching rivals. After one of the few times that the Trojans beat Stanford by a big score (McKay won seven of the nine meetings, but most were close), he was questioned about running up the score, and for once McKay's wit deserted him. 'I'd like to beat Stanford by two thousand points,' he exploded. (Ironically, several years later, when McKay was coaching a weak Tampa Bay team in the NFL, he publicly accused Ralston's Denver Broncos of 'pouring it on.')

Whatever the reason, it was no secret that John McKay simply did not like John Ralston.

Most people did. Ralston didn't have McKay's jokebook, but he was an open, polite man who rarely displayed anger in public. As a coach he was rarely demonstrative—not a Woody Hayes, kicking down markers and swinging on photographers, nor an emotional orator in the Knute Rockne mold. Rather, he was a sound tactical mind and a master organizer.

Before the 1971 Rose Bowl, this writer was approached by a Midwest newspaperman who opened the conversation by saying, 'John Ralston isn't much of a coach, is he?'

'Well,' I couldn't resist replying, 'he's here (in the Rose Bowl), so he must have done something right. What makes you think he's a poor coach?'

'It seems to me,' the Midwesterner said, 'that all he knows how to do is recruit and hire good assistants.'

It wasn't *all* Ralston knew how to do, but he did do those things very well, and at Stanford—as in all major football programs in this modern era—that's 90 percent of the battle.

Stanford had swallowed a bitter pill when it hired Ralston—he was an alumnus of arch-rival California, where he had played linebacker on Pappy Waldorf's Rose Bowl teams. But Jack Curtice had completed five years as Stanford coach and although his last team in 1962 had gone 5–5, his overall record was 14–36 including a miserable 0–10 in 1960. After the colorful Cactus Jack, Ralston seemed as if he'd be more at home behind a corporate desk, but Stanford was tired of losing. In his last official act as athletic director before turning the job over to Chuck Taylor, Al Masters hired Ralston as head football coach.

John had been successful as head coach at Utah State, but he was not an immediate success with the Indians. His 1963 team

At left: **A fanatic Trojan following—including a security guard** *(below center)***—roars its approval as USC's Shelton Diggs (number 20, on the turf) rolls in the limelight of a two-point conversion during John McKay's fifth and last Rose Bowl win; 18–17 over Ohio.**

Great Stanford quarterback Jim Plunkett *(opposite)* combined personal integrity, football smarts and a terrific passing game to lead the West in passing for three years in a row, break the NCAA total offense record by more than 1300 yards (7887 yards career total) and win the Heisman in 1970. *Above:* Stanford receiver Randy Vataha.

went 3–7, although it did beat Notre Dame on national television 24–14. But that was the only losing season he had in nine years (although there were three 5–5 seasons) and his overall record was a very creditable 55–36. Far more important, he lost the Big Game to his alma mater California only once, and he wound up his tenure by taking Stanford to two Rose Bowls—their first in nearly 20 years—and winning them both.

Ralston began to serve notice on the Pac-8 in 1968, when the Cardinal went 6–3–1 and took Rose Bowl-bound USC to the wire before losing 27–24 on a Ron Ayala field goal with 3:09 left in the game (O J Simpson carried 47 times for 220 yards in that game). The following season the record was 7–2–1 and this time Stanford got even closer to the champion Trojans; it took a 34-yard Ayala field goal on the last play of the game to pull out a 26–24 win.

Stanford entered the 1970 season with some fine personnel—outstanding receivers in Randy Vataha and tight end Bob Moore; a solid offensive line anchored by John Sande, perhaps the most underrated center in the country; the 'Thunder Chickens' defense, so named by tackle Pete Lazetich because 'we needed some identity,' and including linemen Bill Tipton and Larry Butler and linebackers

Ron Kadziel and Jeff Siemon (called by Ralston 'the best I ever coached' and later a long-time pro star with Minnesota). And most of all, the Indians had the quarterback—Jim Plunkett.

Plunkett's was an amazing, and heart-warming, story. The son of blind parents, he grew up in near-poverty conditions and spent most of his high school time working to help provide for his family. Nevertheless, he threw 19 touchdown passes his senior year at James Lick High in San Jose, and the recruiters started to gather; but Jim, a good student, narrowed it immediately to California or Stanford in order to stay near home. With the political demonstrations at Berkeley grabbing headline space, he chose Stanford.

In his freshman year he underwent surgery for a tumor in his neck, and fortunately it was benign. He played in the last three games with the freshman team but Stanford had proven quarterbacks returning to the varsity, and Ralston suggested a position change—perhaps to defensive end, where Plunkett had played in a high school all-star game.

'Coach,' Plunkett said, 'tell me what I've got to do. I want to play quarterback.'

He spent the summer on a construction job, and after work would throw literally hundreds of passes every day. When he came back for the 1967 season, Ralston said, 'We couldn't believe it was the same guy.'

Plunkett redshirted that year, but there was no further talk of moving him to defense. In his first varsity appearance (in 1968), he completed 10 of 13 passes for 277 yards and four touchdowns in a 68–20 rout of San Jose State. His football future was assured—and so was Stanford's.

As a sophomore he threw for a conference-record 2156 yards, and 14 touchdowns. The following year it was 2673 yards and 20 touchdowns, and both of those were Pac-8 marks.

That 1969 season produced some great games for Stanford. There was the last-second loss to USC. There was an incredible aerial battle with Purdue in which Plunkett completed 23 of 46 for 355 yards and four touchdowns and the Boilermakers' Mike Phipps was 28–for–39 for 429 yards and five TDs; neither of them threw an interception, and Purdue finally won 36–35. And there was the Big Game with Cal.

Plunkett (on his way to a 381-yard passing day) took Stanford to a 17–0 lead before seven minutes had elapsed, and it looked as if the rout was on. But the Bears—with unheralded Dave Penhall passing for 321 yards—battled back gamely, cutting the deficit to 20–14 by halftime. Two minutes into the fourth quarter it was 23–14, but Penhall hit Ken Adams for 55 yards and Jim Fraser for 37—both touchdowns, and suddenly the underdog Bears were ahead 28–23. With five minutes left in the game, Plunkett obviously would come out throwing—but instead he marched Stanford 80 yards almost entirely on the ground, and Bubba Brown blasted over from the four-yard line for a 29–28 Cardinal win.

Because of his redshirt year, Plunkett could have turned professional after his junior year; and with a family to support, nobody could have blamed him. But he didn't: 'We are always telling kids not to drop out, to finish school, to set targets and work toward them,' he said. 'What would they think if I were to drop out now for professional football?'

The 1970 season was a great one for collegiate quarterbacks—Archie Manning, Joe Theismann, Brian Sipe, Pat Sullivan, Lynn Dickey, Ken Anderson; in the Pac-8 Dan Fouts was at Oregon and Sonny Sixkiller of Washington led the nation in passing; and Dan Pastorini was down the road at Santa Clara. But Plunkett wasn't likely to be overlooked. He threw for 2715 yards to set a Pac-8 mark for the third straight year, his 7887 career yards broke the NCAA total offense record by more than

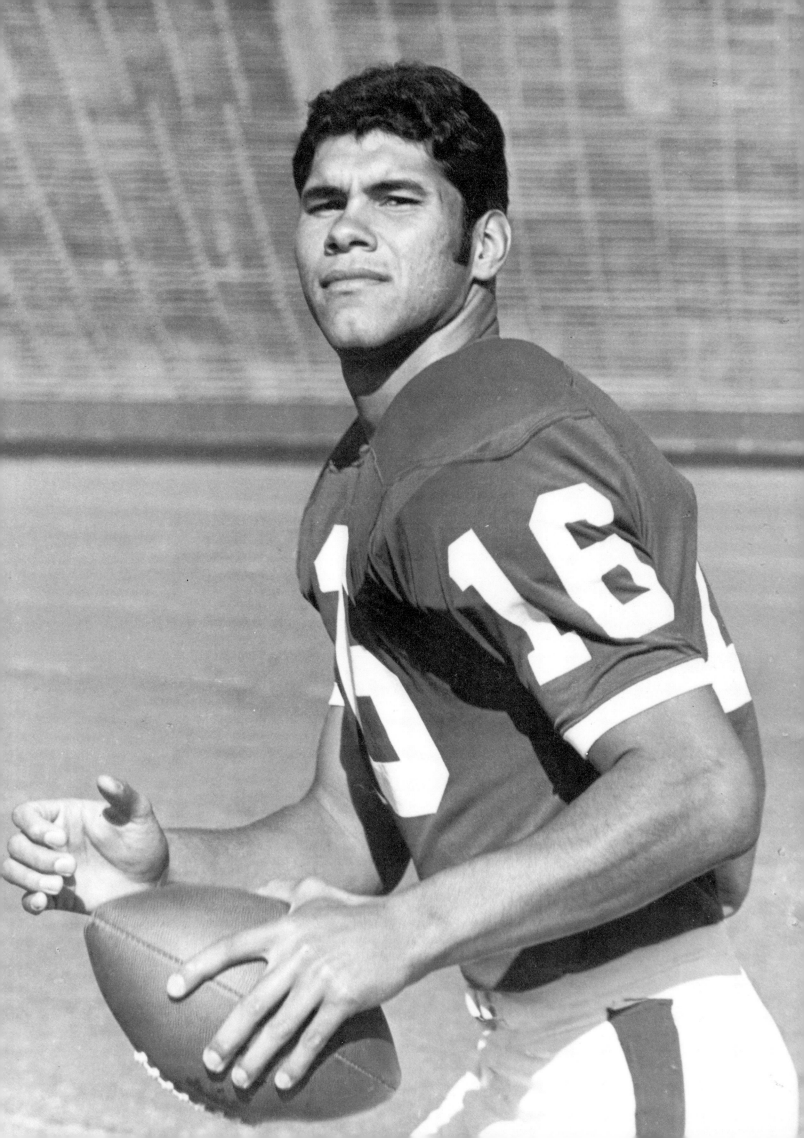

Stanford won back-to-back Rose Bowls—in 1971 (27–17 over Ohio), with MVP Jim Plunkett; and in 1972 (13–12 over Michigan) with MVP Don Bunce (*at left*); and helping Bunce with that effort was Rod Garcia, shown *above* kicking the game-winning field goal.

1300 yards, he took his team to the Rose Bowl and he won the Heisman Trophy: he was the fifth Pacific Coast player in nine years to be acclaimed college football's best.

Manning was Plunkett's chief rival for the award, and his Mississippi backers were going all-out—there were Archie Manning dolls, posters, even a song about him. But Manning broke his hand in mid-year. The telegram that he received from Plunkett is an indication of the fine gentleman Jim Plunkett always has been: 'Sorry to hear about your broken arm (sic),' it read. 'It's a shame you couldn't end your career the way you have always played—brilliantly.'

Stanford compiled an 8–3 regular-season record that year, losing only to Purdue and—after the conference title had been clinched with a 29–22 comeback win over Washington—to Air Force and California in the last two games. The Rose Bowl opponent was Ohio State, ranked second or fifth in the nation (depending on which poll you subscribed to), but nevertheless an 11-point favorite over the eighth-ranked Cardinal.

The Buckeyes, with their usual powerful ground game, rallied from a 10–0 deficit to take a 14–10 halftime lead but Stanford scored twice in the fourth quarter for a 27–17 victory—the last touchdown coming (fittingly enough) on a Plunkett pass to Vataha. Sande totally dominated Ohio State's Outland Trophy winner (nose guard Jim Stillwagon), and Plunkett was 20–for–30 for 265 yards and was named player of the game.

The following year Plunkett was gone, and so was a large part of his supporting cast. But many of the Thunder Chickens were back—Stanford led the Pac-8 in every defensive department in

1971—and Ralston had had the foresight to redshirt quarterback Don Bunce, who now came out for his senior year and proved a versatile and talented replacement for Plunkett. 'I don't think there was any pressure on me because I was following Plunkett,' Bunce said. 'The only pressure I felt was that I only had one year in which to do the things I wanted to do.'

He made it a good one. The Cardinal again went 8–3 during the regular season and faced Michigan in the Rose Bowl, again as an underdog. Michigan was 11–0, had scored 409 points to just 70 for the opponents, and the only wonder was that the Wolverines weren't rated any higher than sixth.

The key play was a masterpiece of trickery. With Michigan leading 10–3, Stanford went into punt formation at its own 33-yard line, but the ball was snapped to Jim Kehl, the blocking back. He handed the ball forward between the legs of Jackie Brown, who stood there while Kehl ran to the left as if he still had the ball—then Brown, who had scored two touchdowns against Ohio State the year before, swept to the right and raced 31 yards through the befuddled Michigan defense. Two plays later Brown ran 24 yards for the touchdown that tied it at 10–10.

Stanford stopped a Wolverine drive at the one-yard line in the third quarter, but a safety gave Michigan a 12–10 lead with just 3:18 left in the game. The Thunder Chickens then stopped Michigan at the Cardinal 22 with 1:48 to play. Bunce—who threw for 290 yards in the game—completed five of six passes, marched Stanford down the field and with just 16 seconds remaining, Rod Garcia booted a 31-yard field goal for a 13–12 victory.

That was Ralston's last game—with nothing else left to accomplish at Stanford, he resigned to take a professional job. The champion's mantle went back to USC and remained there until 1975.

Pac-10: The Seventies and Eighties

If anybody expected Southern California to quietly abdicate its throne when John McKay left, he had to think twice. John Robinson immediately took the Trojans back to the Rose Bowl, and in the next seven years he produced 67 wins, two more Rose Bowl victories, two other bowl appearances and two more Heisman Trophy-winning running backs.

But there were several other fine young coaches beginning to make their mark in the Pacific-8 Conference, and before too much longer two of them especially—Terry Donahue at UCLA and Don James at Washington—would begin to steal the thunder from USC.

The first to threaten Trojan dominance, however, were Dick Vermeil of UCLA and Mike White of California. They were similar in many respects—both young, blond natives of Northern California, and both tremendously intense about their football.

When Tommy Prothro had retired at UCLA after the 1970 season, the Bruins hired the colorful Pepper Rodgers, who had been known to lead his team onto the field doing cartwheels. His first season, the Bruins finished 2–7–1 and even lost to California, for only the fourth time in 22 years. But UCLA then went 8–3 and 9–2, losing to USC both years and finishing second in the Pac-8 both years; in 1973 the Bruins were ranked ninth in the nation.

Rodgers moved on at that point and Vermeil took over, with immediate success. In 1974 the Bruins were 6–3–2; the following year they were 8–2–1 in the regular season, tying Air Force and losing to Washington 17–13, and to Ohio State in the fourth game of the year 41–20. Keep that Ohio State score in mind!

California also had a fine year in 1975. White, who had been a Bear captain in 1957, later was an assistant there and then under John Ralston at Stanford. He was by then considered one of the more innovative offensive minds around, especially in the passing game. When Ralston resigned at Stanford after the 1971 Rose Bowl season, White was offered the job—but at the same time, Ray Willsey, also a Cal alumnus, finished his eight-year tenure at Berkeley. The Bears had not had a losing season since 1966, but neither had they had a big year; the closest was 7–3–1 in 1968. California, too, wanted White.

White chose his alma mater, and Stanford immediately hired Jack Christiansen, a former pro and one-time San Francisco 49ers coach—and the Indians had become the 'Cardinal.'

White took two years to build a team, and he built it around passing. 'When I played for Pappy Waldorf at Cal the offense was run-oriented,' Mike said many years later, after making the Big Ten pass-conscious and leading Illinois to a Rose Bowl. 'When I first started at Stanford under John Ralston we were run-oriented. It took us five years to figure out we couldn't beat the USCs and UCLAs by running.'

In 1972 White had two young quarterbacks, Vince Ferragamo and Steve Bartkowski; it was Ferragamo whose fourth-down pass to Steve Sweeney on the final play beat Stanford 24–21 in another of those incredible Big Game finishes. But, following the 1973 season Ferragamo transferred to Nebraska, and White had to talk Bartkowski (who had announced he was giving up football in favor of baseball) into returning. The Bay Area Rapid Transit system was new then, and California's slogan was 'Ride BART to the Rose Bowl.' The Bears didn't get quite that far, but they did finish 7–3–1 and Bart—the quarterback, not the train—led the nation in passing.

Against Stanford in 1974 Bartkowski threw for 318 yards, and with 26 seconds remaining he put the Bears ahead with a pass to Steve Rivera—in almost exactly the same spot in the corner of Memorial Stadium's south end zone as Sweeney's catch two years earlier. But he'd left too much time; Stanford's Guy Benjamin completed a couple of key passes—including one to tight end Brad Williams, who made a great play by dragging two tacklers out of bounds at midfield with two seconds remaining. Mike Langford then kicked a 50-yard field goal to win for the Cardinals 22–20. *San Francisco Examiner* columnist Wells Twombley (who had left the press box just before the end to interview what he thought would be the victorious Bears) wrote, 'A funny thing happened on the way to the winner's dressing room …'

In 1975 Bartkowski was beginning a long and successful career with the Atlanta Falcons, yet White put together the most balanced offense in college history that year—2522 yards rushing, 2522 yards passing—without him. Joe Roth was possibly the finest quarterback California ever had, and that covers a lot of territory; Chuck Muncie was a 230-pound running back with

John Robinson *(at right)* **took over at USC in 1976, and continued Trojan dominance of national football, including the Rose Bowl.**

Chuck Muncie (*above*, number 42), Cal's swift 230-pound back, lets his feet fly in a yardage spree against Stanford in 1975. Cal beat the Cardinal 48–15, even without the help of QB Steve Bartkowski, by that time an Atlanta Falcon, and whose uniform had been very ably filled by Joe Roth (number 12 *at right*, in the 1975 Big Game).

sprinter's speed who rushed for 1460 yards and was the Heisman runner-up; Rivera was an All-American receiver who led the conference in both 1974 (56 catches) and '75 (57), and sprinter Wesley Walker on the other end averaged 30 yards a catch. The defense was suspect, but the offense was awesome.

California lost to UCLA 28–14, but then came back in the next two weeks with a 28–14 win over USC for the Trojans' first loss of the season, and a 27–24 win over a fine Washington team as Roth riddled the Husky pass defense (which to that point had allowed only 70 yards a game) for 380 yards and four TDs. The Bears then walloped Stanford 48–15, to clinch at least a share of the Pac-8 title. Then they sat back—and waited.

The USC-UCLA game had been delayed until 5pm the following Friday— television's contribution to rush hour in Los Angeles. If the Bruins won, they would be in the Rose Bowl; if they lost or tied, California would get the title outright.

The Trojan tailback was Ricky Bell, taking dead aim at the NCAA single-season rushing title; the quarterback was Vince Evans, a 31 percent passer who in that game threw 14 straight incompletions; once, when USC reached the Bruin 25 yard line late in the game, coach John McKay called four straight passes— all incomplete. Bell finished with 1875 yards, just six short of the national record, and UCLA won 25–22. The conference now allowed its teams to go to other bowl games, but by that late date all were filled; Cal, with its potent offense and its 8–3 record, stayed home. USC, 7–4 and with four straight losses, went to the Liberty Bowl and beat Texas A&M 20–0, in McKay's last game.

UCLA was a fine team, of course. The Bruins had a superb running back in Wendell Tyler (1388 yards and a 6.7 per-carry average), and a great athlete at quarterback in John Sciarra. Sciarra was not the passer Roth was, but he ran the option well and was an outstanding leader. When Vermeil later coached Philadelphia in the NFL, he drafted Sciarra as a defensive back— but often put him at quarterback when the Eagles were in running situations close to an opponent's goal line.

All-American Ricky Bell *(right)*, USC's very hot receiver, led the 'Pac-8' in yardage for 1975-1976. Charles White replaced the injured Bell in his last college game, the 1977 Rose Bowl, and 'just kept going.' Current USC coach John Robinson *(above)* coached them both.

The Bruins were ranked 14th in the nation going into the Rose Bowl; their opponent was Number One Ohio State, the same Buckeyes who earlier had beaten UCLA by three touchdowns. 'But we were a better team by the end of the season,' Vermeil insisted. Indeed, the Bruins won easily 23–10. 'They kicked the hell out of us,' one Ohio State assistant coach said, but that was the only comment from the Buckeye dressing room; the irascible Woody Hayes refused to meet with the press or to let his players talk to anyone. No wonder Woody was mad: it was the sixth loss in seven Rose Bowls for the Big Ten, and the fourth in five games for Ohio State.

John Robinson, who had been (among other things) an assistant with the Oakland Raiders under Al Davis, took over at USC in 1976, and he wasn't left devoid of talent. He had three consensus All-Americans that year—Ricky Bell (who led the Pac-8 in rushing for the second straight year with 1417 yards), tackle Gary Jeter and safety Dennis Thurman on a defensive team that led the conference. The only thing he needed to rebuild was his quarterback, Vince Evans. To that end, he hired Paul Hackett, a

young assistant at California who had had a large hand in developing Ferragamo, Bartkowski and Roth, and he helped turn Evans into a 54 percent passer who threw only six interceptions all year.

USC lost the first game to Missouri 46–25, but from that point on, not only played solid defense but scored a lot of points, winning 10 straight games and the conference title.

UCLA also had a new coach. Terry Donahue, although he never weighed more than 190 pounds, had been a tough defensive tackle on the Bruins' 1966 Rose Bowl-winning team. Unlike the witty, outgoing Robinson, Donahue seemed quiet and almost shy in public. Yet, when he ascended to the head chair after five years as a UCLA assistant, he was only 32 years old.

He was an immediate success. In his first 10 games the Bruins had nine wins and a tie (with Ohio State), and they were piling up the statistics; against Washington State, for example, they intercepted four passes by Jack Thompson (who was on his way to breaking Jim Plunkett's conference passing records), and exploded all over the Cougars for a 62–3 victory. UCLA went into the USC game ranked Number Two in the nation, but in one 20-minute stretch in the second half, the Trojans held UCLA to 17 yards in five possessions while scoring 17 points themselves to take a 24–0 lead, and finally won 24–14. UCLA then lost to Alabama 36–6, in the Liberty Bowl to fall out of the Top Ten, but their new coach was obviously a force to be reckoned with.

The Rose Bowl matched USC with Michigan (which led the nation in total offense and scoring but, as usual, couldn't throw the ball) and the Trojan defense limited the Wolverines to 156 yards rushing on the way to a 14–6 win. Bell was hurt on his fourth carry, but freshman Charles White replaced him and dazzled the Rose Bowl crowd of 106,182 with a 122-yard performance.

The nation would hear a lot more about Charles White, said O J Simpson after that game, 'Me, Anthony Davis, Ricky Bell—I think Charles may erase all our names.' No one could accomplish that, but White did go on to win a Heisman Trophy.

Meanwhile, Washington's Huskies were beginning to growl. Don James, a former University of Miami quarterback, had been a successful coach at Kent State before moving to Seattle. 'Defense, field position and the kicking game—that's what I was brought up on,' was the way he described his coaching style. His special teams became almost legendary. 'I swear Washington is the only team anywhere with a kicking unit that can actually pour it on the opposition,' Jim Walden of arch-rival Washington State said.

Like Donahue, James was soft-spoken and straightforward; unlike Donahue, he did not have instant success. His first two teams went 6–5 and 5–6, and his 1977 team lost three of the first four games, to Mississippi State, Syracuse and Minnesota. But then the Huskies, behind quarterback Warren Moon, began to score points at a rapid rate and won six of the last seven regular-season games, losing only to UCLA. It was a strong conference that year: Stanford was 8–3 and USC, UCLA and California all were 7–4, but only the Bruins had beaten Washington. When USC's Frank Jordan kicked a 36-yard field goal to beat UCLA in the finale, the Huskies were in the Rose Bowl.

Ironically, UCLA later forfeited to Washington; so, in fact, did Mississippi State, which has to be one of the rare times that a college team won two games by forfeit in the same year.

On the field, however, the Huskies were 7–4 and considered no match for Michigan. Sound familiar? The result was getting to be familiar, too; the Wolverines couldn't stop the pass, Moon threw for one touchdown and scored two himself on short runs, and Washington led 27–7 going into the fourth period. Michigan rallied then and cut it to 27–20, but two Husky interceptions in the final minutes kept it there.

Two other Pac-8 teams went to bowl games that year. USC got four touchdown passes from Rob Hertel and outslugged Texas A&M in the Bluebonnet Bowl 47–28, and Stanford went to the Sun Bowl.

There were some other shocks in the Pac-8 in 1977, and two of the biggest came out of Berkeley. Joe Roth, California's brilliant quarterback, had played well enough to get some All-American mention in 1976; no one outside of the team knew that he was quietly, courageously battling cancer. Following the 1976 season he played in the Japan Bowl all-star game in January; scant weeks later, tragically, he was dead.

But another shock of a much different nature was coming for California followers. The Bears had fallen to 5–6 after their co-conference championship in 1975, but came back in 1977 with a 7–4 record (8–3 after UCLA forfeited their game). Mike White (who lived and breathed football) and athletic director Dave Haggard (who also had 20 other sports to worry about) clashed philosophically, and White was fired and replaced by his offensive coordinator, Roger Theder.

Stanford had fired Jack Christiansen a year earlier, just before the 1976 Big Game—whereupon his emotional players went out and upset Cal 27–24, and then carried their deposed coach off the field on their shoulders. It saved Chris' string of never having a losing season in his five years there. His replacement was a former Cal and Stanford assistant who, considering he stayed only two years and didn't win a title or go to a Rose Bowl, had a dramatic impact on the conference.

His name was Bill Walsh. He had been on the staff at Berkeley from 1960–62 and at Stanford from 1963–65, and then had gone into the pro ranks, most notably as the offensive coordinator of the Cincinnati Bengals. He was brilliant at devising of-

Above: Soft-spoken Washington coach Don 'Special Teams' James *(above)* and his quarterback Warren Moon *(right)* upset highly-touted Michigan 27–20 in the 1978 Rose Bowl. Moon looks like he *lives* at QB in the photo *at right.* James and team returned in 1981 (lost 23–6) and in 1982 (won 28–0). Washington won two games by forfeit in 1977.

fenses, especially those built around the pass, and at teaching them to his players; Don James once said that his staff had begun charting all the different offensive sets Stanford used in a game, 'and when we got to 60 we stopped counting.'

'It takes three things (to be a great coach),' former Cardinal passing star John Brodie once told Leonard Koppett. 'You have to really know football, in all its aspects; you have to know how to organize talent, and you have to be able to communicate that knowledge and that organization. That's where Walsh is strongest—communication. He's got the other two also, and that makes him exceptional.'

In a conversation while watching a Shrine East-West practice after Walsh's second season, Lynn Stiles, then coach at San Jose State, put it more succinctly: 'If I was an NFL team owner or general manager, I'd just hire Bill Walsh and then sit back and wait three or four years to go to the Super Bowl.' Stiles turned out to be a prophet; the San Francisco 49ers grabbed Walsh just days after that and in three years he had turned a terrible team into a Super Bowl winner.

Stanford always had had great passing, it seemed. Bobby Garrett in 1953, Brodie in 1956, Dick Norman in 1959 all had led the nation; Jim Plunkett had set national career records. Since 1950, Cardinal quarterbacks had led the conference 13 times. But Walsh's attack surpassed even that standard: for three straight years, Stanford's quarterbacks led the nation in passing, the first time that had ever been done.

Though Stanford has had a long dearth of Rose Bowls (at this point, since its two wins in 1971–72), the team with the Cardinal-colored uniforms had a three-year succession of NCAA passing champions at quarterback, including 1977 consensus All-American Guy Benjamin *(at upper right)*; Steve Dils *(below, immediate right)*; and Turk Schonert *(below left)* (who carried the tradition in 1979—after playmaking genius and quarterback-building coach Bill Walsh *(above)* went to the pros). Stanford placekicker Ken Nabor *(extreme lower right)* was an All-American candidate in 1977.

In 1977 it was Guy Benjamin, in 1978 Steve Dils, in 1979—after Walsh had gone to the 49ers and his offensive coordinator, Rod Dowhower, had been named head coach—it was Turk Schonert.

Walsh also brought in a little freshman running back named Darrin Nelson. Nobody had paid much attention to Nelson out of high school because of his size—he might have been five feet eight, but he might not; the program said he weighed 170 pounds, but as a freshman 145 probably was closer to the truth. But put the football in his hands and he did truly amazing things. Following a game against California in which he somehow escaped from a tackle behind the line of scrimmage and scored a touchdown, Bear defensive tackle Rich Miller said: 'When I got there, I hit everything where he used to be. I was like a runaway train going through an empty tunnel. That Nelson moves laterally better than most guys run straight ahead out of the starting blocks; he's the toughest guy I've ever faced to get a good shot at. It's embarrassing to try to tackle him sometimes.'

As a freshman in 1977, Nelson became the first player in college history to run for 1000 yards and catch 50 passes the same year. He then did it again as a sophomore in 1978; he almost did it a third time in 1980 (he sat out 1979 with an injury); and

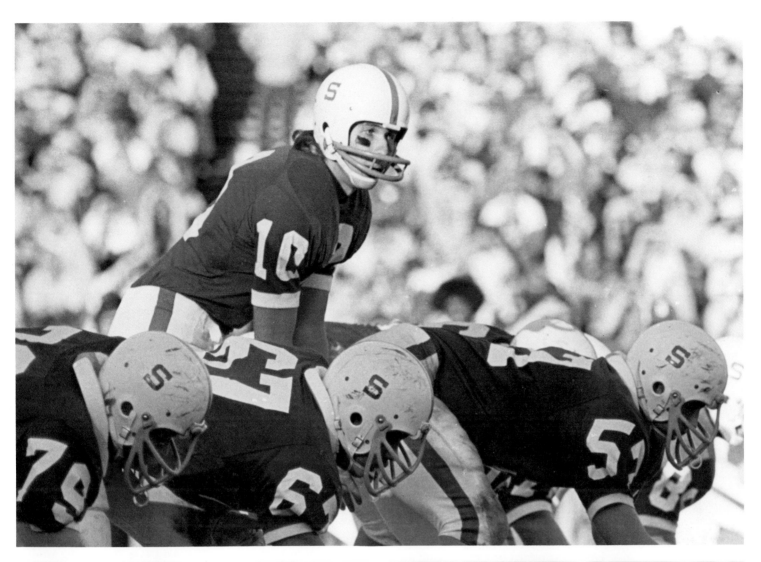

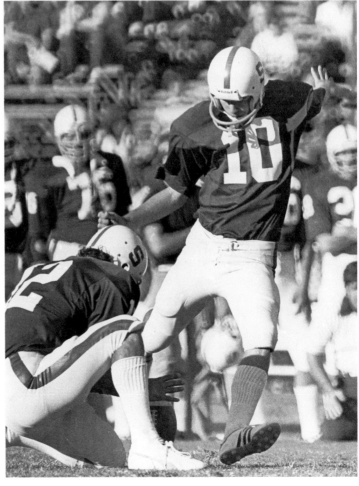

he did do it in 1981. Nobody else ever had done it before; Darrin Nelson did it three times. He wound up not only as Stanford's all-time leading rusher with 4033 yards, but its leading receiver, with 214 catches. He still holds the NCAA record for all-purpose running (rushing, pass receiving, kick returns) with 6885 yards.

That potent offensive combination overcame a shaky defense and led Stanford to an 8–3 record in 1977, including a 32–28 upset of UCLA when, with Benjamin hurt, Dils came in to complete 24 of 37 for 287 yards and Nelson ran for 189 yards. The Cards were rewarded with a Sun Bowl date against favored Louisiana State; Benjamin threw three touchdown passes and Stanford had little trouble registering a 24–14 win. The following year the Cardinal was 7–4, with the three conference losses (to UCLA, Washington and USC) coming by a total of 10 points, and was invited to the Astro-Bluebonnet Bowl, again as an underdog to seventh-ranked Georgia. The Bulldogs jumped to a 22–0 lead early in the third quarter, but in the next six minutes and 13 seconds Benjamin threw three touchdown passes, two to All-American Ken Margerum and one to Nelson, and Ken Naber's fourth-quarter field goal won it for Stanford 25–22.

In 1978 it wasn't new coaches who commanded attention, but new schools; Arizona and Arizona State joined the conference, turning it into the Pacific-10.

Arizona State had an immediate impact on the conference, although it would be nine years before they got to the Rose Bowl. The Sun Devils had built a real dynasty in the Western Athletic Conference under coach Frank Kush—in 20 years at the helm, Kush had had only one losing season (4–7 in 1976), had won nine or more games seven times and, despite playing in a conference that didn't get much attention, had been in the Top Ten four times, including 1975 when ASU was 12–0 and Kush was named Coach of the Year.

The Pac-8 became the Pac-10 with the addition of Arizona and Arizona State in 1978. _Above:_ The Sun Devils' Scottsdale, Arizona haven. The ASU team, shown bedeviling a Huskies receiver _at right,_ was itself bemused and bedraggled in the 1979 transcripts scandal.

In 1977, Arizona State's final year in the WAC, the Devils were 9–3, won the league title and battled fourth-ranked Penn State to the wire in the Fiesta Bowl before losing 42–30.

The Sun Devils' introduction to the Pac-10 was an embarrassment—after winning two non-league games in 1978, they went to Pullman, Washington and were crushed by Washington State 51–26. But those red faces didn't last long. Following two more non-league wins, ASU hosted Southern California, which was 4–0 and ranked Number One after beating top-ranked Alabama two weeks earlier. Arizona State not only won, it won easily 20–7, behind a brilliant 307-yard running and passing performance by quarterback Mark Malone. It was the only loss the Trojans were to suffer all year.

Arizona State finished its first Pac-10 season with a second consecutive 9–3 record, including a Garden State Bowl win over Rutgers. But trouble was brewing in Tempe.

In 1979 the volatile Kush, who had a reputation as a tough taskmaster, was sued by a former player who claimed that the coach had slapped him when he punted badly, then tried to force him to relinquish his scholarship. In the ensuing hubbub of claims, denials and half-truths and outright lies, Kush was fired in mid-year and replaced by interim coach Bob Owens. In addition, the Sun Devils were in the middle of a scandal involving bogus credits and forged transcripts, and were forced to forfeit five of their six wins that season.

It was not just Arizona State that was tampering with the rules; this was to grow into the worst and most wide-spread scandal in West Coast football since the breakup of the old Pacific Coast

Conference in 1959. Just weeks before the 1980 season began, the presidents and chancellors of the Pac-10 schools voted unanimously to make five schools—USC, UCLA, Oregon, Oregon State and Arizona State—ineligible for the 1980 football title and for any post-season play. In addition, UCLA forfeited all its football games for 1977, Oregon State for 1977 and '79 and Oregon for 1977–79. USC was allowed to keep its league football title for 1979, but lost the 1978 NCAA track title and was barred from the 1980 Pac-10 and NCAA track championships, and Oregon suffered some penalties in swimming.

On the field, however, that had little impact. From the time Stanford had last gone to the Rose Bowl on 1 January 1972, for the 14 seasons until Arizona State broke the string on 1 January 1987, only three schools represented the Pacific-8—or Pacific-10—in the Rose Bowl: USC, Washington and UCLA.

Washington had interrupted USC's string of titles in 1977, but only temporarily. In 1978 the Trojans lost only once (the 20–7 upset by Arizona State), capped the season with a 17–10 win over Michigan in the Rose Bowl—Bo Schembechler's fifth straight defeat at Pasadena—and finished up ranked Number One nationally by UPI; AP ranked USC Number Two behind Alabama, despite the fact that the Trojans had beaten 'Bama early in the year.

The Rose Bowl matched two superb defenses, and the difference was Charles White. This time it wasn't his running, although he did gain 99 yards, but a disputed touchdown in the second quarter that gave Southern Cal a 14–3 lead and ultimately provided the difference in a 17–10 victory. White leaped into the end zone—but without the ball; replays showed he had fumbled before crossing the goal, but the officials ruled it a touchdown.

Schembechler was beside himself, but the following day he said graciously, 'Southern Cal is the best team in America. I've seen them all.... The Trojans whipped Alabama convincingly, they're better than 'Bama.' The Associated Press wasn't listening.

In 1979 the Trojans went 10–0–1 in the regular season, suffering only a 21–21 tie with Stanford. USC had four All-Americans, including quarterback Paul McDonald, linebacker Dennis Johnson, guard Brad Budde—who won the Lombardi Award as the nation's best lineman—and White. Living up to the onus placed upon him by O J Simpson three years earlier, White averaged 186.4 yards per game to lead the nation in rushing and, for the second straight year, in all-purpose running as well. He set a Pac-10 career record of 6245 yards rushing, and finished his four years ranked second on the all-time NCAA list with 5598 yards (the NCAA did not include bowl game yardage, and White, remember, had been in four of them). In all, he gained more than 100 yards per game in 31 games, 10 of them in 1979, and broke or tied 22 NCAA, Pac-10, USC and Rose Bowl records. He was a unanimous All-American choice in both his junior and senior years, and a logical choice for the Heisman Trophy.

He went out in a blaze of glory, in one of the most exciting Rose Bowls of all time. Ohio State, now coached by Earle Bruce and led by sophomore quarterback Art Schlichter, also was unbeaten. Despite a great goal-line stand in the first half, the Trojans trailed 16–10 when they got the ball with 5:21 remaining. The ensuing USC drive went 83 yards; White gained 71 of them. With 1:32 left in the game he leaped over from the one-yard line—this time remembering to bring the ball—to give USC

Charles White *(at top left)* was selected as the Rose Bowl's 'Player of the Game' for both the USC 17–10 win over Michigan in 1979 and the Trojan 17–16 win over Ohio in 1980. In addition to his normal superhuman feats, Trojan tailback White won the Heisman Trophy in 1979 *(at right)*, and that's enough to make any football player smile. *At left:* USC's All-American offensive guard Brad Budde.

Marcus Allen *(above and left)* **began his USC career as a blocking fullback keeping the heat off Charles White; took over as a runner when White left; set 14 NCAA records—including a one-year mark of 2342 yards rushing and 11 200-yard career games—and of course, won the Heisman in 1981.** *At right:* **Washington's Danny Greene catches a 39-yard TD pass against USC in 1983.**

a 17–16 victory. Despite a case of the flu, White had carried the ball 39 times and rushed for 247 yards, both Rose Bowl records.

The Trojans finished second in both polls, again to Alabama, and that was John Robinson's last title. He had three more fine seasons (8–2–1 in 1980, 9–3 in 1981—including a 26–10 Fiesta Bowl loss to Penn State—and 8–3 in 1982), then 'retired' from coaching to a job in the USC administration. That lasted literally only a few weeks before Robinson, realizing where his first love lay, accepted the head coaching job of the Los Angeles Rams.

If John was through with the Rose Bowl after the 1979 season, however, he wasn't finished with that other Southern California staple, the Heisman Trophy. In 1981 Marcus Allen, who had begun his football life at USC as a blocking fullback for White, set 14 NCAA records and tied two others, including most yards rushing in a single season (an incredible 2342, the first runner ever over 2000 in one year), highest per-game average (212.9 yards), and most 200-yard games in a career (11), season (eight) and in a row (five).

Let that sink in—he *averaged* more than 200 yards a game. And just to keep the defense honest, he also led the Trojans in receiving in both his junior and senior years, with 30 and 34 catches respectively.

The first half of the 1980s, however, belonged primarily to two teams, the Huskies and the Bruins.

Beginning in the 1979 season, Don James' Washington teams went to eight consecutive bowl games through 1986, including the Sun Bowl in 1979 (a 14–7 win over Texas) and 1986 (a 28–6 loss to Alabama), two consecutive Rose Bowls, the Aloha Bowl two years in a row (a 21–20 win over Maryland in 1982, then a 13–10 loss to Penn State), the Orange Bowl and the Freedom Bowl (a 20–17 win over Colorado after the 1985 season).

The 1980 Washington team was a strange one, and perhaps the greatest testimony to James' coaching ability. The Huskies placed just one man on the first-team All-Conference—placekicker Chuck Nelson. They were drubbed by Oregon 34–10 in the first conference game of the year. They lost to a mediocre Navy team 24–10. And yet, when the dust had died down, Washington had won its last four games, including a 20–10 win over a very good USC team despite 216 yards by the Trojans' Marcus Allen.

It would have been a little too much to expect the Huskies to win the Rose Bowl, too, and although they outplayed fourth-ranked Michigan in the first half, the Wolverines finally got Bo Schembechler his first Rose Bowl win in six tries 23–6.

The 1981 Washington team was stronger. Again the Huskies failed to place a single man on the All-Conference offensive team, but they had several on defense, including All-American

**Coach Don James' Huskies went on to eight consecutive bowl games from 1979–86—which clues us in that James is not 'going to jump' from the platform in the 1979 photo *at right;* he's just getting a bird's eye view of play formations. Among those eight bowls were a 23–6 Rose Bowl savaging by Michigan's Wolverines in 1981 *(left),* and a 1979 14–7 corraling of the U of Texas Longhorns *(below).*

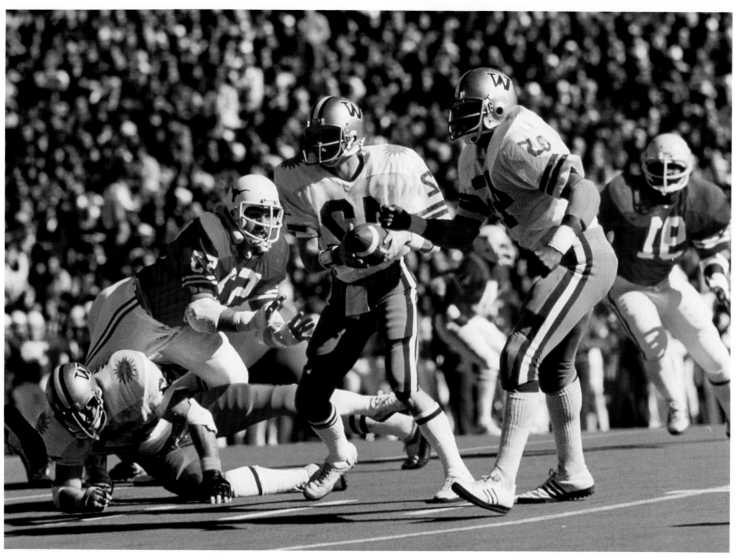

These pages: Looking like a bunch of overexcited puppies, the Huskies (below) did indeed jump all over Iowa, fetching Iowa coach Hayden Fry the sad news of Washington's rather frisky administration of a 28–zip neck-wringing to the once-hawkish Hawkeyes.

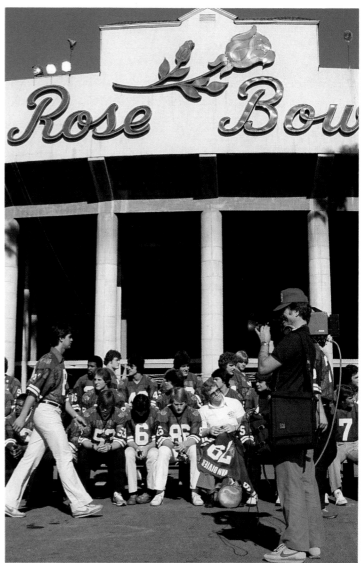

At left: **Triple jeopardy: Number 28 starred in the Huskies' 28–0 Rose Bowl shutout; the first such shutout in 28 years! Also know as Jacque Robinson, 28 burned up the field for 142 yards in that game against Iowa.** *Above:* **A rather dejected-looking 1981 Huskies Rose Bowl team seems to have premonitions of their impending loss to Michigan.**

corner back Ray Horton. It was the closest race in league history. Washington State was in the Race for the Roses itself, but lost to the Huskies 23–10 in the season finale. At the same time, George Achica was blocking a last-second field goal try by UCLA to give USC a 22–21 win over UCLA (which had beaten Washington); the Huskies finished with a 6–2 conference mark, and Arizona State, USC, UCLA and Washington State all were 5–2. USC, UCLA and Washington State all went to other bowls, but all lost—the Trojans to Penn State in the Fiesta Bowl, WSU to Brigham Young in the Holiday Bowl 38–36 and UCLA to Michigan in the Bluebonnet Bowl 33–14.

At Pasadena the Husky defense took charge, registering the first Rose Bowl shutout in 28 years, and a freshman running back named Jacque Robinson ran for 142 yards in a 28–0 win over Iowa.

Final-game upsets by Washington State kept Washington out of the Rose Bowl in each of the next two years, although in 1982 they finished ranked seventh in the nation; however, in the strongest overall showing by the Pac-10 yet, UCLA was rated fifth and Arizona sixth, and USC(8–3) and California (7–4) also had solid teams. The three Top Ten teams went to bowls, and this time they all won, UCLA in the Rose Bowl, Washington in the Aloha Bowl and Arizona State, which had won its first nine

The high Washington team spirit shows in the faces of the Huskies players *at right,* whose uniforms show the signs of yet another intense day on the gridiron. This (no, 'Spuds,' not a linebacker) cheerleader *(above)* speaks the minds of many Huskies fans.

under coach Darryl Rogers but then lost to Washington and Arizona, in the Fiesta Bowl where it beat Oklahoma 32–21.

The 1984 season was the Huskies' best yet—but, ironically, they didn't go to the Rose Bowl. They were highly-rated from the beginning and spent some time in the Number One spot before losing to 10th-ranked USC 16–7 late in the season. That gave the Trojans, who finished 8–3 under coach Ted Tollner, the Rose Bowl bid despite two season-ending losses to UCLA and Notre Dame. Southern California, which had been on NCAA probation the previous two years as a result of the transcript scandal, turned in a brilliant defensive effort in Pasadena, converting two intercepted passes into touchdowns and twice stopping key Ohio State drives, one at the Trojan one-yard line, on the way to a 20–17 victory over the Buckeyes.

UCLA won the Fiesta Bowl 39–37 over Miami on that same New Year's Day, but the big game was that night in the Orange Bowl. Quarterback Hugh Millen, who had lost his starting job earlier in the season, came off the bench to pass for one touchdown and set up another as Washington rallied with 14 points in the final six minutes to beat Oklahoma 28–17. Jacque Robinson, whose career since his starring role as a freshman in the Rose Bowl had had its ups and downs, rushed for 135 yards and became the first player ever to be named MVP in both the Rose and Orange Bowls.

The loss cost Oklahoma the Number One ranking, and the Huskies were given top spot in a couple of lesser polls, but in one of the more controversial selections in the history of the ratings, both AP and UPI chose Brigham Young as Number One and Washington as Number Two.

Huskies
University of Washington
Seattle, Washington

Beavers
Oregon State University
Corvallis, Oregon

Ducks
University of Oregon
Eugene, Oregon

Golden Bears
University of California at Berkeley
Berkeley, California

Cardinal
Stanford, University
Palo Alto, California

Bruins
University of California at Los Angeles
Los Angeles, California

Trojans
University of Southern California
Los Angeles, California

USC

UCLA

ougars
ashington State University
lman, Washington

Sun Devils
Arizona State University
Tempe, Arizona

●

Wildcats
University of Arizona
Tucson, Arizona

That Wild Win

While Washington and USC were grabbing the headlines, Terry Donahue was building a dynasty in Westwood the way he did everything—quietly.

In his first four years, the soft-spoken former defensive tackle won 29 games, lost 15 and tied two—and yet, his predictable running game and his lack of personal flash had UCLA boosters on his back. 'In Los Angeles, it's important to have an exciting team,' Donahue said later. 'You need to be entertaining. That's why we became more passing-oriented; we were winning, but we weren't winning with enough flair.'

That was just Donahue's way. 'People may expect a flashier guy, maybe like (former USC coach) John McKay,' one of Donahue's players, Craig Rutledge, said several years later. 'But when I think of coach Donahue, I always think of quiet, businesslike, very focused, cautious about what it will take.'

Los Angeles fans are hard to please—as Ted Tollner found out at USC a few years later—so following his only losing season (5–6 in 1979), Donahue threw out his playbook, hired former Pacific and Army head coach Homer Smith as offensive coordinator, put in a passing game and finished 9–2. However, back-to-back losses to Oregon and Arizona and the fact they didn't play Washington that year kept the Bruins out of the Rose Bowl. The following year they were 7–4–1, including the Bluebonnet Bowl loss to Michigan, but beginning in 1982 Donahue guided UCLA to three Rose Bowls, a Fiesta Bowl and a Freedom Bowl in four years—and the Bruins won them all.

The 1982 team probably was the best. Quarterback Tom Ramsey had a brilliant year; he completed 61.4 percent of his passes (191 for 311), for 2824 yards and 21 touchdowns to lead the nation in passing efficiency, and was named Co-Player of the Year in the Pac-10 with All-American quarterback John Elway of Stanford. The Bruins tied Arizona in their conference opener 24–24, and lost to Washington 10–7, but finished with a 20–19 win over USC and took a 9–1–1 record into the Rose Bowl against Michigan. Ramsey's touchdown and a field goal by freshman John Lee, who was destined for great things, gave the Bruins a 10–0 halftime lead and they coasted on to a 24–14 victory.

The 1983 Bruins started off miserably, although an incredibly difficult schedule might have had something to do with that; the first four games were against Georgia, which finished that season ranked Number Four in the nation; Arizona State, coming off a 10–2 season; Nebraska, the second-ranked team at the end of the year, and Brigham Young, Number Seven. When that ordeal was over, UCLA had three losses and one tie, 24–24 with ASU, and the experts had written them off. But the Bruins won six of

the last seven, and when they beat USC 27–17, while Washington was being upset by Washington State, they had their second consecutive Rose Bowl bid.

Mike White, who had shared the Pac-8 title while coaching California in 1975, had helped bring the passing game to the Big Ten and with that added weapon, things were supposed to be better for the Midwest at Pasadena. It was worse. The Illini were routed, 45–9, as Rick Neuheisel threw three touchdown passes for the Bruins and defensive backs Don Rogers, an All-American, and Lupe Sanchez helped shut down Illinois' own talented quarterback, Jack Trudeau.

After a 1984 9–3 season (including their Fiesta Bowl win), the Bruins finished 1985 with an 8–2–1 record and another conference title. They obviously had not lost their Rose Bowl touch; Iowa and All-American quarterback Chuck Long were crushed 45–28 as UCLA freshman Eric Ball, replacing injured Gaston Green, romped for 227 yards and four touchdowns. The following year, they finished the regular season 7–3–1. Ball was hurt for much of the year but a now-healthy Green rushed for 266 yards (the most ever by one player in a major college bowl game), scored three touchdowns and passed for another as UCLA buried Brigham Young 31–10 in the Freedom Bowl at nearby Anaheim.

Five straight bowl appearances, five straight wins, a record of 86–33–6 for his first 11 years as a head coach—Terry Donahue was indeed a coach for the '80s.

But the Pacific-10 was making its mark everywhere. Following the 1985 season five teams went to bowl games, the most ever from the conference; besides the Bruins' Rose Bowl win, Washington captured the Freedom Bowl over Colorado 20–17; Arizona tied Georgia 13–13 in the Sun Bowl; Arizona State was nipped by Arkansas 18-17 in the Holiday Bowl, and USC fell to Alabama 24–3 in the Aloha Bowl. The following year was even better—six Pac-10 teams in bowl games. Besides Arizona State's first Rose Bowl appearance, UCLA's Freedom Bowl win and Washington's loss in the Sun Bowl, Arizona captured the Aloha Bowl. Surprising Stanford, which had finished 8–3 under Jack Elway, had to play without injured passing star John Paye and, despite a second-half rally, fell to Clemson in the Gator Bowl 27–21; and USC, in Ted Tollner's final game, never got started and was beaten by Auburn in the Citrus Bowl 16–7.

There were other coaches besides Donahue and James who made their mark. Pullman, Washington, for example, was some-

UCLA's Terry Donahue *(at right)* coached his Bruins to big Rose Bowl wins over Michigan, Illinois and Ohio in 1983, '84 and '86.

UCLA's Gaston Green rushed for 266 yards—the most ever by a single player in a major college bowl game—in the 1987 Freedom Bowl 31–10 stomping of Brigham Young. Green shows his stuff in the photo *above*—and *at left* against UCLA's arch rival, USC.

thing of a football wasteland; there had been some good coaches there—Jim Sweeney, Jackie Sherrill, Warren Powers—but it was extremely difficult to lure good players there. Sweeney managed just one winning season in eight years; Sherrill and Powers lasted only one season each before moving on to more appealing locales.

But Jim Walden, who took over for Powers, planned to stay awhile. His first three years were respectable, and in 1983 he compiled an 8–3–1 record, including a 17–17 tie with UCLA and losses only to USC, Washington and seventh-ranked Brigham Young in that wild Holiday Bowl—the Cougars' first bowl bid in 49 years. WSU had the league's leading rusher that year in Kerry Porter, with an even 1000 yards, but in 1984 he was hurt and the burden fell on Rueben Mayes, a junior from the unlikely little town of North Battleford, Saskatchewan. Mayes, who went on to immediate stardom with the New Orleans Saints of the NFL, responded with 1637 yards rushing, second in the nation only to Keith Byars of Ohio State. With Porter and the All-American Mayes both returning in 1985, as well as All-Coast quarterback Mark Rypien, the Cougars had incredible firepower and were counted on for big things, but Porter got hurt again during the season, Mayes didn't untrack again until mid-year—although he again led the league with 1236 yards—and Washington State finished a disappointing 4–7.

At Tempe, Arizona, unheralded John Cooper, who came from Tulsa to replace Darryl Rogers when Rogers went to the NFL's Detroit Lions after the 1984 season, took the Sun Devils to the

These pages: Washington State's Kerry Porter is here the focus of three Oregon defenders' attentions as he blasts toward the goal line, ball in hand. Porter led the league in 1983 with 1000 forward yards, and in 1985, he and All-American Reuben Mayes were the Cougars' speed, agility and just plain old *motivation.*

At right: Arizona State's fine quarterback Jeff Van Raaphorst readies his offensive team for another pitchforking attack during the Sun Devils' 1987 Rose Bowl rascalry against befuddled Michigan. *Above:* Gerald Riggs makes haste for the 1981 Sun Devils. *At left:* Cougars coach Jim Walden, gathering his WSU forces in 1981.

Holiday Bowl in his first year and then, in 1986, guided ASU to a 9–1–1 regular-season record and the first Rose Bowl appearance by either of the Pac-10's two Arizona 'newcomers.'

There was nothing new about the result at Pasadena, however. Michigan came into the game ranked Number Four nationally with just one loss, and the Wolverines took an early 15–3 lead. But if Michigan, with quarterback Jack Harbaugh, had learned how to pass the ball, it still was having trouble keeping the other team from doing likewise; ASU quarterback Jeff Van Raaphorst passed for 193 yards and two touchdowns to rally the Devils to a 22–15 win.

'We come out every year and get beat by seven points,' said a disgusted Schembechler afterwards—which just about summed up recent Rose Bowl history. It was Schembechler's seventh Rose Bowl loss in eight tries and the Pacific-10's sixth win in a row—and 12th win in 13 years.

The 1986 season was not such a success for two other coaches in the Pac-10. Ted Tollner, despite beating four Top Ten teams and finishing with a 7–4 record and a New Year's Day bowl bid, was fired by Southern California. The biggest reason probably was a 1–7 record in his four years against the Trojans' two biggest rivals, UCLA and Notre Dame; his '86 team lost to both of them in embarrassing fashion, 45–25 to the Bruins and 38–37 to Notre Dame on a last-second field goal after the Trojans had blown a 23–9 lead early in the second half.

The Trojans immediately hired Larry Smith to succeed Tollner. Smith had taken over an Arizona program that was a shambles seven years earlier; when he left for Los Angeles, he had a 48–28–3 record, six straight winning seasons, three consecutive wins

High fives and then into the game: The U of Arizona team *(above)* **gets excited before they break huddle and continue play** *(right)***; one of the reasons they can get excited these days is coach Larry Smith** *(left)***, who set them straight before taking over at USC.**

over arch-rival Arizona State—including the only loss suffered by the Rose Bowl-bound 1986 Sun Devils—and was fresh off the Wildcats' win in the Aloha Bowl. Smith became the first Southern California football coach since Howard Jones in 1925 who had not had some previous connection with the Trojans.

The other coach to be fired was Joe Kapp at California, which brings us, finally, to two men whose paths crossed in probably the most bizarre football game in history: John Elway, a quarterback who just could be the best ever to play the college game; and Kapp, a former quarterback who became one of the game's most unusual coaches.

John Elway had enrolled at Stanford in the autumn of 1979. The son of a football coach, Elway had it all—size, intelligence, an incredible rifle arm, the ability to throw long even when off-balance and the speed and strength to scramble and turn losses into gains.

Stanford already had two other fine young quarterbacks, Grayson Rogers and Babe Laufenberg, in addition to senior Turk Schonert, who would lead the nation in passing that year. Early in fall practice that season, a group of sportswriters were standing on the sideline, watching the quarterbacks warm up and chatting with Ken Margerum, the Cardinal's All-American end.

'I guess it's going to be a pretty good battle at quarterback next year, when Schonert's gone,' one of the writers remarked.

'No, it's not,' the outspoken Margerum responded. 'That guy out there (indicating Elway) is going to be the best there is.'

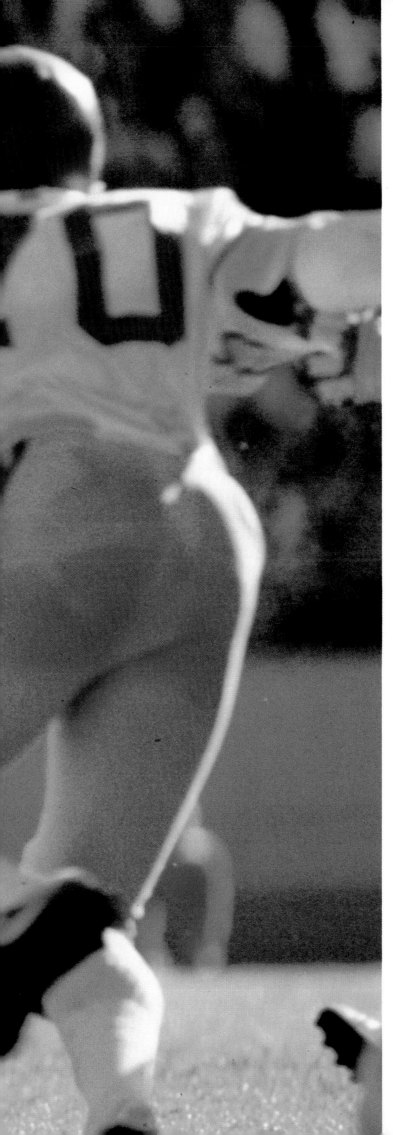

In the photo *at left,* John Elway displays all the cool it takes to be a great quarterback—sizing up his pass opportunities even as a Trojan warrior closes in. Elway had a career yardage at Stanford of 9070 yards, third highest in NCAA history, and was the Number One pick in the 1982 NFL draft. *Above:* USC's 'Tommy Trojan.'

He was right. Although he had Darrin Nelson with him for part of his career at Stanford, Elway did not have the supporting cast of USC or UCLA or Washington, not by a long shot. The Cardinals went 5–5–1 under Rod Dowhower in Elway's freshman year and 6–5, 4–7 and 5–6 under Paul Wiggin, the former Stanford All-American and All-Pro and former Kansas City Chiefs head coach.

Heaven only knows what it would have been without Elway and Nelson. In a 1980 game against Washington State and the talented Jack Thompson, for example, Stanford won 48–34—defense was not a Cardinal strong point—and Elway was 29-for-36 for 379 yards; Nelson had 369 yards all-purpose (running, receiving, kick returns) in the same game. And so it went.

As a sophomore, Elway set a Pac-10 record for total offense of 2939 yards—and as a senior he broke it, with 3104. He broke Jim Plunkett's conference career yardage mark with 9070 yards, second in NCAA history only to Brigham Young's Jim McMahon (9723, a mark later broken by Doug Flutie of Boston College). Elway also had 9349 yards passing, again second to McMahon; his 77 touchdown passes was third all-time, behind McMahon (84) and Joe Adams of Tennessee State (81); his 62.1 percent completion mark, on 774 completions in 1246 attempts, is a national record, and he threw only 39 interceptions. And even more important than the numbers, he had the ability to make plays that no one else could make. He was the Number One pick

in the NFL draft, choosing a million-dollar contract from the Denver Broncos over a rich baseball offer from the New York Yankees.

Laufenberg and Rogers, meanwhile, had seen the handwriting on the stadium wall; both transferred after Elway's freshman season.

Following Elway's graduation, Stanford fell to 1–10 and Paul Wiggin was fired. His replacement was the San Jose State head coach, a guy by the name of Jack Elway. 'Usually it's the millionaire fathers who send their sons to Stanford,' one Cardinal player wisecracked. 'This is the first time I've heard of a millionaire son sending his father here.'

Of all John Elway's college games, the most memorable was one he lost—his last, the 1982 Big Game against California—the stuff that nightmares are made of.

Roger Theder had lasted only four years as Cal's head coach; in the first two the Bears went 6–5 and 6–6, the latter including a 28–17 loss to Temple in the Garden State Bowl, but they tailed off to 3–8, then 2–9. Many, including Theder himself, felt Cal was on the verge of a big year, but Dave Maggard fired him the day after a 42–21 drubbing by Stanford in 1981, and then made the boldest move of his career as athletic director.

He hired Joe Kapp, the former Cal star who had quarterbacked the Bears to their last Rose Bowl 24 years before.

Kapp had had a colorful career since. Virtually ignored in the NFL draft as a running quarterback—he had led the PCC in rushing, remember—he went to the Canadian Football League,

Marching bands, cheerleaders and razzmatazz—here to stay in Pac-10 football. Washington's marching band *(left)* tunes up for a half-time celebration; the Ducks' yellow and green adorns the snazzy marching band *below*; and a USC cheerleader *(right)* lends her rather Nordic but *all American* good looks to urge the Trojans on.

Stanford QB John Paye gets ready to fire a pass over the heads of a savage Bear attack in the 1986 Big Game, which was one of Joe Kapp's happier moments—Cal upset the Card 17-11.

At left: Cal coach Joe Kapp exhorts wide receiver Keith Cockett during Cal's 1985 Big Game loss to Stanford, 24–22. Capp was fired in 1986, with Bruce Snyder taking over as head Bearkeeper. *Above:* Stanford line coach Dick Mannini gives his defenders a talking to; things looked grim as Stanford went down to Cal in 1986.

where he collected a flock of passing records and a scar on his cheek, reportedly in a barroom brawl. He moved to the NFL with the Minnesota Vikings, earning their respect by trying to run over opposing linebackers. In two years, he had the Vikings in the Super Bowl; and became the only man ever to play in a Rose Bowl, a Grey Cup (the Canadian championship game) and a Super Bowl. Later, he sued the NFL over the binding reserve clause, losing the suit but winning the admiration of many pro players.

Kapp had made a comfortable living from real estate, movie production and occasional acting (in such forgettable epics as 'The Longest Yard,' with another ex-football player, Burt Reynolds).

What he had not done, ever, at any level, was coach.

But perhaps Kapp's strongest trait is loyalty—especially to the University of California. He didn't just want to coach; he wanted to coach the Golden Bears. And the Bears right about then needed someone like Joe; someone who had always been a winner and a competitor, and someone who could immediately rally the disgruntled fans.

Reaction around the league was predictable; most opposing coaches wouldn't say flat out that Kapp would fall on his face, but though many professed admiration for the man, they openly resented the fact that he had not worked his way up through the ranks. When California finished with a 7–4 record, losing only to USC and Numbers Five, Six and Seven UCLA, Arizona State and Washington, his peers voted Kapp conference Coach of the Year.

But enthusiasm can take one only so far. What had been a solid staff of assistants broke up when several took jobs with the new USFL, and although Kapp recruited well, the Bears fell to 5–5–1; then to 2–9, 4–7; and in 1986, another 2–9 record. The Bears, an 18-point underdog to bowl-bound Stanford, pulled off one of the biggest upsets in Big Game history in that 1986 finale, winning 17–11 and carrying a teary Kapp off the field on their shoulders. But it was too late; Kapp had been fired three weeks earlier and would be replaced by Bruce Snyder, an assistant coach with the Los Angeles Rams.

Kapp's last Big Game as coach brought back memories of his first, in 1982—but aside from Cal upsetting a bowl-bound Stanford, it wasn't the same: *nothing* will ever be the same as that 1982 Big Game.

Although both teams had 6–4 records, it was Stanford, with the exciting Elway, that had a bowl bid promised—if it won the Big Game as expected. It was a magnificent effort by both sides, filled with brilliant and exciting plays, but it looked as if California would win when Stanford, trailing 19–17 with less than two minutes left, faced a fourth down and 17 yards to go situation at its own 13-yard line.

Elway had been superb—for the day he completed 25 of 39 passes for 330 yards and both touchdowns, without an interception—and again he was equal to the task. He rifled a fourth-down pass deep over the middle to Emile Harry, 29 yards and a first down, and the Cardinal, raised from the dead, took the momentum and marched upfield. With just four seconds remaining, Mark Harmon kicked a field goal, Stanford led 20–19, and the jubilant players rushed onto the field to celebrate.

But hold it! There still were four seconds left, and this was, after all, the Big Game. Cal's special teams captain, Richard Rodgers, gathered the kick receiving team around him and uttered one simple order: 'Don't anybody go down with the ball.'

In the Pacific Coast's long history, there have been many times of jubilation. Whether for a single play, or for a twist of fate such as the Big Game of 1982, *which the Stanford Band helped Cal to win,* **Pac-10 players** *(left)* **and fans** *(above)* **have many reasons to cheer.**

After Stanford was penalized for delay of the game with their prematue celebration, Harmon kicked off from the 25-yard line, squibbing the ball down to the Bear 43. Defensive back Kevin Moen grabbed it, ran it back to the Stanford 48 and then was hemmed in by tacklers. However, he lateraled the ball to Rodgers, and Rodgers immediately lateraled to freshman Dwight Garner, who apparently was piled up right there, at the 48. The Cardinal band, flushed with victory began to march exuberantly onto the field.

But there was no whistle. As Garner fell, he lateraled to Rodgers, and after running two yards, Rodgers flipped it to Mariet Ford. Ford raced to the 25-yard line and then, almost lost in a sea of red-jacketed Stanford bandsmen, threw an apparently blind pass back over his shoulder.

And suddenly, amazingly, there was Moen again, picking the ball out of the air and racing into the end zone, flattening a Stanford trombone player as he leaped jubilantly into the air.

Nobody was sure just what had really happened, and all eyes went to the referee. After what seemed like hours, he threw his arms into the air. Touchdown! California had won 25–20.

The radio and TV announcers were in a frenzy, trying to describe the indescribable. The Cal side was delirious, the Stanford side literally stunned. Wiggin, one of the finest gentlemen the game has ever seen, and Stanford athletic director Andy Geiger stormed to the officials' dressing room in a fury. In the TV truck just outside the stadium, sportswriters watched replay after replay—and came away as confused as ever.

It was the strangest finish in the history of the game.

It was Pac-10 football.

Pac-10 Conference Champions

Year	School								
1916	Washington	1932	USC	1946	UCLA	1959	Washington	1975	UCLA/California
1917	Washington State	1933	Oregon/Stanford	1947	USC	1960	Washington	1976	USC
1918	California	1934	Stanford	1948	Oregon/California	1961	UCLA	1977	Washington
1919	Oregon/Washington	1935	California	1949	California	1962	USC	1978	USC
1920	California	1936	Stanford	1950	California	1963	Washington	1979	USC
1921	California	1937	California	1951	Stanford	1964	Oregon State/USC	1980	Washington
1922	California	1938	California/USC	1952	USC	1965	UCLA	1981	Washington
1923	California	1939	USC	1953	UCLA	1966	USC	1982	UCLA
1924	Stanford	1940	Stanford	1954	UCLA	1967	USC	1983	UCLA
1925	Washington	1941	Oregon State	1955	UCLA	1968	USC	1984	USC
1926	Stanford	1942	UCLA	1956	Oregon State	1969	USC	1985	UCLA
1927	Stanford/USC	1943	USC	1957	Oregon	1970	Stanford	1986	Arizona State
1928	USC	1944	USC	1958	California	1971	Stanford		
1929	USC	1945	USC			1972	USC		
1930	Washington State					1973	USC		
1931	USC					1974	USC		

Pac-10 Standings

The Pac-10 began as the **Pacific Coast Conference (PCC)** in 1916 with only four universities represented. They were Cal, Oregon, Oregon State and Washington. By 1924 the conference had added Stanford, USC, Idaho, Washington State and Montana, to total nine members. UCLA joined in 1928, while Montana dropped out after 1949.

In 1959 the conference was back down to five members—Washington, USC, UCLA, Cal and Stanford—and was renamed the **Amateur Athletic Western Union (AAWU)**. From that point it began to grow again, as seen in the following table, until it was named the **Pacific 8** in 1968. In 1978, with two new members, Arizona and Arizona State, it became the **Pacific 10 (Pac-10)**, and then simply the **Pac-10**.

AAWU Standings

Columns: Conference Games (W L T Pts Opp) — All Games (W L T)

1959
Team	W	L	T	Pts	Opp	W	L	T
Wash	3	1	0	68	29	10	1	0
USC	3	1	0	69	60	8	2	0
UCLA	3	1	0	91	51	5	4	1
Calif	1	3	0	38	92	2	7	1
Stan	0	4	0	58	115	3	7	0

1960
Team	W	L	T	Pts	Opp	W	L	T
Wash	4	0	0	100	25	10	1	0
USC	2	1	1	65	56	4	6	0
UCLA	2	2	0	68	35	7	2	1
Calif	1	3	0	38	92	2	7	1
Stan	0	4	0	34	97	0	10	0

1961
Team	W	L	T	Pts	Opp	W	L	T
UCLA	3	1	0	78	39	7	4	0
USC	2	1	1	65	39	4	5	1
Wash	2	1	1	44	34	5	4	1
Stan	1	3	0	35	70	4	6	0
Calif	1	3	0	22	87	1	8	0

1962
Team	W	L	T	Pts	Opp	W	L	T
USC	4	0	0	99	23	11	0	0
Wash	4	1	0	97	35	7	1	2
WSU	1	1	0	42	32	5	4	1
Stan	2	3	0	67	94	5	5	0
UCLA	1	3	0	36	77	4	6	0
Calif	0	4	0	35	115	1	9	0

1963
Team	W	L	T	Pts	Opp	W	L	T
Wash	4	1	0	96	58	6	5	9
USC	3	1	0	97	45	7	3	0
WSU	1	1	0	32	31	3	6	1
Calif	1	3	0	32	31	4	5	1
Stan	1	4	0	74	103	3	7	0

1964
Team	W	L	T	Pts	Opp	W	L	T
OSU	3	1	0	74	36	8	3	0
USC	3	1	0	88	58	7	3	0
Wash	5	2	0	84	65	6	4	0
UCLA	2	2	0	85	97	4	6	0
Stan	3	4	0	100	95	5	5	0
Oregon	1	2	1	42	38	7	2	1
WSU	1	2	1	57	82	3	6	1
Calif	0	4	0	61	93	3	7	0

1965
Team	W	L	T	Pts	Opp	W	L	T
UCLA	4	0	0	134	56	8	2	1
USC	4	1	0	125	32	7	2	1
WSU	2	1	0	46	42	7	3	0
Wash	4	3	0	156	136	5	5	0
Stan	2	3	0	47	106	6	3	1
Calif	2	3	0	50	112	5	5	0
OSU	1	3	0	60	78	5	5	0
Oregon	0	5	0	55	111	4	5	1

1966
Team	W	L	T	Pts	Opp	W	L	T
USC	4	1	0	101	44	7	4	0
UCLA	3	1	0	55	38	9	1	0
OSU	3	1	0	85	62	7	3	0
Wash	4	3	0	114	102	6	4	0
Calif	2	3	0	76	102	3	7	0
Oregon	1	3	0	42	47	3	7	0
WSU	1	3	0	40	94	3	7	0
Stan	1	4	0	43	67	5	5	0

1967
Team	W	L	T	Pts	Opp	W	L	T
USC	6	1	0	182	47	10	1	0
UCLA	4	1	1	193	90	7	2	1
OSU	4	1	1	87	53	7	2	1
Stan	3	4	0	88	121	5	5	0
Wash	3	4	0	82	106	5	5	0
Calif	2	3	0	79	106	5	5	0
Oregon	1	5	0	60	119	2	8	0
WSU	1	4	0	62	190	2	8	0

Pac-8 Standings

1968
Team	W	L	T	Pts	Opp	W	L	T
USC	6	0	0	114	90	9	1	1
OSU	5	1	0	179	92	7	3	0
Stan	3	3	1	152	129	6	3	1
Calif	2	2	1	99	85	6	3	1
Oregon	2	4	0	82	138	4	6	0
UCLA	2	4	0	103	156	3	7	0
WSU	1	3	1	87	95	3	6	1
Wash	1	5	1	61	118	3	7	0

1969
Team	W	L	T	Pts	Opp	W	L	T
USC	6	0	0	129	66	10	0	1
UCLA	5	1	1	217	72	8	1	1
Stan	5	1	1	204	81	7	2	1
OSU	4	3	0	100	120	6	4	0
Oregon	2	3	0	64	82	5	5	1
Calif	2	4	0	101	123	5	5	0
Wash	1	6	0	84	191	1	9	0
WSU	0	7	0	69	233	1	9	0

1970
Team	W	L	T	Pts	Opp	W	L	T
Stan	6	1	0	220	101	9	3	0
Wash	4	3	0	233	176	6	4	0
Oregon	4	3	0	152	166	6	4	1
UCLA	4	3	0	204	168	6	5	0
Calif	4	3	0	166	123	6	5	0
USC	3	4	0	194	163	6	4	1
OSU	3	4	0	129	171	6	5	0
WSU	0	7	0	112	331	1	10	0

1971
Team	W	L	T	Pts	Opp	W	L	T
Stan	5	1	0	162	98	9	3	0
OSU	3	2	0	123	129	5	6	0
Wash	3	3	0	128	99	8	3	0
USC	2	2	1	91	100	6	4	1
Oregon	2	3	0	118	143	5	6	0
WSU	2	4	0	130	157	4	7	0
UCLA	1	3	1	79	107	2	7	1
Calif †	-	-	-	---	---	6	5	0

† – Games did not count in Pac-8 standings

1972
Team	W	L	T	Pts	Opp	W	L	T
USC	7	0	0	243	59	12	0	0
UCLA	5	2	0	242	137	8	3	0
WSU	4	3	0	168	164	7	4	0
Wash	4	3	0	128	160	8	3	0
Calif	3	4	0	163	208	3	8	0
Oregon	2	5	0	108	184	5	6	0
Stan	2	5	0	136	135	6	5	0
OSU	1	6	0	76	218	2	9	0

1973
Team	W	L	T	Pts	Opp	W	L	T
USC	7	0	0	240	124	9	2	1
UCLA	6	1	0	302	104	9	2	0
Stan	5	2	0	181	161	7	4	0
WSU	4	3	0	179	190	5	6	0
Calif	2	5	0	168	272	4	7	0
Oregon	2	5	0	151	130	2	9	0
OSU	2	5	0	113	159	2	9	0
Wash	0	7	0	128	322	2	9	0

1974
Team	W	L	T	Pts	Opp	W	L	T
USC	6	0	1	226	69	10	1	1
Stan	5	1	1	133	115	5	4	2
Calif	4	2	1	184	148	7	3	1
UCLA	4	2	1	130	108	6	3	2
Wash	3	4	0	184	177	5	6	0
OSU	3	4	0	126	126	3	8	0
WSU	1	6	0	112	195	2	9	0
Oregon	0	7	0	49	216	2	9	0

1975
Team	W	L	T	Pts	Opp	W	L	T
UCLA	6	1	0	215	123	9	2	1
Calif	6	1	0	235	132	8	3	0
Wash	5	2	0	160	122	6	4	1
Stan	5	2	0	188	166	6	5	0
USC	3	4	0	122	94	8	4	0
Oregon	2	5	0	114	182	3	8	0
OSU	1	6	0	83	183	1	10	0
WSU	0	7	0	109	213	3	8	0

1976
Team	W	L	T	Pts	Opp	W	L	T
USC	7	0	0	234	81	11	1	0
UCLA	6	1	0	260	100	9	2	1
Stan	5	2	0	179	174	6	5	0
Calif	3	4	0	115	124	5	6	0
Wash	3	4	0	141	142	5	6	0
WSU	2	5	0	139	227	3	8	0
Oregon	1	6	0	79	215	4	7	0
OSU	1	6	0	87	210	2	10	0

1977
Team	W	L	T	Pts	Opp	W	L	T
Wash	6	1	0	283	103	9	3	0
Stan	5	2	0	151	171	9	3	0
USC	5	2	0	193	104	8	4	0
UCLA	5	2	0	192	129	7	4	0
Calif	3	4	0	125	156	7	4	0
WSU	3	4	0	164	164	6	5	0
Oregon	1	6	0	94	248	2	9	0
OSU	0	7	0	84	198	2	9	0

Pac-10 Standings

1978
Team	W	L	T	Pts	Opp	W	L	T
USC	6	1	0	182	81	12	1	0
UCLA	6	2	0	197	131	8	3	1
Wash	6	2	0	215	119	7	4	0
ASU	4	3	0	164	180	9	3	0
Stan	4	3	0	182	131	8	4	0
Calif	3	4	0	124	204	6	5	0
Arizona	3	4	0	148	140	5	6	0
Oregon	2	5	0	121	135	2	9	0
OSU	2	6	0	92	229	3	7	1
WSU	1	7	0	193	268	3	7	1

1979
Team	W	L	T	Pts	Opp	W	L	T
USC	6	0	1	244	99	11	0	1
Wash	6	1	0	165	98	10	2	0
Arizona	4	3	0	139	136	6	5	0
Oregon	4	3	0	139	136	6	5	1
Calif	5	4	0	217	142	6	6	0
Stan	3	3	1	158	146	5	5	1
ASU	3	4	0	209	134	6	6	0
UCLA	3	4	0	160	182	5	6	0
WSU	2	6	0	153	255	4	7	0
OSU	1	7	0	101	315	1	10	0

1980
Team	W	L	T	Pts	Opp	W	L	T
Wash	6	1	0	198	119	9	2	0
UCLA	5	2	0	175	107	9	2	0
USC	4	2	1	178	94	8	2	1
ASU	5	3	0	224	156	7	4	0
Oregon	4	3	1	189	170	6	3	2
Stan	3	4	0	214	196	6	5	0
Arizona	3	4	0	131	202	5	6	0

	W	L	T	Pts	Opp	W	L	T
WSU	3	4	0	185	163	4	7	0
Calif	3	5	0	149	223	3	8	0
OSU	0	8	0	77	290	0	11	0

1981

	Conference Games					All Games		
	W	L	T	Pts	Opp	W	L	T
Wash	6	2	0	185	147	10	2	0
ASU	5	2	0	226	131	9	2	0
USC	5	2	0	178	106	9	3	0
WSU	5	2	1	183	128	8	3	1
UCLA	5	2	1	223	124	7	4	1
Arizona	4	4	0	151	151	6	5	0
Stan	4	4	0	270	202	4	7	0
Calif	2	6	0	132	204	2	9	0
Oregon	1	6	0	85	185	2	9	0
OSU	0	7	0	75	330	1	10	0

1982

	Conference Games					All Games		
	W	L	T	Pts	Opp	W	L	T
UCLA	5	1	1	218	148	10	1	1
Wash	6	2	0	222	145	10	1	1

	W	L	T	Pts	Opp	W	L	T
ASU	5	2	0	148	91	10	2	0
USC	5	2	0	236	106	8	3	0
Arizona	4	3	1	226	182	6	4	1
Calif	4	4	0	135	207	7	4	0
Stan	3	5	0	239	228	5	6	0
WSU	2	4	1	122	178	3	7	1
Oregon	2	6	0	73	182	2	8	1
OSU	0	7	1	84	234	1	9	1

1983

	Conference Games					All Games		
	W	L	T	Pts	Opp	W	L	T
UCLA	6	1	1	211	158	7	4	1
Wash	5	2	0	175	91	8	4	0
WSU	5	3	0	152	156	7	4	0
USC	4	3	0	151	128	4	6	1
Arizona	4	3	1	226	157	7	3	1
ASU	3	3	1	188	128	6	4	1
Oregon	3	3	1	82	114	4	6	1
Calif	3	4	1	179	173	5	5	1
OSU	1	6	1	85	245	2	8	1
Stan	1	7	0	128	226	1	10	0

1984

	Conference Games					All Games		
	W	L	T	Pts	Opp	W	L	T
USC	7	1	0	148	107	9	3	0
Wash	6	1	0	190	103	11	1	0
UCLA	5	2	0	159	121	9	3	0
Arizona	5	2	0	148	104	7	4	0
WSU	4	3	0	232	187	6	5	0
ASU	3	4	0	157	92	5	6	0
Oregon	3	5	0	156	196	6	5	0
Stan	3	5	0	170	214	5	6	0
OSU	1	7	0	81	202	2	9	0
Calif	1	8	0	104	219	2	9	0

1985

	Conference Games					All Games		
	W	L	T	Pts	Opp	W	L	T
UCLA	6	2	0	231	120	9	2	1
Arizona	5	2	0	134	103	8	3	1
ASU	5	2	0	162	101	8	4	0
Wash	5	3	0	169	134	7	5	0
USC	5	3	0	184	96	6	6	0
Oregon	3	4	0	172	166	5	6	0

	W	L	T	Pts	Opp	W	L	T
WSU	3	5	0	180	176	4	7	0
Stan	3	5	0	148	227	4	7	0
OSU	2	6	0	87	278	3	8	0
Calif	2	7	0	146	212	4	7	0

1986

	Conference Games					All Games		
	W	L	T	Pts	Opp	W	L	T
ASU	5	1	1	203	122	10	1	1
UCLA	5	2	1	245	137	8	3	1
Wash	5	2	1	232	141	8	3	1
Arizona	5	3	0	224	149	9	3	0
Stan	5	3	0	182	124	8	4	0
USC	5	3	0	172	155	7	5	0
Oregon	3	5	0	168	246	5	6	0
WSU	2	6	1	174	278	3	7	1
Calif	2	7	0	116	269	2	9	0
OSU	1	6	0	87	202	3	8	0

Composite Pac-10 Standings since 1978 (8 seasons)

	Conference				All Games			
	W	L	T	Pct	W	L	T	Pct
Southern Cal	43	13	2	.759	67	24	3	.729
Washington	45	15	0	.750	71	24	0	.747
UCLA	41	16	3	.708	64	25	5	.707
Arizona State	33	23	1	.588	60	33	1	.644
Arizona	32	25	2	.551	50	36	4	.578
Washington St	25	34	2	.426	38	48	3	.444
Stanford	24	36	1	.402	38	50	1	.433
Oregon	22	35	2	.390	33	51	4	.398
California	23	42	1	.356	35	53	1	.399
Oregon State	7	54	2	.119	13	72	3	.165

All Time Won-Lost Records of PAC-10 Teams (through 1985)

	W	L	T	Pct
USC	571	219	49	.710
Stanford	528	301	47	.630
Arizona State	388	223	22	.630
Washington	496	284	47	.628
UCLA	377	248	35	.598
Arizona	352	275	24	.559
California	382	313	32	.547
Oregon	386	362	47	.515
Washington State	360	351	43	.506
Oregon State	373	374	47	.499

Pac-10 Heisman Trophy Winners

Marcus Allen (USC), 1981; Terry Baker (OSU), 1962; Gary Beban (UCLA), 1967; Mike Garrett (USC), 1965; Jim Plunkett (Stanford), 1970; OJ Simpson (USC), 1968; Charles White (USC), 1979

Rose Bowl Scores

1902
Michigan 49
Stanford 0
1916
Washington State 14
Brown 0
1917
Oregon 14
Pennsylvania 0
1918
Mare Island 19
Camp Lewis 7
1919
Great Lakes 17
Mare Island 0
1920
Harvard 7
Oregon 6
1921
California 28
Ohio State 0
1922
California (tie) 0
Washington & Jefferson 0
1923
USC 14
Penn State 3
1924
Washington (tie) 14
Navy 14
1925
Notre Dame 27
Stanford 10
1926
Alabama 20
Washington 19
1927
Stanford (tie) 7
Alabama 7

(Pac-10 schools are in boldface)

1928
Stanford 7
Pittsburgh 6
1929
Georgia Tech 8
California 7
1930
USC 47
Pittsburgh 14
1931
Alabama 24
Washington State 0
1932
USC 21
Tulane 12
1933
USC 35
Pittsburgh 0
1934
Columbia 7
Stanford 0
1935
Alabama 29
Stanford 13
1936
Stanford 7
SMU 0
1937
Pittsburg 21
Washington 0
1938
California 13
Alabama 0
1939
USC 7
Duke 3
1940
USC 14
Tennessee 0
1941
Stanford 21
Nebraska 13
1942
Oregon State 20
Duke 16

1943
Georgia 9
UCLA 0
1944
USC 29
Washington 0
1945
USC 29
Tennessee 0
1946
Alabama 34
USC 14
1947
Illinois 45
UCLA 14
1948
Michigan 49
USC 0
1949
Northwestern 20
California 14
1950
Ohio State 17
California 14
1951
Michigan 14
California 6
1952
Illinois 40
Stanford 7
1953
USC 7
Wisconsin 0
1954
Michigan State 28
UCLA 20
1955
Ohio State 20
USC 7
1956
Michigan State 17
UCLA 14
1957
Iowa 35
Oregon State 19

1958
Ohio State 10
Oregon 7
1959
Iowa 38
California 12
1960
Washington 44
Wisconsin 8
1961
Washington 17
Minnesota 7
1962
Minnesota 21
UCLA 3
1963
USC 42
Wisconsin 7
1964
Illinois 17
Washington 7
1965
Michigan 34
Oregon State 7
1966
UCLA 14
Michigan State 12
1967
Purdue 14
USC 13
1968
USC 14
Indiana 3
1969
Ohio State 27
USC 16
1970
USC 10
Michigan 3
1971
Stanford 27
Ohio State 17
1972
Stanford 13
Michigan 12

1973
USC 42
Ohio State 17
1974
Ohio State 42
USC 21
1975
USC 18
Ohio State 17
1976
UCLA 23
Ohio State 10
1977
USC 14
Michigan 6
1978
Washington 27
Michigan 20
1979
USC 17
Michigan 10
1980
USC 17
Ohio State 16
1981
Michigan 23
Washington 6
1982
Washington 28
Iowa 0
1983
UCLA 24
Michigan 14
1984
UCLA 45
Illinois 9
1985
USC 20
Ohio State 17
1986
UCLA 45
Iowa 28
1987
Arizona State 22
Michigan 15

INDEX

AAWU (see Academic Association of Western Universities)
Academic Association of Western Universities (AAWU) 110, 112, 118, 120, 123, 127, 128, 131, 133
Aiken, Jim 90, 108
Alabama, University of 69, 80
Albert, Frankie 72, *74*, 75, 76, 77, 78, 102
Allen, Marcus 158, *158*, 161
Allison, 'Stub' 45, 63, 66, *66*, 68, 80
Alustiza, Frank 60
Andros, Lee 110,128
Arizona State University 8, 10, 128, 154, *155*, 170, 173, 176, *176*, *177*, 179, 189
Arizona State University Stadium 154, *154*, 156, 165, 170, 176
Arizona, University of 154, 165, 170, *179*
Arnett, Jon *103*
Bagshaw, Enoch *18*, *19*, *20*, 30, 40, *44*, 45, 64
Baker, Terry 118, 120, *121*
Baldwin, Burr 82, *82*
Bartkowski, Steve 144, 146
Bears (see California, University of)
Beavers (see Oregon State University)
Beban, Gary 123, 128, *132*, 133, *134*
Bell, Ricky 146, 148, *149*
Benjamin, Guy 144, 152, *153*, 154
Bezdek, Hugo 21, *22*, 30, 31, 32
Big Five Conference 109
Big Four Conference 110
Big Nine Conference 82
Big Ten Conference 104, 112, 120, 123, 136, 144, 170
Boilermakers (see Purdue University)
Bottari, 'Vallejo Vic' 68, *68*
Brigham Young University 173
Brodie, John 96, 102, 107, 150
Brown University *18*, *19*, 20
Bruins (see University of California at Los Angeles)
Buckeyes (see Ohio State University)
Budde, Brad 156, *156*
Bunce, Don *142*, 143
Cal (see California, University of)
California, University of 7–15, 16–23, 24–33, 34–45, 46–53, 54–63, 64–71, 72–79, 80–93, *80* 94–103, 104–111, 112–127, 128–143, 144–169, 170–191, *180*, *181*, *186*, *187*, *188*
Cal-Stanford Big Game 6, 10, 12, 14, 29, 29, 30, 40, 42, *42*, 43, 51, 57, *57*, 59, *60*, *62*, 64, 66, 69, 72, 75, 83–86, 96, 140, *146*, *147*, 185, *186*, *187*, 189, *189*
Calhoun, Shelby *82*
Cameron, Paul 97, 98, *100*, 101, 102
Camp, Walter *9*, 10, *10*, *11*, 12, 26, 36, 72
Cardiac Kids 128 (see also Washington State University)
Cardinal (see Stanford University)
Cardinals (see Stanford University)
Carmichael, Al 98, *99*
Casanova, Len 90, *105*, 106, *106*, 108, *108*, 109, 123
Case, Ernie 82, *82*
Chapman, Sam *69*
Christiansen, Jack 144, 150
Clark, Don 115, 118, *118*
Coach of the Year award 82, 83, 94, 96, 154, 187
Cockett, Keith *188*
Coffee, Junior 123
Cougars (see Washington State University)
Crabtree, Jack 106
Cravath, Jeff 79, *79*, 80
Crowley, James 'Sleepy Jim' 39, *39*
Cureton, Hardiman *103*
Curtice, 'Cactus Jack' 110, 139
Cutihy, Zeb *84*, *85*
Davis, Anthony 136, *137*, 148
Dietz, William 20, 22
Diggs, Shelton 139, *139*
Dils, Steve 152, *153*, 154
Dobie, Gilmour 6, 16, *17*, 18, 21, 22, 23, 24, 45
Donahue, Terry 144, 148, 170, *171*
Dowhower, Ron 152, 183
Drury, Morley 46, 50, *50*
Ducks (see Oregon, University of)
Duke University 72, 78
Edwards, Glen 'Turk' 54
Elliott, Peter 109, 123
Elway, Jack (Sr.) 185
Elway, John 170, 179, *182*, 183, *183*
Evashevski, Forrest 107, 110
Fears, Tom 82, *82*
Fehring, William 'Dutch' *82*
Flying Wedge *14* (see also Harvard University)
Four Horsemen 37, *39*, 62 (see also Notre Dame University)
Freedom Bowl 173
Frei, Jerry *108*
Fry, Hayden 162
Fry, Wes 83, 84, *85*
Gallarneau, Hugh *74*, 75, 77
Garcia, Rod *143*
Garrett, Bobby 102, 150
Garrett, Mike 118, 123, *126*, 127, *127*, 128, 133, 134
Georgia, University of 79
Georgia Tech University 52, *52*
Gifford, Frank 94, 97, *97*
Gophers (see Minnesota, University of)
Grayson, Bobby *58*, 62, *62*, 63, *63*
Green, Gaston 170, *172*, *173*
Greene, Danny *159*
Halas, George 22, 70, 72
Hall of Fame, College Football 21, 34, 48, 54, 58, 59, 62, 64, 75, 80, 90
Hamilton, 'Bones' 58, 59, *59*, 60, 62, *62*, 63 *63*
Hammer, Bill *108*
Harvard University 6, *9*, *14*, *22*, *23*, 36, 72
Hawkeyes (see Iowa, University of)
Hayes, Woody 103, 106, 109, 115, 136, 148
Heffelfinger, W W 'Pudge' 10
Heinrich, Don 92, 98, 107
Heisman, John W 8, 133
Heisman Trophy 70, 79, 89, 90, 102, 107, 112, 115, 118, 120, 121, 123, 127, 133, *133*, 134, 136, 140, 143, 144, 146, 148, 156, *157*, 158
Henderson, 'Gloomy Gus' *30*
Hill, Jess 94, 96, 97, 101, *101*, 106, 115
Hollingbery, Babe 46, 54, *55*, 62, 69, 80
Hoosiers (see Indiana, University of)
Horrell, Edwin 'Babe' *30*, 46, 57, 69, *69*, *72*, 79, 80, 82
Huskies (see Washington, University of)
Idaho, University of 80, 101, 108
Illini (see Illinois, University of)
Illinois, University of 82, *82*, 83, 96, 97, 123, *124*, *125*, 144, 170
Indiana, University of 82, 131
Indians (see Stanford University)
Ingram, Bill 42, 57, *57*, 62, 63, 64, 66, *66*
Iowa, University of 106, 107, 110, 134, *162*, *163*, 170
James, Don 'Special Teams' 144, 148, 150, *150*, 161, *161*, 170
Jensen, Jackie 84, 85, *87*, 89, 102
Jones, Howard 30, 46, *47*, *48*, 50, 51, 52, 54, 57, 58, 63, 64, 68–70, 78, 79, 97, 179
Jones, Jimmy *136*
Kapp, Joe 107, 109, 110, *110*, 179, 185, *186*, *187*, *188*, 189
Kerkorian, Gary 85, 94, 96, *96*
Kmetovic, Pete 72, *74*, 75, 77, 78
Knox, Ronnie 103, 104, 106
Krueger, Al 69, 70, *71*, 73
Kush, Frank 154
La Brucherie, Bert 80, 82, *82*, 101
Layden, Elmer 39, *39*
Lindskog, Vic *75*
Lom, Benny 51, 52, *52*
Longhorns (see Texas, University of)
Mannini, Dick *189*
Manske, Ed 'Eggs' 83, *84*, *85*
Margerum, Ken 154, 179
Markov, Vic 64, *66*
Mathews, Ned *82*
Mathias, Bob 94, *96*
Mayes, Rueben 173, 174
McColl, Bill 94, 96, 97, *97*
McElhenny 'Hurryin' Hugh' 89, 90, 92, *92*, *93*, 94, 97, 98, 112
McKay, John 90, *90*, *108*, 112, 115, 118, *119*, 127, 128, *129*, 131, 134, *134*, 136, 139, 144, 146, 170
McKeever, Mike 115, 118
McKeta, Don 115, *115*, *116*, *117*
Memorial Stadium, Berkeley *32*, *33*, 36, 83
Michigan State University 82, 102, 107, 110, 123, 127, 137
Michigan, University of 12, 85, 90, 94, 98, 134, 136, 143, 148, 150, 156, *160*, 161, 165, 170, 176
Miller, Don 39, *39*
Minnesota, University of 115, *116*, *117*, 128, 140, 148
Monachino, Jim 85, 86
Montana, University of 85, 101
Moomaw, Donn 101, 102, *102*
Moon, Warren 148, *151*
Morrison, Marion (see Wayne, John)
Moscrip, 'Monk' 58, *59*, 63
Muller, Brick 24, 26, *26*, *27*, 29, *29*, 30, 45
Muncie, Chuck 144, *146*
Nabor, Ken *153*, 154
Nave, Doyle 69, 70, *71*
Nebraska, University of 74, 134
Nelson, Darrin 152, 154, 183
Nevers, Ernie 32, 36, 37, *37*, 39, 40, *41*, 46, 62, 63, *63*
Norguard, Al 59, *60*
Northwestern University 85
Notre Dame 39, *39*, 48, 50, 51, 54, 57, 62, 64, 68, 69, 82, 96–98, 102, 112, 115, 118, 123, 127, 128, 131, 133, 134, 136, 140, 176
Odell, Howie 92, *92*
Ohio State University 82, 85, 104, 106, 107, 108, 109, 110, 115, 123, 133, 136, 139, 143, 148, 156, 166, 170
Ohio, University of 139, 143, 156
Olzewski, Johnny 85, 86, 89, *89*, 90, 94, 96, 98
Oregon State University 6, 18, *22*, 50, 54, 64, 69, 75, 78, 79, 80, 102, 103, 104, 106, 107, 108, 115, 118, 120, 123, 128, 131, 134, 156
Oregon, University of 6, 18, *18*, *19*, *22*, *22*, *23*, 45, 63, 64, 69, 75, 80, 84, 90, 102, 104, 106, 107, 108, 109, *109*, 110, 115, 118, 120, 123, 156, 161, 170, *174*, *175*, *180*, *181*, *185*
Owens, Jim 'Jumbo' 112, *113*, 115, *115*, 120
Pac-8 Conference (see Pacific-8 Conference)
Pac-10 Conference 154, 156, 165, 170, 176, 183, 191
Pacific Coast Conference 6, 18, 20, 24, 32, 34, 40, 45, 46, 54, 57, 64, 70, 79, 80, *80*, 82, 84, 85, 86, 92, 94, 98, 103, 104, 106, 110, 112, 154
Pacific-8 Conference 133, 140, 144, 148, 150, 152 (see also Pac-8 Conference)
Paul, Don 82, *82*
Paye, John 170 *186*, *187*
Pennsylvania, University of *18*, *19*
Phelan, Jimmy 24, 64, *64*, *65*, 69
Plunkett, Jim 140, *141*, 143, 150, 183
Pollock, 'Mushy' *68*
Porter, Kerry *174*, *175*
Powers, Todd *180*, *181*
Price, Clarence 'Nibs' 24, 51, 54, 57, 83, *84*, *85*
Princeton University 6, *12*
Prothro, Tommy 102, 103, 104, *105*, 106, *106*, 107, 118, 120, *120*, 123, 128, 144
Purdue University 128, 140, 143
Purple Gang, The 115 (see also Washington , University of)
Ralston, John 139, 140, 143, 144
Redman, Rick *122*, 123
Remington, Charles 9, *10*
Remington, Frederick *10*
Reynolds, Robert 'Horse' 58, 63
Richter, Les 85, 86
Riegels, Roy 51, 52, *52*
Riggs, Gerald *176*
Rix, Leland *180*, *181*
Robinson, Jackie 69, *70*
Robinson, Jacque *164*, 165, *165*, 166
Robinson, John 144, *145*, 148, 158
Roche, Jack *108*
Rockne, Knute 34, 37, 39, 48, *49*, 50, 54, 57, 139
Roosevelt, President Theodore *14*, 15, *15*
Rose Bowl 7–15, 16–23, 24–33, 34–45, 46–53, 54–63, 64–71, 72–79, 73, 80–93, *81*, 94–103, 104–111, 112–127, 116, *117*, 128–143, *124*, *125*, *131*, *137*, *142*, *143*, 144–169, *160*, *161*, *164*, *165*, 170–191, *177*
Roth, Joe 144, *146*, *147*, 150
Rugby football 6, *9*, 12, 14
Sanders, Harry 'Red' 101, *101*, 102, 103, 104, 106, 108
San Jose State University 108, 140, 150, 185
Schabarum, Pete 85, 86, *86*
Schembechler, Bo 134, 156, 176
Schloredt, Bob 112, *114*, 115
Schmidt, Victor O 104, 106
Schonert, Turk 152, *152*, 179
Schwartz, Perry 66, 68, 82
Sears, Jim 97, *98*, *99*
Shaughnessy, Clark 72, *73*, 74, 75, 78, 82
Simpson, O J 118, 131, *131*, 133, 134, *134*, *135*, 140, 148, 156
Sinkwich, Frank 79, *79*
Smith, Andy 24, *24*, *25*, 26, 29, 32, 36, 45, 46, 51, 66
Smith Larry 176, *178*, 179
Snyder, Bruce 189
Stagg, Alonzo 12, *12*, *13*, 14, 21, 22, 34, 72
Standlee, Norm *74*, 75, 77
Stanford-Cal Big Game (see Cal-Stanford Big Game)
Stanford University 7–15, *12*, 16–23, 24–33, 34–45, 46–53, 54–63, *62*, 64–71, 72–79, *76*, *77*, 80–93, 94–103, 104–111, 112–127, 128–143, 144–169, *152*, *153*, 170–191, *182*, *183*, *186*, *187*, *189*
Stiner, Alonzzo 'Lon' 68, 78, *78*, 79
Stuhldreher, Harry 39, *39*
Sturzenegger, A J 'Sturzy' *82*
Sun Devils (see Arizona State University)
Sutherland, Jim 107, 120
Swann, Lynn 136, *137*
Taylor, Chuck *74*, 82, 94, *95*, 96, 101, 107, 139
Tessier, Bob 83, *84*, *85*
Texas, University of *161*
T-formation 70, 72, *74*, 75, *76*, 78, 79, 107, 109, 118
Thornhill, Claude 'Tiny' 58, *58*, 59, *62*, *63*, 64, 66, 72
Thorpe, Jim 12, 37, *37*
Thunder Chickens 140, 143 (see also Stanford University)
Thunder Team 66, 69 (see also California, University of)
Thundering Herd 45 (see also University of Southern California)
Tollner, Ted 166, 170, 176
Top Ten Teams 128, 165, 176
Trojans (see University of Southern California)
UCLA-USC Big Game 97, 133, *134*, 139, 144, 146, 148
UCLA (see University of California at Los Angeles)
University of California at Los Angeles (UCLA) 20, 40, 57, 63, 64, 66, 69, 70, 75, 78, 79, 80–93, *80*, 94–103, 104–111, 112–127, 128–143, 144–169, 170–191, *171*, *172*, *173*
University of Southern California (USC) 7–15, 16–23, 24–33, 34–45, 46–53, 54–63, 64–71, 72–79, 80–93, *84*, *85*, 94–103, 104–111, 112–127, 128–143, *138*, *139*, 144–169, 170–191, *182*, *183*, *185*
USC (see University of Southern California)
USC-UCLA Big Game (see UCLA-USC Big Game)
Van Brocklin, Norm 90, *91*
Van Raaphorst, Jeff 176, *177*
Vataha, Randy 140, *140*, 143
Vermeil, Dick 144, 146
Vow Boys 40, 50, 52, 54, 57, 58, *58*, 59, 63, 64, 66, 72, 94
Walden, Jim 148, 173, *176*
Waldorf, Lynn Osbert 'Pappy' 80, 83, *83*, 84, *84*, 85, *85*, 86, 90, 94, 96, 103
Walsh, Bill 150, *152*
Warburton, Irving 'Cotton' 50, *50*, 51, 59, 86
Warner, Glenn 'Pop' 20, 29, 30, 34, *35*, 36, *36*, 37, 39, 40, *42*, 45, 46, 48, 51, 57, 58, 62, 72
Washington, Kenny 69, 72
Washington State University 6, 20, 22, 46, 48, 54, 57, 62, 64, 66, 75, 78–80, 89, 90, 101, 107, 108, 110, 118, 120, 123, 128, 131, 148, 154, 165, 170, 173, *174*, *175*, 176, 183
Washington, University of 7–15, 7, 16–23, *18*, *19*, 24–33, 34–45, 46–53, 54–63, 64–71, 72–79, 80–93, *80*, *93*, 94–103, 104–111, 112–127, *116*, *117*, *124*, *125*, 128–143, 144–169, *155*, *160*, *161*, *162*, *163*, *164*, *165*, *166*, *167*, 170–191, *184*
Waterfield, Bob 79
Wayne, John 51, *51*
White, Charles 148, *148*, 156, *156*, *157*, 158
White, Mike 107, 144, 150 170
Wiggins, Paul 107, *107*, 183, 185, 191
Wild Bunch 134 (see also University of Southern California)
Wildcats (see Northwestern University)
Wilson, George *45*, 46
Wisconsin, University of 85, 98, 112, 120
Wolverines (see Michigan, University of)
Wonder Team 24, *24*, 26, *26*, 29, 30, 32, 34, 45, 66, 82 (see also California, University of)
Wow Boys *74*, 75, *76*, *77*, 78, 80 (see also Stanford University)
Yale University *9*, *10*, *12*, *14*
Yary, Ron 118, 128, *130*
Yost, Fielding H 'Hurry-Up' 12, *12*, *13*